Evelyn Waugh Revisited

An Exploration of His Comic Vision and Art

Ravi K Dhar

Think Tank
Books

Title: Evelyn Waugh Revisited
Author: Ravi K Dhar
Published by: Think Tank Books in 2022
Address: RZ-26/27B, Ashok Park, West Sagarpur, New Delhi - 110046
Website: thinktankbooks.com
Email: editorial@thinktankbooks.com

Image of The Mother by Henri Cartier Bresson
https://artcritique.files.wordpress.com/2013/07/divine-mother.jpg, Public Domain, https://commons.wikimedia.org/w/index.php?curid=44956597

Cover image of Evelyn Waugh by Carl Van Vechten (1880–1964) - This image is available from the United States Library of Congress's Prints and Photographs divisionunder the digital ID cph.3a42832.This tag does not indicate the copyright status of the attached work. A normal copyright tag is still required. See Commons:Licensing for more information., Public Domain, https://commons.wikimedia.org/w/index.php?curid=43620

ISBN: 978-81-947561-6-3
Price: INR 699/-
Retail price listed is only for the Indian subcontinent.
Selling price may vary elsewhere.

Dedicated to

The Mother

Foreword

The English Novel has continued to develop after James Joyce and Virginia Woolf; it has, in fact, emerged with greater diversity and complexity. Wyndham Lewis has set himself against all that is represented by Joyce, Lawrence and Virginia Wolf; Orwell has documented the social and political realities; Joyce Carey has written to restore some of the traditional concepts within the framework of modernism. But the novels of Graham Greene and Evelyn Waugh are perhaps the most remarkable.

Waugh like Greene deals with Catholicism, morality, and the conflict between good and evil; and both are 'entertaining' writers. But Waugh's world, unlike that of Greene, is pervaded by gaiety. This, however, does not prevent the reader from having a glimpse into the acute sense of boredom, lack of emotional stability and absence of ethical concerns in Waugh's novels. Waugh weaves an extremely intricate pattern of the paradox of fun and gloom; he presents a highly sophisticated kind of comedy; and he is perhaps the wittiest novelist of his generation. Though, in his later novels, fun gives way to devotion, he does not cease to become witty and paradoxical. Indeed, he is an artist in creating novels of paradox, and his themes emerge through the dialectical juxtaposition of seriousness and triviality, laughter and gloom devotion and irreligiosity.

Dr. Dhar's study of Waugh may be regarded as an exploration into the meaning of this paradoxical pairing of opposites in Waugh. Therefore, he examines the philosophical basis of Waugh's novels. His contention is that Waugh's novels are philosophical in their attitude to change and progress. This very attitude shapes Waugh's comic vision of life, and this makes his works universal. There may be many useful approaches to the study of Waugh, but the approach that touches the heart of Waugh's novels and reveals his genius is the study of his comic vision of life.

Dr. Dhar has successfully shown that Waugh's comic vision of life is often close to sublimity. This he has done by concentrating on the symbolic image of the "wheel of life." The movement towards the hub of the wheel of life indicates man's willingness to conform to Divine Order and Harmony which alone makes for progress. Progress through secular change is bound to be a futile and illogical quest. Dr. Dhar says "if the image of wheel of life defines Waugh's comic vision of life adequately, it also endows it with an equally expressive form. While the absurdity of secular change is underlined by a circular plot in the lesser comedies, the purposefulness of religious change is conveyed by a linear plot in the greater comedies."

Dr. Dhar's work is the outcome of a long and painstaking research. This meticulous study of Waugh's novels will certainly contribute to a deeper understanding of Waugh's novels.

S. K. Das, PhD
Former Professor & Head
Dept. of English
Calcutta University, Kolkata

Acknowledgements

The book, **Evelyn Waugh Revisited: An Exploration of His Comic Vision and Art,** was initially conceived as a doctoral thesis. I had the good fortune of working it out under the guidance of two eminent Professors of English, Prof. S. Homchaudhuri, the then Dean, School of Languages, North-Eastern Hill University, Shillong, India, and Prof. B. Mazumdar, my friend and colleague at the then Nagaland Campus of the North-Eastern Hill University, Shillong. Each of the two men contributed in their own ways to the shaping up of this book. Dr. S. Homchaudhuri, a Shakespearean scholar, played a key role in making me understand the significance of having a clear roadmap of research. Dr. B. Mazumdar was more of a comrade-in-arms than a guide; he helped me access the rich resources of National Library, Calcutta and would sit with me to critically rip open each of my drafts to garnish it with reason and stylistic nuances. I would also like to acknowledge here the support that I received from National Library, Calcutta, for the honeycomb of information it made available to me at a time when the information super-way of Internet was unheard of in India.

I would also like to thank here Mr. Neeraj Nain, my Assistant, for being generous enough to volunteer to type this book in his off-duty hours and that too for gratis.

Finally, a word of thanks to my illustrious student, Gaurav Sharma, who is not only a celebrated author himself but also the publisher of this book. It is he who has, like a son, always urged me to keep writing and never let the ink of my pen dry up. This book would possibly have never seen the light of the day but for his painstaking effort.

Ravi K Dhar
January 2022

Contents

Chapter 1

Introduction

This book seeks to inform the readers with the ways in which Evelyn Waugh, an early twentieth century novelist, shapes his comic art and vision with his unique understanding of the nature and significance of change and progress in life. The usage of the qualifier, 'comic', calls for an explanation here in the context of its application to Waugh. But before it may be done, it is essential to understand the attitude out of which it is born. This, in effect, takes us into the area of historiography, as Waugh understood it. The onward march of time leaves in its wake a trail of change. Whether this change is progressive in character or not has been a topic of much debate among historians. Two irreconcilable approaches are, however, discernible: one progressive and the other, cyclical. The first approach, traceable to theories of Enlightenment, runs through the thought of both Humanist and Romantic historiographies. The second, advanced by cyclical historiographers like Arnold Toynbee, John Dewy and Oswald Spengler, disputes the overwhelming faith in the inevitable progress of mankind. It regards change as cyclical and hence, the idea of progress, a delusion in the long run. Himself a former student of history at Oxford, Waugh inclines to the latter belief.

He maintains: "Progress, as it has been understood since the eighteenth century, has proved a disappointment. For every gain, there has been a compensating, or even preponderating loss. Former 'progressives' suspect that they have gained all that is attainable and are in danger of losing it, while others believe that for a century the 'spirit of the age' has been moving in a wrong direction."[1]

---

[1] Evelyn Waugh, "Commentary for T.A.Mc Iverny's *The Private Man*", *A Little Order*, ed. Donat Gallagher (London: Eyre Methuen, 1977) 40.

While Waugh shares with the latter contempt for the false claims of progress, he differs from them in two major respects. Change, according to the cyclical historiographers, travels along a spiral-shaped path which, in spite of obliterating all chances of betterment, does not prevent one from touching a new point at the end of one revolution. Waugh's notion of change rules out even that possibility. He believe that the circuitous course of change brings one back to one's original position at the end of each revolution.

The second major point of difference lies in their points of view. While the cyclical historiographers view change from the secular angle, Waugh surveys it from the religious as well as the secular angle. The realization of progress depends on the individual concerned. If he seeks to achieve it through secular change, he shall be caught in the futility of circuitous change. But, if he wishes to do so through religious change, he shall move along a linear path, starting from the unstable circumference and ending at the ever-stable transcendental hub of the wheel of life. The end of such a spiritual odyssey promises hope and regeneration. It is this idea of progress that is central to Waugh's attitude to change and progress.

That is why Waugh writes: "I believe that man is, by nature, an exile and will never be self-sufficient or complete on this earth; that his chances of happiness and virtue, here, remain more or less constant through the centuries and, generally speaking, are not much affected by the political and economic conditions in which he lives; that the balance of good and evil tends to return to a norm."[2]

As Waugh's comic vision and art are rooted in both these attitudes of change, it is useful to understand the word 'comic' in the context of both. The comic vision of life that emerges out of the secular attitude to change is of the nature of absurdity. The man, who attempts to achieve progress though secular change, is caught in the demonic circle of meaninglessness and futility. The

---

[2] Evelyn Waugh, "Conservative Manifesto", *The Essays, Articles, and Reviews of Evelyn Waugh*, ed. Donat Gallagher (London: Methuen, 1983) 161.

'comic' here connotes absurdity, in the sense in which Eugene Ionesco defines it as 'that which is devoid of purpose, ... Cut off from his religious, metaphysical, and transcendental roots, man is lost; all his actions become senseless, absurd, useless.'[3]

However, in order to understand the comic nature of the persons deluded by the apparently progressive nature of secular change, we also need to define the word 'comic', after the manner of Plato in **Philebus**, as 'a vice which gets its name from a certain habit of mind, and is that particular form of this vice which exhibits the contrary of the state of soul spoken of in the inscription at Delphi.'[4] Put more precisely, it may be said that comic characters suffer from a 'foolish false conceit of themselves'.[5]

By mistaking change for progress, the comic character exposes himself to our ridicule. Yet, our ridicule is never allowed to touch the borderline of condemnation, as the comic writer also makes us sympathise with the ignorance of the comic character. This saves characters in a comedy from becoming the butt of satiric ridicule. Plato plays up the significance of sympathy in 'comic catharsis' when he distinguishes between those suitable for 'the singular blending of pleasure with pain' and those who are not.' [6] In a somewhat similar strain, Northrop Frye maintains that the comic catharsis 'raises sympathy and ridicule'[7]. It may, therefore, be said that comedy unlike satire, elicits the sympathy of the reader for the person ridiculed. Reacting to Bergson's suggestion that the comic is unfeeling,

---

[3] Eugene Ionesco, "Dans les Armes de la Ville", *Cahiers de la Compaignie Madeleine Renaud Jean-Louis Barrault* October 1957 in Martin Esslin, *The Theatre of the Absurd* (Harmondsworth: Penguin, 1972) 23.

[4] Plato, "Philebus", *Comedy: Developments in Criticism* ed. D. J. Palmer (Houndmills: Macmillan Education, 1984) 25.

[5] Palmer 26.

[6] Palmer 26.

[7] Palmer 73.

Eric Bentley too observes: "Precisely that anti-emotional attitude which Bergson attributes to the comic in general belongs… to farce in particular. Farce, not comedy, is 'unfeeling'. Conversely, the bitterness and sadness that so readily come to the surface constitute our first, best evidence that in comedy feeling is not only present but abundant."[8]

In marked contrast with the comic vision that emerges from secular attitude to change is the comic vision that is forged by the religious attitude to change. Gone is the ennui and futility of an absurd world. It is replaced by hope and meaningfulness of life imparted by the regenerative character of religious change. No wonder then that the superior vision of life realized here also has a sublimating effect on the meaning of the word 'comic'. In view of this development in Waugh, I have redefined the word 'comic' here on the lines of Northrop Frye and Eric Bentley. Frye seeks to restore to the comic art the grandeur which the classical notion of comedy had taken away, when he observes that the 'ritual pattern behind the catharsis of comedy is the resurrection that follows the death, the epiphany or manifestation of the risen hero.'[9] This is precisely the pattern that emerges in those of Waugh's novels, which unfold his ultimate comic vision of life. That such a view of comedy is often ignored by critics who argue, on the lines of Aristotle, that comedy deals with low action performed by low characters should not deter us from endowing the comic with grandeur and splendour.

Eric Bentley has rightly observed: "Yet, if comedy begins in the kitchen and the bedroom, it can walk out under the stars. It can attain to grandeur. If this is not generally admitted, it is only because any comedy that has grandeur is immediately stamped as Not a Comedy."[10]

---

8 Palmer 143.

9 Palmer 78.

10 Palmer 143.

Echoing Frye, he maintains that the 'comic dramatist's starting point is misery; the joy at his destination is a superb and thrilling transcendence.' [11]

In the comic vision of this kind, the comic character, by transcending the limitations that render him ridiculous, attains grandeur and splendour both in his conduct and personality. The word 'comic', thus, undergoes a semantic volte-face in its application to character here. It no longer signifies foolish conceit. Instead, it connotes freedom from ignorance and admission to the wonderland of truth and meaningfulness. Eric Bentley has, therefore, rightly remarked, 'Now the art of comedy is an undeceiving, an emancipation from error, an unmasking, an art, if you will, of denouement or untying.'[12]

Evelyn Waugh represents the post-modernist tradition in modern British fiction. In marked contract with the avant-garde movement, it emphasized solving "the problems of 'structuring' history in literature... in rather a different way – for instance, by allowing the concern with crisis and change to become part of the matter of literature, rather than as a feature of its experimental form" [13] Ronald Firbank stood for Waugh as a shining example of this change in fictional style. In an essay on Firbank, Waugh explains how the former solved the problem of representation in fiction.

He remarks: "Other solutions are offered of the some problem (representation in fiction), but in them the author has been forced into a subjective attitude to his material; Firbank remained

---

[11] Palmer 140.

[12] Palmer. 146.

[13] Malcolm Bradbury, *The Social Context of Modern English Literature* (New York: Schocken Books, 1971) 97.

objective and emphasized the fact which his contemporaries were neglecting that the novel should be directed for entertainment."[14]

Taking a cue from his literary ideal, Waugh preferred to retain the classical attitude of objectivity toward his work for the sake of entertaining his readers rather than confusing them in a subjective maze. This did not, however, adversely impact upon his concern with communicating his personal vision. The recurrent use of symbolic images and a highly stylized plot convey the author's comic vision of life amply.

However, a prominent stream of literary criticism has tended to condemn Waugh for his supposed lack of values owing to its inability to see though his objective style. Waugh is treated as a splendid entertainer devoid of any significant attitude to life that can earn him place among the literary greats. This attitude is discernible among both, the reviewers and the critics. Among the reviewers, Gerald Gould[15], Arnold Bennett[16] and Desmond Shawe-Taylor[17] are appreciative of Waugh's brilliant sense of humour but not of the equally profound philosophical point of view that informs it. Similarly, Eric Linklater and Ernest Oldmeadow not only fail to understand Waugh's comic vision but also castigate him for reasons that are not supported by facts in the novels. The former accuses Waugh of being 'so abominably subversive as to mock the idea of progress'[18] and the latter contends that his novels are 'a disgrace to anybody professing the Catholic name'[19]. John Brophy[20]

---

[14] Evelyn Waugh, "Ronald Firbank: Life and Letters", *A Little Order*, ed. Donat Gallagher (London: Eyre Methuen, 1977) 80.

[15] Gerald Gould, "Observer", *Evelyn Waugh: The Critical Heritage*, ed. Martin Stannard (London: Routledge & Kegan Paul, 1984) 81.

[16] Stannard 82.

[17] Stannard 195.

[18] Stannard 129-130.

[19] Stannard 136

[20] Stannard 199

is candid enough to confess his inability to locate the moral centre of Waugh's comic vision. In considering 'Europe a more effective background…than the other continents' in Waugh, Derek Verschoyle[21] disregards Waugh's preoccupation with the idea of change and progress that shapes his comic vision and art. Though Waugh's early novels received rave reviews from Rose Macaulay, yet they too are myopic in getting at the significance of Waugh's comic novels. She is of the opinion that Waugh is one of those gifted writers who 'step aside, turn an oblique glance on the world they know, reject it, and, half deliberate, half instinctive, compose one of their own making, a would within a world, in which they can move and invent with greater felicity, sureness and ease'.[22] Her praise does more harm than good. By dissociating Waugh from the world of reality, she deprives the comic vision manifest in his novels of any sound metaphysical basis. Her dissatisfaction with the Catholic novels, in which Waugh reveals the philosophical basis of his comic vision and art, is understandable in the context of her desire that 'he should speedily retrace his steps' to the 'baroque circus tent' of his imagination.[23] A survey of recent criticism reveals that Waugh's art of objective narration continues to act as a Kafkaesque castle for a number of critics also.

Louis O. Coxe opines: "A high moral purpose, working in the fury and mire of human veins, and low shifts men stoop to: this is the double theme of classical comedy and satire, and it is just here, I believe, that Mr. Waugh fails for all his real virtues of wit and style."[24]

Even though Gilbert Highet accepts Waugh's works as examples of successful satire, he does not attribute any definable set of values to them. He argues quite unacceptably that both virtue and vice are ridiculed in Waugh. He remarks: "The main point of

---

[21] Stannard 201

[22] Stannard 90

[23] Stannard 90-91.

[24] Louis O. Coxe, "A Protracted Sneer", *New Republic,* CXXXI Nov 28, 1954, 20.

this is the double-edged satire that the good are dull and stupid, and that the beautiful and rich are corrupt and ruthless: the world is not governed by moral principles, or even by orderly reason, but by chance and the power of the absurd."[25]

Highet overlooks the fact that the absurdity found in Waugh's comic universe owes not to a lack of principles but to man's decision to abjure them and to lead a secular life of self-delusion. By suggesting that Waugh writes "at once social chronicle and fantasy in a spirit of comic delight that absolves him from consistent moral presentation"[26], Malcolm Bradbury takes up a familiar stand. Though A.E. Dyson grants success to Waugh in 'the fineness of his style', yet he deprives his works of any morally coherent comic vision, when he argues: "Much of his success depends on the fineness of his style; 'fine style' thought of in the old fashioned way, as felicity of utterance, wit, charm, rather than as vital union of form and moral content. His *bons* mots deserve to be repeated exactly. Take away the verbal precision, and you crash down too violently on the meaning."[27]

Martin Green mistakenly observes that Waugh is 'both for and against everyone, or rather no one'.[28] By arguing thus, he muddles up the moral issues in Waugh's comic vision of life. Though James F. Carens recognizes the positive aspect of the works beginning with **Brideshead Revisited**, he does not do so in the case of the earlier novels, which he regards as 'generally negative and destructive; and, consequently, Waugh is criticized for lacking a

---

[25] Gilbert Highet, *The Anatomy of Satire* (New Jersey: Princeton University Press, 1962) 195.

[26] Malcolm Bradbury, *Evelyn Waugh*, Writers and Critics Series, No. 39, (Edinburgh: Oliver and Boyd, 1964) in Jeffrey Heath, *The Picturesque Prison: Evelyn Waugh and His Writing* (London: George Weidenfeld & Nicolson Ltd., 1982) 58.

[27] A. E. Dyson, "Evelyn Waugh and the Mysteriously Disappearing Hero," *The Crazy Fabric* (London: Macmillan, 1966) 187.

[28] Martin Green, *Transatlantic Patterns* (New York: Basic books, 1977) 84.

high moral purpose and writing satire without a moral centre.'[29] Graham Martin's analysis suffers from the same malady that has plagued the preceding ones. He fails to see 'any alternative position in whose terms the attack (on modern civilization) can be understood'.[30] Therefore, he contends, 'Except in a kind of brilliant faking, Waugh never goes beyond the external accuracy of observation which served him in the satires.'[31] His indictment is, perhaps, one of the best examples of how one of Waugh's artistic strengths, his objective style, turns into an artistic weakness, in the eyes of some critics. They ignore that language and the form of fictional work can be made to reveal the author's personal vision of life even without direct authorial intrusions. That Waugh could do so speaks of his firm and commendable grasp over the technicalities of his art.

While the impenetrable objectivity of Waugh's fictional style has led some critics to the point of denying the presence of 'an implied author' in his works, his much too vocal public persona has misled others to superimposing the views of Waugh, the man, on Waugh, the 'implied author'. Waugh's personal life style and stray remarks betrayed a predilection for the antiquated rather than the modern. His biography by Christopher Sykes records how he preferred to stay in imposing gothic houses rather than in a modern one. But Waugh was not unaware of this shortcoming in his own self. In **A Little Learning**, he confesses to having fallen a victim, early in his life, to the Englishman's confusion of the antiquated with the sublime.[32]

---

[29] James F. Carens, *The Satiric Art of Evelyn Waugh* (Seattle: University of Washington Press, 1966) 70.

[30] Graham Martin, "Novelists of Society: Evelyn Waugh, Graham Greene, C. P. Snow," *The New Pelican Guide to English Literature*, Vol. 7, ed. Boris Ford (Harmondsworth: Penguin, 1984) 482.

[31] Ford 485.

[32] Evelyn Waugh, *A Little Learning* (Harmondsworth: Penguin, 1984) 44.

But critics have preferred to stonewall the significance of this introspective condemnation and Waugh is shown to be playing up the importance of old English values as enshrined in the obsolescent institution of chivalry. He is, thus, misunderstood to be representing in modern English literature, a reactionary trend to the valuelessness of modern times. As Martin J. Stannard has rightly observed, 'In an age of egalitarianism, Waugh has often seemed a redundant elitist'.[33] Prominent among the reviewers who have followed this line of critical approach are Donat O'Donnell, J.B. Priestley, David Pryce-Jones, V.S. Pritchett, Gore Vidal and Simon Raven. Donat O'Donnell argues that 'the main emotional constituent of Mr. Waugh's religion – using the term in a wide sense - is a deep English romanticism.'[34] Similarly, J.B. Priestley notices in Waugh an attempt to bolster redundant aristocratic values apart from those enjoined by Roman Catholicism. He observes that he 'is an author pretending to be a Catholic landed gentleman'.[35] David Pryce-Jones stresses that 'it is the old order that matters to Evelyn Waugh'[36] and that he tries 'to enlist (in his works) our sympathy for the old order, our sorrow at the financial and moral collapse of the aristocracy...'[37] In a way, V.S. Pritchett accepts the idea of class-snobbery in Waugh, when he tries to play down its significance by observing, 'To object to his snobbery is as futile as objecting to cricket, for every summer the damn game comes round again whether you like it or not.'[38] Gore Vidal argues that Waugh indulges in 'romantic day dreams which are not only quite as unpleasant as the things he satirises, but tend in their silliness to undermine his authority as critic.'[39] Though Simon Raven recognizes the significance of Roman Catholicism as a symbol of

---

[33] Stannard 1.

[34] Stannard 256.

[35] Stannard 389.

[36] Stannard 273.

[37] Stannard 273.

[38] Stannard 425.

[39] Stannard 439.

order and goodness in Waugh, yet he too imputes aristocratic values to him.[40] Waugh was justifiably stung by these reviews. A cardinal principle of literary criticism is violated here. The man with whom the works are associated is substituted for the artist-narrator who created them. Consequently his works are condemned for what they themselves reject.

A survey of the somewhat comprehensive criticism reveals the continuation of this tendency in a good number of critiques on Waugh. It goes to Stephen J. Greenblatt's credit that he should have focused attention, perhaps for the first time, on the significance of the wheel-imagery in understanding the comic vision of life in Evelyn Waugh.[41] But, it is precisely in doing so that he errs. Though there can be no two opinions about the primacy of the wheel-imagery noticed by him, his inference from it is unacceptable. He misconstrues the circular motion of the wheel to imply the meaninglessness of action or change merely in modern times. As a result, he too localizes the moral centre of Waugh's comic vision in 'the value structures of the past'[42]. He argues that the circular motion of the wheel in Waugh is symbolic of an example of the upper-class novel and attributes to it the limited and fragmentary vision of such a novel. He also detects an ambivalent attitude towards the upper classes in Waugh's novels: 'the need to defend at certain crucial points, an upper-class world which is also satirized'[43]. Bernard Bergonzi, in his initial appraisal of Waugh, adopts the right stand. In his review of **A Handful of Dust**, he had rightly maintained that "in its treatment of the doomed Gothic hero – not yet a Catholic hero – it points forward to such ambitions later novels as **Brideshead Revisited** and, in particular, the **Sword of Honour** trilogy where Guy Crouchback, a more complex and

[40] Stannard 448.

[41] Stephen J. Greenblatt, "Evelyn Waugh," *Three Modern Satirists: Waugh, Orwell, and Huxley* (New Haven: Yale University Press, 1965) 6.

[42] Greenblatt 6.

[43] Terry Eagleton, "Evelyn Waugh and the Upper Class Novel", *Exiles and Émigrés* (London: Chatto & Windus, 1970) 209.

developed version of Tony Last in the early novel… realizes the insufficiency of the gentlemanly ideal and is stripped of his romantic illusions."[44]

But in **The Situation of the Novel**, Bergonzi seems to have changed his stand altogether. He argues here: "The total pattern of Waugh's work reveals a consciousness that is indeed dedicated to looking backward, to reliving the past and trying to preserve its values, and which ultimately is unable to resist the pressures of modernity, although it never willingly surrenders to them."[45]

The thrust of the analysis by Jeffrey Heath is on showing how Waugh's own search for a refuge that promises order and harmony from the cramping confines of an irrational and chaotic world gets carried over into his novels. "His search was so urgent that it inevitably carried over into his novels, where it became a major motif, and if we examine the refuges in Waugh's fiction we may discern a pattern which illuminates the core of his work and personality."[46]

Accordingly, he classifies his fiction into two segments: the one written before **Brideshead Revisited** and that written after it. While in the former, 'Waugh's protagonists typically find solitary refuges which are false', 'in the fiction of later date they discover the correct refuge which has been adumbrated by the false ones; the Household of the Faith'.[47] The adoption of a biographical approach, however, tells upon his critical insights. Like Terry Eagleton, he discerns in Waugh an ambivalent attitude towards the

---

[44] Stannard 159.

[45] Bernard Bergonzi, "Looking Backward," *The Situation of the Novel* (London: Macmillan, 1979) 117.

[46] Heath 2.

[47] Heath 2.

objects of his comic ridicule. He presumes that 'Waugh disapproves of what delights him, and is fascinated by what he deplores.'[48]

S.M. Pandeya, in a more recent analysis, argues after Peter Green, [49] that the romantic nostalgia for the *ancien regime* provides the moral centre to Waugh's comic vision and art. Pandeya[50] bases his argument on a passage in **Decline and Fall** that reads: "'English spring', thought Paul. 'In the dreaming ancestral beauty of the English country'. Surely, he thought, these great chestnuts in the morning sun stood for something enduring and serene in a world that has lost its reason and would so stand when the chaos and confusion were forgotten?"[51] Its interpretation by David Lodge[52] aptly invalidates Pandeya's stand.

The preceding analysis of criticism on Waugh may foster the impression that criticism has run completely amuck in the case of Waugh. But it is not so. There has been a steady stream of literary criticism that has recognized the moral centre of Waugh's comic vision and art in the Roman Catholic values of life, as opposed to any secular values. Accordingly, the merits and demerits of Waugh's comic vision and art, as unfolded aesthetically, have been pointed out and his literary achievement been assessed. Traces of it can be found even in the early reviews. John Bayley, F.J. Stopp, and Brigid Brophy best represent this section of reviewers.
John Bayley emphasizes the primacy of Roman Catholicism in Waugh, when he remarks that both 'Evelyn Waugh and Graham

---

[48] Heath 58.

[49]Peter Green, "Du Cote de chez Waugh", A Review of English Literature, II, Apr. 1961: 90.

[50] S. M. Pandeya, "The Early Novels of Evelyn Waugh," Studies in Modern Fiction (New Delhi: Vikas Publishing House, 1983) 76.

[51] Evelyn Waugh, *Decline and Fall* (Harmondsworth: Penguin, 1984) 123-124.

[52] David Lodge, *Evelyn Waugh* (New York: Columbia University Press, 1971) 10.

Greene are writers who use their Catholicism as a weapon and probe; they explore vice and anarchy from a definite standpoint'.[53]

But the point of his argument lies in his hope that "Evelyn Waugh and Graham Greene will not be taken too seriously and will not attract too many disciples'.[54] By calling his concern with the Roman Catholic values of life as partisan, he detracts attention from the aesthetic significance of Waugh's view-point. F.J. Stop has, in a way, set criticism right on this point. He not only draws attention towards the Catholic standpoint of the novels but also warns against judging the artist's achievement in a manner other than aesthetic. He rightly argues: "Lord Marchmain's change of heart and Charles Ryder's conversion, Helena's heroic virtue and her discovery of the fragments of the True Cross… are all matters which are the appropriate subjects of aesthetic delineation. But they are not problems for solution, since the novel is not a spiritual case-history. It is enough for the novelist that such things are humanly possible: his task is limited to making them humanly and poetically probable."[55]

Brigid Brophy too has rightly noticed Waugh's concern with the rejection of the inadequate past and the acceptance of Raman Catholic values. She observes: "Mr. Waugh, after stating that ***Brideshead*** in contrast to the first novel by Waugh, was 'not meant to be funny' declared its 'general theme' to be 'romantic and eschatological': the really extraordinary thing is that precisely the same is true of the general theme of Waugh's novels."[56]

She, however, does not speak of the simultaneous rejection of the modern way of life in Waugh. It is essential to do so in case

---

[53] Stannard 312.

[54] Stannard 312.

[55] Stannard 333. The article by F. J. Stopp, published originally in Month in August 1953, later developed into the book, Evelyn Waugh: Portrait of an Artist (London: Chapman & Hall, 1958) because of Evelyn Waugh's appreciation of its contents.

[56] Stannard 161.

one is to understand the supremacy of Roman Catholic values of life over the temporal ones.

The problem with the reviews on Waugh is that they are either sketchy or inadequate. Detailed attention to this concern in Waugh is more forthcoming in critiques written by Stephen Spender, Christopher Hollis, A.A. De Vitis, David Lodge, and Richard Johnstone. Spender considers the emphasis on Roman Catholicism as self –defeating and an artistic blunder on the part of Waugh. He argues: "It is when he identifies his prejudices with a moralizing religion that qualities anachronistic and absurd in his view of life – intolerance, bigotry and self-righteousness – work against his talent, and even tend to caricature the very ideas he is supposed to be supporting."[57]

Far from undermining his art, the Roman Catholic thrust of Waugh's fiction gives his comic vision and art depth and stability. Christopher Hollis recognizes Waugh's development as a novelist alongside his pre-occupation with perfecting a literary form that could adequately convey his religious interest.[58] But he refrains from showing how this affects ultimately his comic vision and art. A.A. De Vitis takes a provincial view of comedy when he argues that Waugh succeeds only in the so-called early comic novels and not in the 'confines of the traditionally serious (Catholic) novel'.[59] He ignores the sublime heights the so-called traditionally serious novels attain. Also, he overlooks how language and fictional form are made to blend with his comic vision to achieve a unique aesthetic expression. David Lodge's analysis, though brief, is decidedly superior to that of most other critics in this group and also an improvement over Stephen Jay Greenblatt's work. Unlike the latter, he does not commit the mistake of associating the moral centre of Waugh's comic vision with the value structures of the

[57] Stephen Spender, "The World of Evelyn Waugh," *The Creative Element* (London: Hamish Hamilton, 1953) 174.

[58] Christopher Hollis, *Evelyn Waugh* (London: Longmans, Green & Co., 1954) 737.

[59] A. A. De Vitis, *Roman Holliday* (London: Vision Press, 1958) 83

past. He recognizes that Waugh's Christian anti-humanism leaves no room for the acceptance of any secular value system.[60]

But the thrust of his critique is on Waugh's success in the artistic portrayal of the 'myth of decline'. David Lodge's analysis focuses attention only on the degradation that creeps into human society when it tries to achieve progress through secular change. It, therefore, takes a partial view of the vision that emerges from Waugh's works. Though Richard Johnstone has rightly perceived the significance of Roman Catholic values of life in Waugh's comic vision, yet he is concerned more with trying to show Waugh's lack of intellectual conviction in it than in trying to show how it grows out of his work artistically. He argues: "The order imposed here by Waugh's Catholicism is, like Updike's Marxism, no more logically convincing than any of the other means of ordering existence that are dismissed in **Journey to the Border** or in **A Handful of Dust**. The power of the belief springs not from any inherent compelling logic, but from the individual's overwhelming will to believe."[61] By asking for logical necessity in a work of art, he overlooks the fact that a work of art is not a logical treatise but an aesthetic expression of the narrator-author's vision of life.

In order that a true estimate of Waugh's artistic capabilities and achievements may be made, it is of paramount importance that his comic vision and art be understood not only from the Roman Catholic point of view but also in terms of his singular attitude to change and progress. I, therefore intend to show, in the following pages of this book, how Waugh's comic vision of life grows effortlessly and, above all, with artistic facility, out of his singular approach to the concept of change and progress. In trying to substantiate that, I would also like to underline the fact that Waugh's genius is quintessentially comic and not satiric, as many critics have tended to suggest.

---

[60] Lodge 9-10.

[61] Richard Johnstone, The Will to Believe (Oxford: OUP, 1984) 94

The world that confronted Waugh was not only caught up in the cyclorama of change but was also obsessed by it. The sense of change felt by man in the twentieth century has been unparalleled compared to any other age. The world has presented so changing a face that it has been difficult to reconcile with the long and continuous string of changes. Malcolm Bradbury has rightly summed up the modern situation thus: "Living *now* is not at all like living *then*. We live in a world of persistent change, where the past is dead and the present is dying; our pressing imperatives are drawn from a temporal location somewhere between the present and the future. Our problems are persistently novel; and precedent and the past are unpromising guides. And so to be modern is not only to live now, but to live now in a certain way."[62]

What Bradbury emphasizes while defining 'modernity' is the act of living now in a persistently changing environment. Bradbury seems to echo Jung, who maintains in a somewhat similar strain: "the modern man is a newly formed human being: a modern problem is a question which has just arisen and whose answer lies in the future; the exemplary modern man is moving towards a fuller consciousness of the present and finds that the ways of life which correspond to earlier levels of consciousness pall on him."[63]

Behind this unprecedented pace of change lie, however, the hopes and aspirations of the Humanist and Enlightenment historiographers who by their secular utterances have helped man humanize history to the point of seeking fulfilment with its bounds. The urbanisation and democratization that the English and other European societies have undergone in the wake of industrialisation have particularly proved their point right. Progress can be achieved on earth through means totally within man's reach. Man only needs to quicken the pace of change by ushering the world into a technological era.

---

[62] Malcolm Bradbury, The Social Context of Modern English Literature (New York: Schocken Books, 1971) 3.

[63] Bradbury 13.

It is at this very moment of celebration of man's progress through secular change that a strong anti-progressive view of history was shaping itself in the unsettling revelation of Freud's psychological theories and those of the new generation of physicists. Freud belittled the significance of reason in human conduct when he drew attention to the tendency of human mind to rationalize the subliminal desires pressing for satiation. Suddenly, reason lost the pre-eminence it was granted by the Enlightenment theorists and it was reduced to the rank of a handmaid of the powerful irrational unconscious mind. The savage in man stood revealed and man could no longer turn a blind eye to this overwhelming reality. If the reason of man could not be trusted, then how could the notion of secular progress be accepted? The civilized man, by being vulnerable to the same irrational drives of the unconscious mind as the barbarian is, presented a picture of helplessness and stagnation.

The advances in physics compounded this feeling of uncertainty and anti progressiveness. The concern of science with 'models of reality' rather than reality itself came to be recognized. This introduced a note of subjectivity in the hitherto objective science. The knowledge, that science uncovered relative truths and not the absolute one, added to the intellectual confusion. Man began to realize the amorphous nature of a relativistic world. Both science and reason proved inadequate guides to progress that could be lasting and true. The modern age has thus concretised the fears and apprehensions of the cyclical historiographers in a way that no other age has done. That Waugh was not insensitive to this obsession of the age with change is obvious from what he has to say about the nature of its occurrence in rural England: "The process is notorious and inevitable. Expostulation is futile, lament tedious. This is part of the grim cyclorama of spoliation which surrounded all English experience in this century…"[64]

In coming to terms with it, however, he chooses a path which resembles neither that of the progressives nor that of the anti-progressive cyclical historiographers. Even though it is

[64] Waugh, A Little Learning (Harmondsworth: Penguin, 1984) 33

individualistic, yet it is not outside the tradition of Roman Catholic Church. Waugh is one with the cyclical historiographers in rejecting the claim of linear secular change. In his opinion, the quest for progress through secular change is a sheer mirage. He sees a ray of hope for humanity in only the religious transformation of man's outlook and conduct. According to him, man can hope to progress if he gives up the secular outlook and elects religious change as the high road to progress. It is this dual approach to the phenomena of change and progress that informs his profound comic vision of life. It speaks highly of Waugh that he should have been able to outline this metaphysic right in his first major novel, **Decline and Fall**.

The image of the revolving wheel that Waugh invokes here is central to an understanding of the metaphysical basic of his comic vision of life. Its significance is persistently felt in its recurrent use, obvious or concealed throughout the entire length of Waugh's fictional work. The wheel is metaphorically compared to life. At this point, however, a distinction is made between the commonly held notion of life and the one suggested here. This difference is clarified with the help of the imagery of the wheel that is placed in a circular room with seats for spectators. The rotating wheel offers three choices. One can simply be seated in the spectators' gallery and watch the fun, signifying the decision to simply play the role of an objective observer of the action of life. The other choice offered is of jumping on to the wheel and daring to race along its circular motion by overcoming its unsettling motion, signifying the decision to jump into the action of life, braving the instability of change. There is a third option too. After jumping on to the rotating wheel, one could choose to pierce through its mazy motion towards its stable centre, signifying the decision to choose an action that is directed towards peace and stability.

Waugh observes: "People don't see that when they say "life" they mean two different things. They can simply mean existence, with its physiological implication of growth and organic change. They can't escape that even by death, but because that's inevitable they think the other idea of life is too – the scrambling and excitement and bumps and the effort to get to the middle, and when we do get to the middle, it's just as if we never started. It's so odd."[65]

It goes to the credit of Waugh that he expounds his vision of life in a somewhat tongue-in-cheek manner through a character who least qualifies for this role. But, as the narratives in novel after novel testify, this is the presiding imagery around which his works are woven. It, therefore, becomes important to understand the significance of this primary image.

Waugh clearly draws a distinction between three modes of living life. One, in which a person withdraws from the normal business of life and only accepts change inasmuch as it is unavoidable such as the biological processes of life. Such people are indolent and can be found peopling his works in the rural settings, where the laid back life of agricultural economy allows them the luxury of such a withdrawal from the hectic action of life. Waugh calls them static characters. The second mode is one in which people struggle to build empires, big or small, by virtue of their individual industry. Such people can be found peopling his works in the urban settings, where people try to match the breakneck pace of social and economic change with their individual enterprise to steal a march over the other. Waugh calls them dynamic characters. Comic fun arises when a static character strays into the world of change represented by the wheel and tries to ape the ways of the dynamic denizens of the world of secular change. He is rescued only when he realizes that he is unfit for the world he has strayed into.

The philosophical basis of Waugh's comic vision and art, however, runs deeper than that. Apart from the static and the dynamic modes of life, there is a third mode as well. Unlike the first two, the third mode of life does not negate life by withdrawing from its action by seeking refuges like the one offered by the fast disappearing rural economy or engaging in the thoughtless pursuit of success through secular change as glorified in the project of

---

65 Evelyn Waugh, Decline and Fall (Harmondsworth: Penguin, 1984) 208-209.

modernity by the Enlightenment historiographers. It accepts life as it is and seeks to transform it by heading for the transcendental core/hub of the wheel of life, which alone promises true and abiding progress. Just as the hub of the rotating wheel transcends the absurdity of its circuitous motion, Roman Catholicism, the faith of Waugh's own deliberate volition, transcends the absurdity of secular change for it is the temporal representative of eternal and transcendent reality in this life. In the story *Out of Depth*, Rip Van Winkle wakes up after five hundred years of slumber and discovers to his utter surprise that the entire world has changed beyond measure but for the Church. In this utterly changed world, Rip sees one sign of permanence: the Roman Catholic Church. Only it has not undergone any change, the service in Latin continues and the sacrament is administered without any change. Again in **Edmund Campion,** the Jesuit priest expresses similar views in a striking manner.

"'Make the best of Rome', he (Edmund Campion) wrote later to Gregory Martin. 'Do you see the dead corpse of that Imperial city? What can be glorious in life, if such wealth and beauty has come to nothing? But who has stood firm in these wretched changes – what survives? The relics of the Saints and the chair of the Fisherman.'"[66]

Suffice it to say then that the Roman Catholic Church stood for Waugh as an eternal reminder of an immutable reality. Keeping out of the Church means, therefore, losing the eternal perspective of Roman Catholicism and gaining a secular outlook on life, which is akin to racing on a rotating wheel.

Consequently, a person who steps on the wheel of life is confronted with two options. He may either choose to go along with the circular motion of the wheel or else direct his efforts towards the hub of the wheel by cutting through the circular motion of the revolving wheel. The desire to go along with the motion of the wheel implies readiness to participate in secular change for human

---

[66] Evelyn Waugh, *Edmund Campion* (Oxford: OUP, 1980) 61.

betterment and progress. This is what the progressive thinkers have been emphasizing and this is what science has been trying to achieve with its cocksure positivism. However, as the graph of this change indicates such efforts are foredoomed to failure. Progress involves not merely a movement in time and space, as change does, but a considerably perceptible shift in the position of the individual or the society undergoing change that is amenable to value judgment. This, however, is precisely what the circular motion of the wheel does not impart to the secular efforts of man. The wheel of life with its circular motion brings the subject, undergoing change, back to its original position once it completes one revolution. Moreover, no position on the circle of the wheel can be adjudged better than another. Eugene Ionesco's definition of absurdity aptly defines the nature of secular change. Cut off from the transcendental source of his existence, man gropes in the dark when he undertakes to achieve progress through secular change. His fate is as absurd as that of Sisyphus. The fact that the participant in this change, called dynamic character by Waugh, refuses to see the absurdity of his action in the beginning renders him comic. The shattering of the illusion makes his end grim and gives the comic vision unfolded here, a dark tinge. That is way, Waugh has also been called, many times, a writer of black humour. The incipient tragedy within the comic situation obtaining here precludes the censure of the individual. It demands, instead, our sympathy for the person ridiculed. A suitable example of such a dynamic character in Waugh is Seth, the Emperor of Azania, in **Black Mischief**. The novels that unfold the comic vision of absurdity have been classified in this book the 'lesser comedies'. In choosing and using this term for these novels, I have been guided by the quality of vision unfolded in them.

The rejection of the circular motion of the wheel of life for the linear motion directed toward the stable hub of the wheel of life implies a desire to achieve progress not through delusive secular change but through religious change. This is precisely what Roman Catholicism aims at: deflecting men from the 'wasteland' of sin towards the rejuvenating world of prelapsarian reality. As the graph of this change indicates, such an effort is bound to meet with success as the linear course of this change is very much amenable to value judgment. Besides, as the person, undergoing this change, approaches the hub, he has to face less and still less the destabilising impact of the circular motion of the rotating wheel. This means his progress becomes perceptible in the degree of stability he has achieved on the linear course of religious change. The final moment of triumph comes when he reaches the transcendent hub of the wheel of life for no sooner does he reach there than he is liberated from the shackles of the secular world of change. The moment of arrival is accompanied with the bliss of immutable transcendental reality. In Waugh, such an act is conveyed through conversion to Roman Catholicism and a staunch adherence to its doctrine. The best example of such a character in Waugh is Helena. I have called the characters willing to undergo this change, 'spritual elites' for their superiority owes to their superior attitude to life. Some of these characters, however, do not realize this in the beginning. It is then that they become butts of comic ridicule. But no sooner do they reject the path of secular change and embark on that of religious change than they cease to be so. Yet they continue to remain essentially comic characters, for the act of emerging out of ignorance into the light of knowledge is also a part of comedy, as Eric Bentley has also emphasized. The comic vision that is unfolded here is of the nature of resurrection and epiphany. This makes the comic outlook presented here at once Christian and universal in appeal. The sense of joy and transcendence of misery at the end of the comic hero's journey is the hallmark of greater comedies. Accordingly, I have termed the novels which play up this sublime comic vision, 'greater comedies'. These comedies speak of the artistic maturity and insight that Waugh achieved in his literary career and shall, therefore, remain the foundation of any valid evaluation of Waugh as an important twentieth century writer. In trying to gauge the extent of Waugh's ability in conveying his comic vision of life successfully through his comic art, I have been guided more by aesthetic considerations than any other. Primacy has, therefore, been given to the 'implied author' in the literary works rather than the man with whom the works are otherwise associated. This has necessitated a distinction between Waugh as an author and Waugh as a man. The task of doing so is made easier in Waugh as he himself inclined to this literary approach. The words of Pinfold- Waugh in **The Ordeal of Gilbert Pinfold** are revealing in this regard.

"Mr. Pinfold gave nothing away. Not that he was secretive or grudging by nature; he had nothing to give these students. He regarded his books as objects which he had made, things quite external to himself to be used and judged by others."[67]

This, however, does not imply that useful sidelights offered by Waugh's life and utterance have been ignored. It only means that they have been considered for their supplementary value only and so far as they do not damage the argument contained within the works themselves. This has meant reliance on a close textual analysis of the works. Such an approach is particularly rewarding as it concerns itself essentially with the neat and successful aesthetic expression of the comic vision of life in Evelyn Waugh.

The task of aesthetic analysis differs widely from that of a logical analysis. While the latter demands of the writer that he should explain the situation in his works, the former does not. Here, it would be pertinent to point out that that the logic of a work of art is revealed in its skilful use of artistic devices and not in a logical disputation for a work of art is not a piece of argumentative prose but an aesthetic whole. The novel is placed uniquely in this regard. The novelist, as Iris Murdoch has observed, 'has a blessed freedom from rationalism… he has always been … a describer rather than an explainer'.[68] This distinction is particularly useful in Waugh as he, like Ernest Hemingway, believes in using language suggestively and sparingly.

In keeping with the division of Evelyn Waugh's fictional output into 'lesser' and 'greater' comedies, this book undertakes an exposition of his comic vision and art by critiquing his thirteen novels in two chapters. Such a division is rewarding as it enables the

---

67 Evelyn Waugh, *The Ordeal of Gilbert Pinfold* (Harmondsworth: Penguin, 1984) 9.

68 Iris Murdoch in Jonathan Raban, *The Technique of Modern Fiction* (Indiana: University of Notre Dame Press, 1969) 69.

reader to have a glimpse of the myriad manifestations of one kind of vision in different novels at one place and also in tracing the shift in the artist's comic view and art. Accordingly, the second chapter of my book presents how Waugh use his artistic skills in the lesser comedies for successfully conveying a vision of absurdity about a world that has steeped itself in the quest for progress through secular change. The novels studied here are: **Decline and Fall** (1928), **Vile Bodies** (1930), **Black Mischief** (1932), **A Handful of Dust** (1934, **Scoop** (1938), **Put out More Flags** (1942), **The Loved one** (1948), and T**he Ordeal of Gilbert Pinfold** (1957). The third chapter of my book deals with the novels which fall under the title, 'greater comedies'. These are: **Brideshead Revisited** (1945), **Helena** (1950) and **The Sword of Honour Trilogy** which includes three novels: **Men at Arms** (1952), **Officers and Gentlemen** (1955), and **Unconditional Surrender** (1961).

As the names of the novels listed above may have also suggested, my study of Waugh's comic vision and art is limited in its scope to the eleven major novels of Evelyn Waugh: the three novels included in **The Sword of Honour Trilogy** being treated as one. In doing so, I have been guided by the feeling that the other minor works are more in the nature of long short stories rather than novels. Besides, the graph of Waugh's artistic achievement comes through more clearly in the major novels than in the minor fictional works.

My study of Waugh's comic vision and art is based on the Penguin editions of his novel, by and large. The Penguin editions, apart from their easy availability, also mirror truly the real artistic intentions of Evelyn Waugh. Based on the British first editions, which continue to be the authoritative version of almost all Waugh-novels, the Penguin editions make a departure in the case of **Brideshead Revisited** and **The Sword of Honour Trilogy** only. So far as the variations in the latter are concerned, the have been critically evaluated in the analysis of this novel.

Chapter 2

The Lesser Comedies

Central to the comic vision of life manifest in the lesser comedies of Evelyn Waugh is the comic absurdity of a world which has chosen to better its state of existence through secular change. The repetitive nature of secular human endeavours promises no material change in the lot of man. Caught in the vortex of secular change, man returns to his original sate of existence again and again. Out of it grows a sense of comic futility of all secular human efforts. Waugh suggests that if man has to progress, then he must transcend the cycle of repetitive events and touch the hub of the wheel of life where alone life is salvaged from the delusion of secular change. Ignorance of the absurdity of seeking progress through secular change prevents one from seeing this point. Consequently, the person who is taken in by the delusion of bettering his lot through secular change not only renders himself comic but also deprives himself of the opportunity of living life meaningfully. Waugh's comic vision of absurdity, therefore, contrasts sharply with that of Albert Camus, an existentialist. Camus' Sisyphus has no other choice save that of accepting his absurd fate as he is denied the possibility of religious salvation. But Waugh's comic characters have an alternative choice. They can make their lives meaningful by preferring religious change over the secular one. So, there is no attempt in Waugh's lesser comedies to celebrate the absurdity of secular life. Rather, the emphasis is on its rejection. Therefore, even when Waugh explores the absurdity of secular change, his comic vision of life continues to remain poised in the Roman Catholic hub of the wheel of life. This lends the comic vision revealed in the Lesser Comedies an air of absurdity that is different in tone and texture from what is encountered either in the Theatre of the Absurd or the existentialist work of art.

Of the eleven major novels, the three novels included in the war trilogy being treated as one, that Waugh wrote, eight novels contain a vision that is distinctly absurd. This chapter presents an analysis of these eight novels as Lesser Comedies. Each of these novels has been considered separately in the chronological sequence of their years of publication in order that the comic vision of absurdity in each becomes vivid.

Decline and Fall

Decline and Fall (1928), Waugh's first major novel, is set against the backdrop of early twentieth century Britain. The choice of the period of time is not without reason. Early twentieth century represents the high point of the British Empire, held aloft by its colonial conquests and the might of its business and industry. Underpinning this economic and political success story was the Enlightenment faith in the sovereignty of human agency, as opposed to the retrogressive 'pre-historicity' of religious belief. It is at the very zenith of the secular Western civilization that Waugh shows the seeds of decline and fall. Quite evidently, Waugh wishes to hold up to ridicule the progressive notion of secular change as epitomised in the secular advancement of modern Britain. It is pertinent to note here that modern Britain is the child of the 'Enlightenment' belief in the progressive character of secular change. In the works of R.G. Collingwood: "The historiographers of the Enlightenment thought the central point of history.... (to be) the sunrise of the modern scientific spirit. Before that, everything was superstition and darkness, error and imposture. And of these things there can be no history... because there is in them no rational or necessary development" the story of them is a tale told by an idiot, fully of sound and fury, signifying nothing."[69]

It is precisely by showing the omnipresence of these very anti-cultural values in modern Britain that Waugh ruthlessly renders ridiculous the progressive claims of the Enlightenment historiographers. His irony is, therefore, directed at the self-deceptive illusion of the progressive historiographers. Lest this should be mistaken for his sympathy with the antiquated and obsolete code of chivalry, he makes the comic censure through the point of view of a static character, Paul Pennyfeather. He is an

[69] R.G. Collingwood, *The Idea of History* (Oxford: OUP, 1983) 80.

academic who is conditioned by his association with the value of the past. It is difficult for him to outgrow it. He may, therefore, be likened to a person with is merely capable of watching the action of life from the spectators' gallery, but nor of participating in it. By rendering Paul ridiculous again and again, Waugh draws attention to the inadequacy of the value system of the past. Obviously, Waugh is trying to covey that no point on the trajectory of secular change, be it the located in the past or the present, is a desirable state of being. Thus, Waugh conveys forcefully the idea of absurdity implicit in the quest for progress through secular change. This is the vision that is characteristically common to all lesser comedies of Waugh.

With the intention of exposing the luxuriant and unchecked growth of barbarity in modern Britain, Evelyn Waugh focuses his artistic attention on three important segments of British social life: education, high social life and judiciary. Each forms the subject-matter of a separate section in the novel. Commenting on this scheme, Cyril Connolly observes perceptively, 'School life, high life and prison are the three stages, and each is exquisitely comic and plausible.'[70] Waugh exposes the absurdity of the tall claims of progress in each of these phases of British life by making his central character, Paul Pennyfeather, undertake a picaresque journey through them.

Waugh's choice of this artistic form is highly ingenious. The picaresque fiction, right from **Lazarello de Tormes (1554)**, had been employed to 'point out the follies of ordinary life'. Introduced into England by Alaine Rene Le Sage's **The Adventures of Gil Blas of Santillane,** the tradition underwent a major change in the hands of Smollet whose **Roderick Random**_replaced the picaro of loose morals with the one of good breeding. Waugh's use of the tradition here is more in the line of Smollet than in that of Le Sage. Much before him, Charles Dickens too had employed this narrative technique after the manner of Smollet. But Dickens used

---

70 Cyril Connolly, *New Statesman,* 3 November 1928, 126, ed. Martin Stannard, *Evelyn Waugh: The Critical Heritage* (London: Routledge & Kegan Paul, 1984) 86.

it in his early novels. In his later mature phase, Dickens preferred the more compact plot of temporal-cum-logical progression. The lack of logical progression inherent in the picaresque plot helps Waugh in reinforcing the idea of the lack of logical development in the process of secular change. Consequently, his vision of absurdity concerning the secular quest for progress becomes all the more graphic.

Paul Pennyfeather, like the Spanish picaro, is an orphan. The resemblance ends here. Unlike the Spanish picaro, who is a vagabond, he is a student of theology at Oxford. The world of scholarship entails an assessment of social reality but not participation in its changing facade. It is, therefore, static and Paul, by virtue of inhabiting it, can be considered a 'static' character. As the movements of Paul are restricted within the bounds of the static world of scholarship, his acquaintance with the dynamic world of change is minimal. However, by an irony of fate, he is transplanted from his native static world into the alien dynamic world of British society. One night, when all sensible people quit Oxford because of the raucous festivities of the Bollingerites, he, while returning from one of the meetings of the League of Nations, unwillingly encounters this highly dynamic bunch of brats. Coming from the crème de la crème of British society, they are the very epitome of barbarism and savagery. Waugh writes, 'At the last dinner, three year ago, a fox had been brought in a cage and stoned to death with champagne bottles, what an evening that had been!'[71] In the savagery of their festivities, Waugh rips open the thin veneer of the progressive claims of the Enlightenment historiographers and exposes them to comic ridicule. Unaware of the standpoint from which Waugh was hitting out at the hollow claims of progress, Waugh's reviewers mistook it for a valueless, or better still value-free, demolition of the gains of the Western civilization.

One expects that at least those in authority would have shown civilized human behaviour by restoring order on the campus. But far from asserting authority and restoring sanity, they pray to

[71] Evelyn Waugh, *Decline and Fall* (Harmondsworth: Penguin, 1984) 9.

God for them to attack the Chapel so that they could impose penalties on them for this delinquent act. Waugh paints the temples of learning in lurid light when he shows how even the custodians of order on the campus are unredeemed from barbarity. Thus, beneath the thin veneer of civility can be discerned the menacing proportions of barbarity. Waugh's own assertion at another place illustrates this point well.

"Barbarism is never finally defeated, given propitious circumstances, men and women who seem quite orderly will commit every conceivable atrocity. The danger does not come from habitual hooligans; we are all potential recruits for anarchy… Once the prisons of the mind have been opened, the orgy is on."[72] Not only is progressive British society simmering with barbarity, but it is also a victim of inversion and perversion of justice. When Paul is debagged by the high-society barbaric Bollingerites, the custodians of moral order on the campus, the two Dons, watch with relish instead of coming to his help. Eventually, when the two Dons do act, they do so to frame the charge of indecency against Paul and have him sent down unjustly. The incident serves two purposes. One, it helps in revealing the inversion of values that is peculiar to the dynamic world of decadent humanity. Two, it thrusts Paul out of the perilous surroundings of the dynamic world of modern Britain. Paul's sojourn in the dynamic world is essential for the exposure of the decadent nature of modern Britain. Paul's successive reverses at the hands of the dynamic world play up its rampant valuelessness and ruthless barbarity as well as the inadequacy of static ideal in combating these regressive features in British society.

There is no mistake in understanding right in the first novel that Waugh has made certain essential choices. He has decided to give the story a firm historical location and draw on our sense of historical verisimilitude by highlighting the contrary values signified

[72] Evelyn Waugh, "Appendix: Conservative Manifesto", *Robbery under Law,* ed. Donat Gallagher, *The Essays, Articles and Reviews of Evelyn Waugh* (London: Methuen, 1983) 162.

by the 'static' and the 'dynamic' world. While the static world is comparable to the gallery sheltering the spectators of the play of life, the dynamic world is comparable to the ever-changing region of the wheel of life. In the world-view of Evelyn Waugh, the dynamic world is the secular world making a vain bid to achieve progress through an essentially circular secular change.

Next in the line of Waugh's comic fire is the judicial system. Sent down from Oxford, Paul approaches his solicitor-guardian for help. Paul suffers his second reverse at the hands of his 'dynamic' solicitor-guardian who apart from withholding his allowance on the pretext of his shameful misconduct at Oxford, advises him to see life 'in the raw'. Waugh writes suggestively, 'That spring Paul's guardian's daughter had two new evening frocks and, thus glorified, became engaged to a well conducted young man in the office of works.'[73] The hint is obvious. His guardian had defrauded him of his allowance to meet his own personal ends. Waugh's choice of profession for Paul's guardian and his guardian's son in law is a sly comment on the corruption in progressive British society. Unethical to the core, they are symptomatic of the level of instability one finds on the periphery of the rotating wheel. Paul, a static character, is ill-equipped to deal with such highly dynamic characters. Obviously, in his encounter with them, he must suffer total defeat and incomprehension. Having stepped into unfamiliar environs of the dynamic world, he struggles for survival. However, despite all his efforts to comprehend and emulate it, he is unable to so. In the process, neither does he retain his real identity, nor does he become a dynamic character like the others. He becomes, so to say, a shadow of his previous self. The 'disappearance' of Paul is, therefore, accomplished with artistic deftness, unlike what A. E. Dyson maintains, when he observes, 'As the leading character, and minor character, disappear, one feels not only that society doesn't care, but that the author doesn't care himself. The causes of Paul Pennyfeather's mysterious disappearance are neither explored nor

[73] Evelyn Waugh, *Decline and Fall, op. cit.*, 16.

regretted.'[74] Eagleton, in contrast, has shown acute perceptiveness of the functional nature of this change, when he remarks: "The significance of Paul's blankness is twofold. It allows the novel's real concern- the life of upper class society – to emerge 'objectively', as a neutrally descriptive record rather than as part of a more personal, inward, evaluative history; and it deftly prevents their experience from being unduly criticized by the man who is its sacrificial victim."[75]

It is partly on account of this objectivity in the narrative that Dyson is unable to comprehend the change in Paul. The disappearance of Paul as a real character, far from being an artistic weakness, is a sign of artistic strength. No. writer of picaresque fiction had till then effected such a change in the protagonist's identity, and for such a purpose. In this respect, Waugh has made an innovative use of the tradition of picaro.

Paul's picaresque struggle for survival leads him to the doorsteps of Church and Gargoyle scholastic agents. The experiences described here and at Llanabba Castle, Dr. Fagan's model school of vice and disobedience, reflect Waugh's own when he was in a somewhat similar predicament. Asked to apply for a job that demands knowledge of subjects that Paul does not know, he replies: "'But I don't know a word of German, I've had no experience, I've got no testimonials, and I can't play cricket'. 'It doesn't do to be too modest,' said Mr. Levy. Why, only last term we sent a man who had never been in a laboratory in his life as senior Science Master to one of our leading Public Schools…'"[76]

Waugh's caustic comments on British educational system expose the hollowness of an empire that was then at the peak of its

---

[74] A. E. Dyson, "Evelyn Waugh and The Mysteriously Disappearing Hero", *The Crazy Fabric* (London: Macmillan & Co. Ltd., 1966), 190.

[75] Terry Eagleton, "Evelyn Waugh and the Upper Class Novel", *Exiles and Émigrés* (London: Chatto & Windus, 1970), 43.

[76] Evelyn Waugh, *Decline and Fall, op. cit.*, 16.

colonial glory. Lest it may be mistaken for his figment of iconoclastic and diabolic imagination, we need to look at Waugh's own personal experiences in this regard. Paul's experience resembles that of his creator who once found himself in a precisely similar situation. Waugh writes about his own predicament thus: "But, as the scholastic agent remarked, few headmasters were able to find men with all the qualities they demanded and with desperate levity I offered to teach anything which any one might require."[77]

Notwithstanding these resemblances, it would be a gross exaggeration to interpret the entire novel as a pastiche of autobiographical material as, to put it in the words of Waugh himself, 'Nothing is more insulting to a novelist than to assume that he is incapable of anything expect the mere transcription of what he observes.'[78] In the offices of the Church and Gargoyle, scholastic agents, Paul learns about the ridiculously elaborate gradations of public schools. His interview with Dr. Fagan, Llanaba Castle's owner, is also instructive similarly. Upon being prodded to reveal the reason for his abrupt discontinuation of studies at Oxford, Paul confesses the truth.

"'I understand, too, that you left your University rather suddenly. Now… why was that? This was the question that Paul had been dreading, and true to his training, he had resolved upon honesty. 'I was sent down, sir for indecent behaviour.'"[79]

No matter how much he may try to adjust to the serpentine ways of the dynamic world, Paul's innate static character keeps peeping out at critical junctures. A Basil Seal would have held his ground and given nothing away. But, as Paul Pennyfeather lets his static core emerge at such critical encounters, he must pay the price for it. Dr. Fagan uses this confession, not to reject him, but to lower

---

[77] Evelyn Waugh, *A Little Learning* (Harmondsworth: Penguin, 1984), 215.

[78] Evelyn Waugh, "People Who Want to Sue Me"", *Daily Mail*, 31 May 1930, in ed. Donat Gallagher, *Evelyn Waugh: A Little Order* (London: Eyre Methuen, 1977), 10

[79] Evelyn Waugh, *Decline and Fall, op.cit.*, 18

the sum offered for the job. This is another sad but comic comment on the depth of corruption in the British educational system. Like Gilbert Pinfold, Paul is no match for the dynamic characters of the world of secular change. Dr. Fagan's small victory in the interview with Paul shows him up as a 'dynamic' character capable of clinging to the wheel of life in its incessant circuitous motion. It is from such a person that Paul receives his first lesson in the ways of the dynamic world: 'temper discretion with deceit'. This prepares us for the picture of lawlessness to be seen at Llanabba Castle, Dr. Fagan's model school of vice and anarchy. Stephen Jay Greenblatt's remarks about this nursery of vice are worthy of note: "Paul's experience at Llanabba is a marvellous initiation into the savagery of society, for all greed, corruption, doubt, ugliness, hysteria, and callous indifference to suffering are found there in microcosm. The butler, Solomon Philbrick, is a criminal; the school master, Captain Grimes is a bigamist and a scoundrel; the Chaplain, Prendergast, is tormented by "doubts" and has no faith; the owner, Doctor Fagan, is a swindler."[80]

Of all these characters, Captain Grimes brings out best the public school code as he is himself the product of that system. Deciphering it, he says, 'They may kick you out, but they never let you down.'[81] Even though as a student, he has been expelled from his school, yet he was provided with a letter of recommendation that whitewashes his innate indecency, to help him find a job. The parallel with Paul's case is obvious. In both cases, there is inversion as well as perversion of justice. It is in this way that British educational system has made the unsuspecting society a dumping ground for all potential anarchists.

---

80 Stephen J. Greenblatt, "Evelyn Waugh", *Three Modern Satirists: Waugh, Orwell, and Huxley* (New Haven: Yale Univ. Press, 1965), 9.

81 Evelyn Waugh, *Decline and Fall, op. cit.*, 28. In *A Little Learning*, Waugh provides the clue to the person who inspired him to create the character of Captain Grimes. He writes: 'A very surprising man, about ten years my senior, had come to take the place of the disgruntled Scotchman as Second Master; a dapper man of sunny disposition who spoke in the idiom of the army. He later provided certain features of the character, 'Captain Grimes' in my first novel.' (Evelyn Waugh, *A Little Learning, op. cit.*, 227.)

Completely unheroic, Grimes prefers to save his life by electing to undergo the undignified course of court-martial rather than killing himself in all honour. He also has the singular distinction of never sticking to any job for long which he attributes to his 'temperament and sex'. Instability is the basic characteristic of not only individuals like Grimes, but also of the world they inhabit. This grows because of clinging to the wheel of life at its outermost periphery. It is here that the giddiness of motion is felt the most. The inference is quite obvious: the degree of dynamism in a person depends on the distance of his position from the hub ('You see, the nearer you can get to the hub of the wheel the slower it is moving and the easier it is to stay on.'[82]). When Grimes says that he is 'singularly in harmony with the primitive promptings of humanity', he highlights a basic truth about the character of a dynamic person: that despite the high rate of change sweeping over their lives, there is a conspicuous absence of any remarkable progress in their selves. Like the world to which they belong, they do not progress from a state of primitivism to that of culture and civilisation. Grimes, thus offers a good example of the stagnation of human society at the temporal level and Waugh uses him to his great advantage as a tool and also as a potent artistic device to mock at the Enlightenment historiographers' claims of inevitable progress. John Willet expresses similar views when he observes: "There are not many very durable characters in the modern English novel let alone immortals, like Don Juan or Jeeves, but Grimes is now part of our heritage; his language and values, his reflection on the public schools and the honour of the regiment, are marvellous glimpses of a suppressed rich underworld of English life."[83]

The other teacher at Llanabba, Prendergast, is an ex-clergyman of the Church of England, who has given up his benefice after spiritual doubts began to plague his mind. The Bishop to whom Prendergast refers his problems is unable to provide a neat solution to them. His evasion is a sign of the spiritual bankruptcy within the Church of England ('I asked my bishop, he

---

[82] Evelyn Waugh, *Decline and Fall, op. cit.*, 208.

[83] John Willet, *The Times*, 10 March 1966, 13, in ed. Martin Stannard, *op. cit.*, 93.

didn't know. He said that he didn't think the point really arose as far as my practical duties as a parish priest were concerned.'[84]).

Waugh is building up the world in language slowly and steadily and in this persistently developing world, consisting of a devised succession of events, he succeeds in projecting views of disruption found in civilisation, almost the kind of 'inoperancy of the world of spirit' that we find in Eliot's **The Hollow Men.** No longer a priest, he still nurses hopes of becoming one by seeing one day the light that will dispel his doubts.

"'Perhaps one day I shall see Light', he said, 'and then I shall go back to the ministry. Meanwhile Clutterbuck ran past the door, whistling hideously.. 'That's a nasty little boy,' said Mr. Prendergast, 'if ever there was one'."[85]

The atrocious degree of indiscipline in Prendergast's personality instinctively renders the world around him hostile to him. The students delight the most in teasing him. One student even calls him 'Prendy' at the breakfast table while he is saying the grace. Prendergast thus embodies the spiritual instability that is eating into the vitals of British society. Here, it is pertinent to mention that Evelyn Waugh converted to Roman Catholicism soon after writing this novel, anticipating here the central place that he accorded to the Roman Catholic Church instead of the Church of England, in his world view.

In a letter to Paul, his Oxford friend and fellow static character, Potts writes with insight and understating: "...the great problem of education is to train the moral perception, not merely to discipline the appetites... it is in greater fastidiousness rather than in greater self control that the future progress of the race lies. I

---

[84] Evelyn Waugh, *Decline and Fall, op. cit.*, 13

[85] Ibid., 34.

shall be interested to hear what your experience has been over the matter."[86]

Paul's experience is disappointing, for both his colleagues represent values contrary to the ones emphasized by Potts. While Prendergast is a victim of 'moral perplexity', Grimes is given to 'self indulgence'. A society whose educational system is manned by such 'a criminal class' and 'potential recruits for anarchy' can scarcely claim to be a civilized society. It is by drawing attention to such examples of disorder and anarchy that Waugh mocks at the infantile belief of the secular progressive historiographers.

No wonder then that the students reading in such a farcical system of education are audacious and flippant even in front of their mentors. Several anecdotes in the novel show students asserting themselves at the expense of their teachers. Paul's first encounter with these students brings out in sharp focus the comic disorder prevailing in the school. A never-ending chorus of 'Good morning, Sir', greets him as he enters the class for the first time. Waugh writes: "'Oh, shut up', sail Paul. At this the boy took out a handkerchief and began to cry quietly. 'Oh, sir', came a chorus of reproach, 'you've hurt his feelings. He's very sensitive; it's his Welsh blood, you know; it makes people very emotional. Say "Good morning" to him, sir or he won't be happy all day. After all, it's good morning, isn't it sir?'"[87]

The quoted conversation illustrates not only the spirit of light-weight comic fun but it is also charged with significance: the dynamic way of life has found its way even into the attitudes of the students. In order that Paul may wrest initiative from them, he must employ against the dynamic world its own weapons. He does so by asking his students to write an essay on 'self-indulgence', promising to reward the one that is the longest. Such a kind of education, doled out in the public schools makes a mockery of all high

[86] Ibid., 43.

[87] Ibid., 37.

sounding objectives of education, designed to make children responsible members of the society.

Paul's eagerness to learn the depraved ways of a dynamic world shows the growing influence of his dynamic colleagues on him. He even compromises his dignity for the sake of getting the money that Alastair Digby Vane Trumpington offers to him by way of damages for the injury caused to him on the Bollinger night. Potts' displeasure with such a suggestion is reminiscent of the attitude of the vanished static Paul.

"'I fairly let him have it, it, I can tell you, and told him just what I thought of him for making such an insulting suggestion. I asked him how he dared treat a gentlemen like that just because he wasn't in his awful set. He seemed rather taken aback and said: 'Well all my friends spend all their time trying to get money out of me,' and went off.'"[88]

Paul's conduct in the episode under discussion contrasts with that of Potts and parallels Alastair's. The emergence of a new set of relationships indicates that the direction in which Paul is drifting, leads to the dynamic world. These successes delude Paul into considering himself as dynamic as Captain Grimes. However, his encounter with Margot Beste-Chetwynde shatters this belief.

The events at the Annual School Sports further highlight the callous indifference to indiscipline and decorum prevailing among the custodians of discipline. Though they begin on a frivolous note, they culminate in a savage final. Dr. Fagan's penchant for pomp and splendour makes him introduce a revolver for starting the races. By a strange working of fate, it falls into the hands of the drunken Prendergast, who has been made the starter. Instead of shooting in the air, he fires it in Tangent's direction and consequently shoots him in the foot. The barbarity of the action is enhanced by Prendergast's complete indifference to what he has done. Instead, he waxes eloquent on ecclesiastical matters with the vicar who

---

[88] Ibid., 43

cannot help pronouncing him deranged. While his comic capers regale the readers, Tangent's injury strikes a note of concern. It is this element of horror concealed in the comic situations that has earned Waugh fame for writing black humour. Incidents such as these are a comic comment on the extent of disorder and anarchy brewing in the British public school system, held out as the paragon of excellence. Besides, it is also presented as the breeding ground of values that are antithetical to the idea of progress. By revealing the lack of progress through secular change, Waugh slowly builds up his comic vision of absurdity.

Waugh now proceeds to show how a diseased educational system has affected the health of the British society, and with this purpose in mind, he introduces Paul to the very heart of high social life, the Mayfair upper class circle of Margot Beste-Chetwynde. But before Paul meets Margot, he has a meeting with his old 'static' friend, Potts. The meeting is significant as it sheds light on the nature of Paul's consequent disappearance a second time. In Pott's company Paul enters a familiar world, the static world of scholarship, and thereby retrieves his last static personality. Waugh writes: "For an evening at least the shadow that has flitted about this narrative under the name of Paul Pennyfeather materialized into the solid figure of an intelligent, well educated, well-conducted young man, a man who could be trusted to use his vote… with discretion and proper detachment…"[89]

But, once Paul separates from Potts, he again loses his real identity to become a shadow of his real self. The loss of identity is a necessary fallout of his foray into a world which is incomprehensible to him. Being a static character, Paul finds it difficult to match the wit and guile of the dynamic world. Waugh draws attention to this transformation in Paul, when he intrudes into the narrative and observes: "…but next day, he woke up leaving himself disembodied somewhere between Sloane Square and Onslow Square….From the point of view of this story Paul's second disappearance is necessary, because…..Paul would never

---

[89] Ibid., 122

have made a hero, and the only interest about him arises from the unusual series of events of which his shadow was witness."[90]

At King's Thursday, Paul meets Otto Silenus, a young architect whose intellectualism is self-defeating. Yet, it is through him that Waugh enunciates the vision underlying all his works. Waugh's choice of such a character for such an important task is understandable. For one, Waugh was an extremely private person, who zealously guarded his personal space, leading some people, including his reviewers to mistake it for his 'aristocratic snobbery and arrogance'. Besides, Waugh enjoyed playing cat and mouse with his reviewers. No sooner did they feel they were on sure ground than he would spring a surprise upon them. This way, he kept them guessing about the true intent of his works. This was, however, in keeping with his overall artistic point of view that the novelist must never pontificate as he felt that the primary business of a writer was to entertain. Silenus regards the process of 'becoming' vile as it has rendered man unfit both for the static life of a machine and the free life of a monkey. None of the possibilities are in themselves attractive. Waugh is castigating here, in an oblique manner, the evolutionary concept of change.

By now, Paul has started regarding himself as a dynamic person. His success with Margot has assured him of his ability to move about in the dynamic world with some measure of success. It is in this false self-estimation and in his gullibility about the purity of Margot's shady business that he makes a fool of himself. Even after being alerted by Philbrick, the man who knows the underworld very well, and by Potts, who sniffs white slave traffic at Margot's place, he chooses to turn a blind eye to what goes on under his nose. Paul's illusion about Margot's philanthropy is shattered only when he finds himself caught in a bind. Not only does he become the butt of comic ridicule but he also comes face to face with a grim and tragic situation. An interesting characteristic of Waugh's comic style is that the incongruity from which the comic element springs has very great possibility of turning tragic at

90 Ibid., 123

any moment. A small hitch during marriage preparations hastens that. The women recruited by Margot for her shady Latin American Entertainment Co. are held up at Buenos Aires. Due to her insistence, Paul goes to procure their release. As the time at his disposal is too short, he flies all the way to that place, with the tickets booked for the return journey. Enjoying for the first time such a whirlwind tour, Paul feels no less than the lord of the dynamic world. He even pities Potts for doubting the benevolence of his sudden flight to Buenos Aires. Potts, who is working for the League of Nations, is after Paul to dig out vital clues to the shady business carried out at Margot's house. Paul's ignorance of Potts' real intention behind tracking his movements renders him comic only when Paul realizes the gravity of his mistake. Comedy here is blended with the tragic as the fate that awaits Paul is grim and unjustified. His sympathy with Margot's women for having been trapped in a notorious street, irritation with Govt. officials who are non-cooperative and impatience with the League of Nations which hinders his apparently pious work make him look as comic as Don Quixote who sees in all his miscalculations the hand of some sorcerer. It is only after his arrest that Paul begins to understand the reality of his situation. By then it is too late. When Margot learns about her fiancé's arrest, she takes flight, leaving him to suffer for her crimes.

'Paul's blankness' may prevent 'this experience from being unduly criticised'. But it does not in any way mitigate the reprehensibility of Margot's conduct. Eagleton's inference that it shows Waugh's dual approach to upper classes, that of acceptance and rejection, is unacceptable as 'Paul's blankness' merely guarantees the objectivity of condemnation.[91] The second section of the novel, therefore, exposes the sterility and pointlessness of Britain's high social life through the point of view of the rebuffed acquiescent picaro, Paul Penny-feather. Once again the comic vision of absurdity is concretised in the moral valuelessness of high social life. Ignoring this function of the second section, John Willet complains that 'there are sizable bald patches, particularly in the

[91] Terry Eagleton, *op. cit.*, 68

second section of the book. To some extent, this comes from the novel's pattern. The school staff members have to be brought together in prison so as to stress the similarity of the two regimes.'[92]

True, this section includes the chapter, 'Interlude', which breaks off the narrative for a while. Still, instead of detracting attention from the novel, it helps in a better explication of the sub-textual meaning of the novel. Also, this section performs a function much greater than that of allowing the school-staff to reassemble in Sir Lucas Dockery's prison. As already discussed, it shows Britain to have progressed little from its hated barbaric past in so far as its society lacks all civilized values. Indeed, the imbalance and abnormality in human relations projected here seem more than what one can find even in a primitive society. The claims of British colonial superiority thus look comic against the foreground of its vulnerable reality.

Every society has had to face threats to its existent order from the irrational forces of barbarity and savagery. Modern societies have devised the ingenious system of containing these forces in prisons with the help of an efficient judicial system. As Waugh very perceptively remarks, 'There are criminal ideas and a criminal class in every nation and the first action of every revolution, figuratively and literally, is to open the prisons.'[93] The third section of the novel unmasks the criminality hidden beneath the seemingly civilized façade of colonial British Empire and the paragon of industrial enterprise. Paul's trial reduces the system of segregating criminals from the healthy body of British society to the level of a farce. While the real culprit goes scot free, the Judge and Potts are foolishly content with their success in saving the society form the malicious influence of a white slave trafficker by indicting Paul. Like Falder, in John Galsworthy's **Justice,** Paul is a victim of the miscarriage of justice meted out in the British courts of law. It would be delusive to consider such a society progressive and civilized. In the comic farce of Paul's indictment is encapsulated a

---

92 John Willet, *The Times*, 10 March 1966, 13, in ed. Martin Stannard, *op. cit.*, 93-94.

93 Evelyn Waugh, "Appendix: Conservative Manifesto", *op. cit.*, 161-162

scathing comment on the progressive claims of secular change made out by the Enlightenment historiographers.

Paul's picaresque journey leads him violently to the prison of Sir Lucas Dockery. He meets his old friend, Prendergast, here. Prendergast has by now seen the 'Light' that he had been waiting for. He has discovered that in order to be a priest, one need not adhere to any particular Christian theological doctrine. Accordingly, he is now a Modern Churchman in the prison of Sir Lucas Dockery. As has been said earlier, Waugh regarded the Roman Catholic Church as an ever-abiding Rock of Tradition and Faith. So, the sprouting of myriad sects and denominations in Christianity represented for him a process of falling away from the ideal, a drifting away so to say from the hub of the wheel of life. As the emergence of these denominations led to a Babel of voices, confounding the truth of life, he considered them to be a part of the dynamic world. Prendergast's discovery of the light, therefore, epitomizes the perversion of religion that is so often encountered in the dynamic world.

While the Governor, Sir Lucas Dockery, is supposed to be the custodian of physical and mental discipline among the criminals, who are variations on the barbarians of yesteryears, Prendergast is supposed to be the custodian of their spiritual discipline. Both, however, are misfits in their respective roles as they themselves are the epitome of indiscipline. Sir Lucas Dockery can be always seen musing over his future renown for having invented and introduced novel theories of penal reforms. He belongs to that class of people about whom Waugh writes that in the bid to be enlightened and progressive, they have tolerated all shades of opinion and in the process have lost more than gained by the loss of all principles and considered opinions.[94] Upon being told about Paul's preference for solitary confinement, he sees signs of introversion in him. So the next thing Paul is made to do is to socialize with a homicidal carpenter who bears a deep-seated ill will

---

[94] Evelyn Waugh, "Tolerance", *John Bull*, 21 May 1932, in ed. Donat Gallagher, *Evelyn Waugh: A Little Order*, *op. cit.*, 26.

against Prendergast for being a false priest and an infidel. As the carpenter considers himself God's Elect and the Sword of Israel against the infidel, Prendergast's life cannot be safe in his hand. In his vision, he keeps on hearing the command, 'Kill and spare not'. So, when he is equipped with the tools of a carpenter, on the recommendation of the prison Governor who wishes to provide the aesthetic satisfaction of carpentry to him, he becomes a potential source of danger to all. The prison Governor, however, realizes it only after he has sawn off in his cell the head of Prendergast. The comic obsession of the homicidal lunatic with the visions of blood and murder take on a tragic dimension in Prendergast's cold blooded murder. This is the grotesque element that so often permeates Waugh's fiction.

The black comedy enacted in the grotesque death of Prendergast and the tragic defeat of Sir Lucas Dockery's new fangled ideas of prison reforms shows Waugh's antipathy to an individualistic attitude to religion, as is manifest in Protestantism. Waugh's views are analogous to those of the Roman Catholic Church in G. B. Shaw's **Saint Joan,** who is burnt at the stake not for being an atheist but for encouraging a heretical propensity, whose later image may be founded in Waugh's homicidal lunatic. Were every individual free to interpret the scriptures the way he wants, the world would be flooded with a bewildering variety of wild spiritual beliefs. Waugh's later conversion to Roman Catholicism is anticipated here.

Sometime after Prendergast's death, Paul is shifted to Egdon Heath where he is supposed to pass the rest of his seven years' penal sentence. Captain Grimes is already there, but he does not intend to stay there for long. One day, he makes good his escape despite the entire prison guard force being at his back. To shroud their incompetence, they declare him dead. From his newly acquired familiarity with the dynamic world, Paul knows that it is not the truth. Once again Waugh exposes the inability and inefficiency of the judicial system in isolating criminals from the society and the modern British Society is likened to a jungle infested with savages and barbarians. Thus, the myth of progress, epitomized in Britain's advancement is exploded.

The Judicial system is again made to look completely absurd in the fake death of Paul. One day Paul is asked to get ready for an operation of appendicitis, even though he is perfectly alright. He is unable to make out the intention of the prison officials. He is taken to the seaside nursing home of the protean Dr. Fagan, who has by now metamorphosed into a medico from a teacher out of pecuniary considerations. Alastair-Digby-Vane Trumpington is there to arrange the false declaration of Paul's death by a drunken Doctor who is amply rewarded. Paul's fake death is significant from the point of view of his search for identity. Underlying it is the fact of his death as a shadow of his real self. The chapter is appropriately enough titled 'Resurrection', suggesting his phoenix-like rebirth as a real static character from the ashes of his imposed dynamic self. Paul's steps are guided towards this self realization by Otto Silenus, who with a blend of wisdom and insight, tells him:

> "'Now you're a person who was clearly meant to stay in the seats and sit still and if you get bored watch the others. Somehow, you got on to the wheel, and you got thrown off again at once with a hard bump. It's all right for Margot, who can cling on, and for me, at the centre, but you're static… there's a real distinction there, though I can't tell you how it comes. I think we're probably two quite different species spiritually.'"[95]

Stephen Spender[96] appears to have overlooked the significance of this experience in Paul's life when he accuses Waugh of not developing his characters properly. Richard Johnstone also falls into the same error when he writes, 'These picaresque journeys… are quests for knowledge and personal fulfilment; they lead, however, to increasing incomprehension and isolation.'[97] In

---

[95] Evelyn Waugh, *Decline and Fall, op. cit.*, 209.

[96] Stephen J. Greenblatt, *op. cit.*, 108.

[97] Richard Johnstone, "The Catholic Novelist II: Evelyn Waugh", *The Will to Believe: Novelists of the Nineteen-thirties* (Oxford: OUP, 1982), 92.

fact Waugh needs to be commended for having made the picaro, a developing character, when all through the history of picaresque fiction, he had been a stagnant one.

The epilogue re-enacts the action witnessed in the prologue. Paul is back at Oxford, though disguised as a distant cousin of the previous Paul. The Bollingerites are again on the rampage. But Paul is wise enough this time to keep clear of them and avoid being thrust on the wheel of dynamic life. The only person aware of his true identity is Peter Beste-Chetwynde to whom Paul confesses the incompatibility of his static nature with the dynamic nature of Peter's class of people. With the dawning of this realisation, he ceases to be the butt of comic ridicule. In view of Paul's development from a ridiculous shadow character to a thoughtful real person, it is difficult to agree with Stephen Spender, who observes, 'Perhaps one of the things which makes Evelyn Waugh primarily a comic writer is that, with all his observation of manners and behavior, struggle into a character.'[98]

True, Paul does not touch the summit of self realization that Guy Crouchback does. But, he does plumb the depths of his self to discover his true nature and to act accordingly. This movement from incomprehension to comprehension lies at the base of most comedies.

The action of the novel describes a full circle with the re-admission of Paul at Oxford. The situation with which the novel ends is a repetition of that with which the prologue of the novel opened. The circular plot of the novel underscores the metaphor of the wheel of life hinted in the speech of Otto Silenus. The circuitous nature of Paul's picaresque journey reinforces the absurdity of secular change as does the circular motion of the wheel at Luna Park as observed by Stephen J. Greenblatt too- 'The plot of Evelyn Waugh's first novel is not a linear progression, a

---

98 Stephen Spender, "The World of Evelyn Waugh", *The Creative Element* (London: Hamish Hamilton, 1953), 162

series of events which conclude in a true shift from the original condition but a great circle "like the big wheel at Luna Park".'[99]

Waugh does not sit in judgement on the secular world. Nor does he pontificate on its absurdity. He narrates a tale wherein he embeds a metaphor that contains within its folds his comic vision of life. The image of the wheel, pointed out by Otto Silenus, brings out in sharp focus the anti-progressive attitude of the author. The circularity of secular change underlines the comic futility of human endeavour in a world rendered absurd by the exclusion of the true religious impulse from it. This is the vision that informs all the lesser comedies of Waugh.

While evaluating the novel, we should guard against being carried away by the flavour of its 'particular' quality; the sheer temporal progression of events in Paul's life dealing with his comic misadventures. An underling logical connection between these seemingly unrelated incidents lends the novel its universal quality which is that change at the temporal level of reality yields no significant results. Terry Eagleton's assertion that Waugh's fiction is 'unable to pass beyond its own specialized social experience to discern and evaluate the total structure of which it is a part' is, therefore, partial and prejudiced in many ways.[100] If Terry Eagleton fails to see the universality of vision in Waugh's novels, Stephen Spender reads the novel inverted, when he writes, 'But the title has also a subtler irony; for **Decline and Fall** like the novels of Ronald Firbank, deals with a world where there is in reality no Fall, nor Sin, nor Redemption.'[101]

True, the dynamic characters score over the unsuspecting static characters like Paul Pennyfeather and roam with complete impunity, giving the impression of a Before-the-Fall world. But, they also do not escape the stinging edge of Waugh's irony which reveals

---

[99] Stephen J. Greenblatt, *op. cit.*, 12

[100] Terry Eagleton, *op. cit.*, 70.

[101] Stephen Spender, *op. cit.*, 163

the futility of their delusive faith in temporal progress on the wheel of life. The novel shatters the illusions not only of Paul Pennyfeather but also of the progressive historiographers who believe in the superiority of 'modern' Britain and in doing so, renders not only Paul but also the progressives, comic. It is this non-progressive character of secular change that lends the world of Evelyn Waugh an air of absurdity. It is comic in so far as it mocks at man's delusive faith in progress through secular change and grim, in so far as it holds out no hope of salvation from the pointlessness of an incessant circular motion. Thus, the view of life presented here is at once tragic and comic. In a perceptive piece of critical remark Horace Walpole once said, "The world is a comedy to those who think and tragedy to those who feel". There is much truth in understating life as a curious blend of tragedy and comedy. By holding the mirror up to a tragi-comic view of life, Waugh was merely exploring the old theme in a new way and his perception of reality from the point of view of the genre of literature is as old as that of Shakespeare.

Vile Bodies

In **Vile Bodies** (1930), Waugh's second major novel, the focus of artistic attention continues to be the absurdity of seeking progress through secular change. Waugh mocks at the idea of secular progress by showing how an individual who allows himself to be deluded by it returns to his original state of existence despite all his best efforts to improve his lot. The symbolic image of the wheel of life comes through graphically in the various circular images employed by the author for the purpose. Yet, Waugh at no stage precludes sympathy from the object of our ridicule. His delusion demands sympathy rather than outright condemnation. This is what makes Waugh's second major novel a lesser comedy rather than a satire. The comedy is, however, tinged with tragedy in so far as it points to the outbreak of disorder and chaos in the shape of the Second Great War, at the end of the novel. In Waugh's comic view of life, while a movement along the wheel of life generates a sense of ennui and absurdity, the movement away from the hub releases forces of disintegration and instability. A quickening of the pace of secular change thrusts human society to such a state. The comic vision of life revealed in this novel makes both these aspects of secular change explicit.

Culled from Lewis Carrol's **Through the Looking Glass,** the two epigraphs that preface **Vile Bodies** (1930), Waugh's second major fictional work, proclaim ideas that form the very foundation of the apparently ramshackle superstructure of its story. The first epigraph, a dialogue between Alice and the Queen, is an oblique comment on the modernist's single-minded pre-occupation with accelerating the pace of change and labelling that as 'development'. In this dialogue, the Queen tells Alice how rapidly one needs to run in order to get away from one's original position, especially in view of the fact that even to stay put at one's original place one has to keep running ('Now, here you see, it takes all the running you can do, to keep in the same place. If you want to get somewhere else, you must run at least twice as fast as that.'[102]). It goes to Waugh's credit that without intruding into his artistic work, he communicates his idea through literary devices such as this.

Waugh wishes us to understand that notwithstanding the massiveness of human efforts for change, there can be no real progress as long as the change desired is secular. The circuitous course of secular change deprives human effort of all its significance. The only possibility that the Queen holds out is delusive as no person can work twice as hard as his abilities allow. Quite appropriately, the second sentence ends with an exclamation mark. An accelerated pace of secular change has, however, been mistaken in the industrialised world of today for progress. By pointing out the folly of nursing such illusion, Waugh drives home the idea of the non-progressive character of the modern secular world.

The second epigraph, again a dialogue, raises the perennial question of the distinction between illusion and reality. When Alice

---

[102] Lewis Carroll, *Through the Looking Glass,* in Evelyn Waugh, *Vile Bodies* (Harmondsworth: Penguin, 1979), 7.

asserts the reality of her existence by pointing to the fact of her shedding tears, Tweedledum questions the very veracity of her tears ('I hope you don't suppose those are real tears? Tweedledum interrupted in a tone of great contempt.'[103]). The interweaving of these epigraphs helps to direct the attention of the readers to the theme of change and progress running through the sub-text of this novel. S.M. Pandeya, However, overlooks the thematic significance of the second epigraph when he restricts its interpretation to the technical aspect of the novel. He opines: "The first epigraph has a thematic bearing on the book, and the second a technical one ... This (the second epigraph) raises the question as to the nature of reality presented in **Vile Bodies** ...There is no wonder that the contemporary socio-cultural reality presented in Waugh's novels gives the impression of being a fantasy."[104]

The central character of **Vile Bodies**, unlike that of **Decline and Fall**, has a certain goal to achieve: marriage with Nina Blount. However, like Paul Pennyfeather, he belongs to the static world of scholarship and learning: Adam is a creative writer. When the novel begins, he is on board the ship bound for Dover. Waugh creates a microcosmic picture of British society on this ship by having the passengers on it drawn from the various segments of British society. There are the Bright Young Things, representing the youth; a politician, representing the British political class; and two religious leaders, representing the religious leadership of the times. The ship thus acquires the symbolic significance of human society and the rough sea that of the difficulties in the progress of human society.

The roughness of the sea lends a circular motion to the ship which suggests the circular nature of secular change. Waugh highlights the impact of the delusion of secular progress, by showing the sickening effect that the circular motion of the ship has on its passengers. He writes:

---

103 Ibid., 7.

104 S. M. Pandey, "The Early Novels of Evelyn Waugh", *Studies in Modern Fiction* (New Delhi: Vikas Pub House, 1983), 60.

"Sometimes the ship pitched and sometimes she rolled and sometimes she stood quit still and shivered all over, poised above an abyss of dark water; then she would go swooping down like a scenic railway train into a windless hollow and up again with a rush into the gale; sometimes she would burrow her path, with convulsive nosings and scramblings like a terrier in a rabbit hole; and sometimes she would drop like a lift, it was this last movement that caused the most havoc among the passengers."[105]

The pains Waugh takes in comparing the motion of the ship to a scenic railway train, a terrier, a lift, are not without significance. He is establishing in this passage the similarity between the circuitous motion of the wheel of life and that of the ship of human society. The importance of the last sentence cannot also be reduced. It shows the impact that the lifting of the veil of ignorance has when one is brought back to one's original position. The circular motion of the ship thus becomes the central and all pervasive image of the novel.

The modern secular society throws up two types of leadership: the political and the religious. One expects them to steer the society to a state of well-being and progress. The politician in the micro-cosmic British society on board the ship is Walter Outrage. He has drugged himself with worldly temptations and is, therefore, incapable of leading others. Besides, 'he is (only) last week's Prime Minister'. Among the religious preachers present are: Father Rothschild and Mrs Melrose Ape. As her name also suggests, Mrs. Melrose Ape's religion is a sham. She holds the un-Christian opinion that the real religious journey begins only after death.

"'Rough? 'course it's rough. But let me ask you this. If you're put out this way over just an hour's sea sickness..., what are you going to be like when you make the mighty big journey that's waiting for us all? Are you right with God?' said Mrs. Ape. 'Are you prepared for death?'"[106]

---

[105] Evelyn Waugh, *Vile Bodies, op. cit.*, 14.

[106] Ibid., 19-20.

Contrasted with it is the religious attitude of Father Rothschild. "To Father Rothschild, no passage was worse than any other. He thought of the sufferings of the saints, the mutability of human nature, the Four Last Things, and between whiles repeated snatches of the penitential psalms."[107]

Unlike Mrs. Melrose Ape, Father Rothschild makes no distinction between the life before and the one after death. He does not consider the former secular by nature and only the latter, religious. Mrs. Ape belongs to the kind of Christians, about whom Harry Blamires says: "…the Christian has relegated the significance of the eternal to the life that succeeds this one. In doing so, it has enabled itself to come to terms with the secular mind on a false basis. The basis is that here and now Christians and secularists can share the same conceptions, attitudes, and modes of action within the temporal sphere, since the essential difference between them … is one which begins to be applicable only when this life is ended."[108]

Thus, Father Rothschild's Roman Catholicism, in contrast with Mrs. Ape's religiosity, provides the hub to the wheel of secular life depicted in the novel. No wonder, Mrs. Ape has her way with the seasick Bright Young People, representative of the desperate but deluded humanity. Her secular approach to religion, contrasted with Father Rothschild's devotion to the Roman Catholic Church, is easier for the secular minded humanity to understand. Father Rothschild cannot help deplore this tendency. So, when he hears the people on board the ship singing with her, he does not join them. Waugh says, "Father Rothschild heard it and turned his face to the wall'.[109] Thus, the first episode of the novel is indicative of the extent of helplessness of British society by virtue of its pathetic belief in the illusion of secular progress.

---

107 Ibid., 15.

108 Harry Blamires, *The Christian Mind* (London: SPCR, 1974), 69.

109 Evelyn Waugh, *Vile Bodies, op. cit.,* 20.

Waugh continues with the imagery of the circular motion of the ship even after the ship docks in at Dover. The highs and lows of Adam's life describe a pattern not different from those of the ship which brings him to Dover. Adam returns to England in the hope of marrying Nina Blount. It would not be out of place to point out here the religious importance of marriage. In Roman Catholicism, it has a unique sacramental value and therefore, Adam's desire for marriage may be mistaken for his quest for the permanence of the Roman Catholic hub of life. That it is not so, is clear from the monetary considerations that play a vital role in the possibility of his marriage. Thus, Adam's desire for marriage is in no way different from any other secular effort of man. This exposes his endeavours to the absurdity implicit in the circuitous course of secular change.

The ship of Adam's hopes of marriage with Nina takes its first nosedive, when the Customs officials at Dover detain him for search and interrogation. Adam has come back to England with an autobiographical typescript, which he hopes to get published. With the money that he earns out of its publication, he hopes to marry his fiancée, Nina. When the Customs official enquires from him if he has anything to declare, Adam very casually replies that he had nothing but books to declare.

"'It was sometime before Adam could get attended to. 'I've nothing but some very old clothes and some books' he said. But here he showed himself deficient in tact, for the man's casual air disappeared in a flash....
'Yes', said the customs officer menacingly, as though his worst suspicions had been confirmed, 'I should just about say you had got some books."[110]

The Customs Officer's sudden change of tone is beyond Adam's understanding. Being a 'static' character, he little anticipates the reaction of the offensively inquisitive customs officer who considers his brain-child not only 'down right dirt' but also consigns

---

110 Ibid., 23-24.

it to flames. If Adam's lack of understanding of the real nature of the dynamic world renders him comic, the irrational assessment of Adam's scholarly work renders the dynamic customs officers comic too, for he fails to see the real merit of Adam's book. With the loss of the book, Adam's hopes nosedive like the ship which bore him back to England. The circuitous course of Adam's efforts to marry his fiancée manifests in his return to his original state of penury. The ship of Adam's hopes describes a circle, in its rise at the prospect of marriage and fall because of its impossibility after the incident at the Customs.

Waugh draws our attention successfully to the futility of secular progress. A distinction needs to be drawn here between Waugh and the cyclical historiographers like Ibn Khaldun and Oswald Spengler. Ibn Khaldum[111], the fourteenth century Muslim historiographer, makes an allowance for secular progress, at least in the short run, when he compares the growth and decay of " dynasties" to that of living organisms. Oswald Spengler[112] too makes such an allowance, when he traces the course of human history from blatant barbarism through a classical period into a new type of barbarism where everything is commercialised and vulgarized. In contrast, Waugh denies the possibility of secular progress in not only the long run but also short run. Even the hope of such a progress proves to be illusory, as it happens in the case of Adam. Notwithstanding external change, human society never progresses to a state of civilization, so long as the change effected is merely secular.

Henceforth, the impoverished Adam leads the life of a picaro shuttling through the different local circles of British high society with a view to improving his fortunes and consequently, marrying Nina. Adam's picaresque journey takes him first to Shepherds' hotel which is owned by Lottie Crump. Among the people assembled in the hotel is the ex-king of Ruritania. A victim of instability in his own lost kingdom, he is of the opinion that

---

[111] B. Kuppuswamy, *Social Change in India* (New Delhi: Vikas Pub House, 1979), 35-36.

[112] R. G. Collingwood, *op. cit.*, 181.

England too is in the grip of a similar political instability ('And now when I come England and always there is different Prime Minister and no one knows which is which.'[113]). The instability manifest in the political order of British society has deeper roots. It stems out of a perversion of moral values. Waugh conveys it in the conduct of Outrage who, right at that moment, is closeted intimately with Princess Yoshiwara, in contravention of all principles of morality. Waugh is here expressing a view that has long been popular and is still very common among lay readers of fiction. Waugh's representation of reality can be justified, for it communicates philosophical or moral truths in a lively and pleasing manner, and if it meant telling thing which were not literally true, the untruths or for that matter the aberrations of the moral truth can be interpreted metaphorically as way of representing an underlying general truth. In fact, Waugh's Projection of reality may be viewed as a plausible reconstruction of what might well have occurred.

It is at Lottie Crumps' hotel that Adam's hopes describe a second circle. A young man who visits the hotel of this time, challenges any one to perform the trick he can. Adam accepts his challenge for a sum of five hundred pounds Adam performs it not once but twice and wins, in the process, one thousand pounds. The sight of so large a sum fills Adam's mind with the hopes of marrying Nina. The ship of his hope rises once again on the waves of life. Dizzy with excitement, he gives it away to a drunk major who promises to multiply it for him by betting it on a race-horse, Indian Runner . Adam rings up his fiancé to apprise her of his ability to marry her by virtue of the sudden wing fall he has had and the thousands he would have, after winning the bet on Indian Runner. Nina sees through the illusion of Adam's hop of marriage as she is well aware of the poor quality of that horse. So she advises Adam to get his money back from that drunk Major. But before Adam may catch him, he has already made off with his money. Once again m the ship of Adam's desire dips down to the place from where it had risen and once again, Waugh underlines the comic futility of secular change. Though the reader cannot help

[113] Evelyn Waugh, *Vile Bodies, op. cit.*, 41.

laughing at Adam's excessive faith in the illusion of secular progress, yet the reader's ridicule is untainted by malice as he sympathises with the ignorance of the comic character. It is this quality that precludes a Waugh novel from being called a satire.

Waugh's attitude to change shows signs of resemblance with that of the Roman Catholic Church, even though he got converted sometime after the composition of this novel. This attitude of Roman Catholic Church to secular change has been summed up for us by Harry Blamires, who writes thus:

"For the Christian mind earthly well being is not the *summum bonum*, as pain and death are not the worst evil. Eternal well-being is the final aim and end of things here. This means that success and prosperity within the earthly set up cannot be regarded as a final criterion. Nor indeed can happiness within time be regarded as a final criterion."[114]

The Catholic antipathy to 'earthly well-being' should be understood in the perspective of man's fall from the Garden of Eden state. As one sociologist says: "While Christianity laid a basis for the idea of progress in the teachings of redemption, it also put forth the idea of the "fall of man" and the total depravity of the human race and thus left hardly any scope for the notion of possible improvement of Man's condition on earth."[115]

The perspective provides an incontrovertible evidence of Waugh's irony being centred in the morality of Roman Catholic Church.

The theme of disorder and consequent decay of human society regains Waugh's attention when he narrates the events that lead to the fall of Sir Brown's Government. Archie Schwert has invited the Bright Young People to a Savage Party. As the name suggests, the invitees are expected to come dressed as savages: a fact

114 Harry Blamires, *op. cit.*, 83.

115 B. Kuppuswamy, *op. cit.*, 29.

that points to the increasing irrationality and barbarity among youth. Order and civilization have lost their lustre for them. Barbarity fascinates them, as they see novelty in it. The seed of disorder and decay are, therefore, germinating even in the psyche of British youth. It is to such a lot of young anarchists that Sir Brown's government falls a victim. The press takes him unawares when it reports the savage festivities of the Bright Young People at his residence and the parliament dismisses his government on the charges of immorality in private and public affairs, the latter being substantiated with Agatha's shameless treatment at the Customs upon reaching Dover from France. Sir Brown becomes an easy scapegoat of an irrational social system, for neither the censure of the press nor that of the parliament is just or founded on any cause that may be attributed to him. The frequent change of political leadership and that on unreasonable charges shows not only the extent of the impermanence that has crept into the British society but also of the irrationality that has gained sway over all human assessments.

Adam's third attempt to find the means which shall make him acceptable to Nina, takes him to her father, Colonel Blount's house, Doubting All at Aylesbury. Adam's meeting with the Colonel is one of the most hilarious episodes in the novel. Before Adam departs for Aylebury, Nina confirms to her father that Adam would be coming to meet him. But when Adam arrives at Aylebury, the Colonel shuts the door upon him, denying that he had ever invited Adam. When Adam rings the door bell again and asks if he can use the telephone, the Colonel suddenly warms up to him, mistaking him for a vendor of vacuum cleaners.

"'…why don't you come in? Have you come about the vacuum cleaner?'
'No.'
'Funny, I have been expecting a man all the morning to show me a vacuum cleaner. Come in, do. Won't you stay to luncheon?'
'I should love to.'
'Splendid…'

… Colonel Blount picked up a telegram and read it 'I'd quite forgotten,' he said in some confusion. 'I'm afraid you'll think me very discourteous, but it is, after all, impossible for me to ask you to luncheon. I have a guest coming on very intimate family business… To tell you the truth, it's some young rascal who wants to marry my daughter….'"[116]

The Colonel in his ignorance abuses Adam in his face. The latter, however, bears with it, keeping in mind his need. It is only after the Colonel discovers his identity that the comic fun explodes and the novel resumes its serious overtone. The comic episode of Adam's meeting with Colonel Blount illustrates the moral perplexity frequently found in Waugh's novels. Adam's comic meeting with Colonel Blount, encourages Adam to nurse the false hope of marrying Nina when he receives a cheque for one thousand pounds from his future father-in law. Adam's ship of desires rides high on this sudden conquest. Waugh writes: "It does not befall many young men to be given a thousand pounds by a complete stranger twice on successive evenings. Adam laughed aloud in the Rector's car as they drove to the station.[117]

In his high state of excitement, he calls on Nina to acquaint her with his success. Nina, who understands her father much better than Adam, examines the cheque to discover the deception played by her artful father on the static Adam. Her father had signed 'Charlie Chaplin' on the cheque. But, she holds back the knowledge of this deception to enjoy a one-night stand with him. In the morning, she shatters Adam's illusion by revealing the deception played by her father on him. The incident shows up Nina as an artful seductress who cares little for social institutions such as marriage in comparison with the satisfaction of her immediate needs of the flesh. Like her father, she is a dynamic character out to make a kill of static characters like Adam. If Waugh condemns the valuelessness of characters such as the Colonel and Nina, he also reveals the inadequacy of secular values of life in the comic fun

---

116 Evelyn Waugh, *Vile Bodies, op. cit.*, 69-70

117 Ibid., 75

poked at Adam's expense. Besides, the absurdity inherent in the circuitous course of Adam's efforts to have a settled married life with Nina further underlines the inadequacy of the static code of life.

Adam's inability to progress is comparable to Vladimir and Estragon's predicament in Beckett's **Waiting for Godot**. Like Adam waiting for his never-to-materialise marriage with Nina, Vladimir and Estragon wait ceaselessly for the Godot who never turns up. Both Waugh and Beckett deny any notable change in man's lot Yet, while Beckett is a pessimist who considers even the hope offered by religious revelations and teachings false, Waugh does not think so. A movement towards the *sub-specie aeternitatis* reality of Roman Catholicism, symbolized by the hub of the wheel of life, constitutes in Waugh's comic vision and art a step towards progress and freedom from the sterility of modern secular life.

Opportunity knocks once again at Adam's door when he gets to write a column in the **Daily Excess** as Chatterbox. Adam gets it as the previous Chatterbox, Lord Balcairn has burnt his head in the gas-oven after being caught reporting a party from which he was purposely excluded. The manner of his death is a sad comment on the fallen gentry. Adam's quick successes as a Chatterbox raise his hopes of marriage yet again. Now that he is no longer a penniless unemployed person, he hopes to present his case as an eligible suitor for Nina's hand to the Colonel once again. Adam calls on Colonel Blount once again. On his second visit, Doubting All is abuzz with the activity of the Wonder –Film Company which is shooting a film on Wesley. The Director of the film mistakes Adam for a reporter who has come to report the shooting. The Colonel once again fails to recognize Adam. Though Adam tries his best to remind the Colonel as to who he is, the Colonel refuses to recognize him. Adam's efforts to identify himself look absurd in the face of the Colonel's rigid inability to understand. Once again, Adam has to return without being able to seek the Colonel's consent for the marriage. Upon returning to London, he discovers that Nina and her childhood friend, Ginger, have performing his job by proxy. However, in doing so, they have unwittingly violated the prohibitory orders of Lord Monomark against mentioning three names: Espinosa, Count Cincinnatti and green bowler hats. As a result of this mistake, Adam loses his job of 'Chatterbox'. With these two reverses, Adam's ship of desire once again returns to its original place. Marriage has eluded him the fourth time. All his efforts for changing his condition have yielded no result for the circular path of secular change brings the labouring man back to his original position. While the non-progressive character of Adam's life describes a circuitous course round the hub of the wheel of life, the decadence of Britain describes a different kind of course. It is discernible in the increasing disorder, political instability and moral perplexity in British society. Commenting on the disregard for order among the Bright Young People, Father Rothschild remarks:

"'Don't you think', said Father Rothschild gently, 'that perhaps it is all in some way historical? I don't think people ever want to lose their faith in religion or anything else... they are all possessed with an almost fatal hunger for permanence. I think all these divorces show that. People aren't content just to muddle along now-a-days...They say, "If a thing's not worth doing well; it's not worth doing at all." It makes everything very difficult for them.'"[118]

The 'fatal hunger for permanence' among the youth shows how chaos and anarchy have struck roots in the social structure of England. Father Rothschild sees only a catastrophe such as a war, a fit finale to this divisive trend. Welter Outrage, who lacks the penetrating insight of Father Rothschild is alarmed upon hearing war mentioned. He mistakes it for an actual one and remonstrates comically against the withholding of this information from him.

"'What war?' said the Prime Minister sharply. 'No one has said anything to me about a war. I really think I should have been told. I'll be damned,' he said defiantly, 'if they shall have a war without consulting me. What's a cabinet for if there's not more

[118] Ibid., 132

mutual confidence than that? What do they want a war for, anyway?'"[119]

Condemned to the Sisyphean task of meaningless labour on the wheel of life, the dynamic Walter Outrage cannot have the insight which a spiritual elite at the hub of the wheel of life can have. Before the astounding insight of the latter, the former's reliance on worldly knowledge looks comically myopic. Father Rothschild, the only spiritual elite in the novel can thus analyse the outbreak of wars, in a profound manner. Father Rothschild asserts:

"Wars don't start nowadays because people want them. We long for peace, and fill our newspapers with conferences about disarmament and arbitration, but there is a radical instability in our world order, and soon we shall all be walking into the jaws of destruction again, protesting our pacific intentions."[120]

The course of destruction chalked out by Father Rothschild is such that it leads one away from the hub of the wheel of life to the farthest orbit on the wheel. The degree of impermanence, because of the high rate of speed at the outermost orbit, is so high that it is difficult to keep oneself in place there. Obviously, impermanence in world order manifests itself in a catastrophe like war. Progress and decline in Waugh, therefore, need to be understood in the perspective of the direction of change, to or away from the hub. In this respect, Waugh differs from the cyclical historiographers who see progress and decline occurring on the circuitous course of life only. His view parallels the Christian view of progress and decline as a movement towards or away from the permanent values of Christianity. To be Christian must be understood here as having faith in redemption and emancipation from the Original Sin.

The circular car race provides another image to convey the futility of circular secular change. A statue of Fame embraced by

---

[119] Ibid., 133

[120] Ibid., 122

Speed has been kept as the trophy for the car which stands first in this race. Waugh appears to suggest that human efforts are rewarded similarly in the dynamic world. The man who travels the fastest on the wheel of life and reaches the starting point first is, ludicrously enough, adjudged the best in the competition. Though by returning to his original position, he negates the significance of all his efforts, yet he earns fame in the secular world. The incongruity between fact and fiction renders the entire enterprise ridiculously comic. Agatha Runcible's motor car accident, during this race, and her later nightmare of moving round and round at a faster and still faster pace ceaselessly, brings out the absurdity of engaging oneself in secular change. Commenting on the pathetic plight of Agatha Runcible, Rose Macaulay writes:

"Agatha Runcible, whirling to her fatal crash in a fantastic motor race... is a figure perhaps more menacing and exemplary than the Bright Young Person she seems; Mr. Waugh might, with a little less of artistic control, have emphasized this aspect of her, given her in her last moments a spiritual malaise more explicit and profound than her delirium of racing cars."[121]

Though Rose Macaulay reads the obvious meaning, the 'menacing and exemplary' fate of Agatha, she is unable to see the 'spiritual malaise' it implies. Apparently, it stems out of her inability to understand the symbolic significance of the circular car race. In contrast, Stephen Jay Greenblatt[122] does not miss the profound implication of Agatha's nightmarish end, as he considers her 'delirium dream' to be the 'central image of Vile Bodies. Greenblatt, however, reduces the symbolic significance of the image of circle when he restricts it to the process of change taking place in modern times only while, according to Waugh, the image of circle of wheel stands for the entire continuum of time or life. This error of judgment impels him to see the moral centre of Waugh's irony

---

[121] Rose Macaulay "Evelyn Waugh", Horizon, 14 December 1946 in ed. Martin Stannard, op. cit., 118

[122] Stephen J. Greenblatt, op. cit., 14

within the temporal perspective of life, in the "value structures of the past".[123]

It is during this race that Adam happens to meet the drunk Major yet again. The Major had duped Adam earlier of his money. To make recompense for that, he offers to return the money at a much enhanced value of thirty five thousand pounds. This raises Adams hopes of becoming rich enough to marry Nina yet again. However, as the Major does not have the sum upon his person at that moment and as he has lost even his money-purse, he wonders if Adam would help him. Adam obliges him by borrowing from Archie Schwert. The next day, Adam goes to the drunk Major's hotel to get the huge sum of thirty five thousand pounds from him and be a rich man to indulge his desires. But, when he reaches the hotel, he learns that the drunk Major has already left the place. The ship of Adam's hopes nosedives yet again. Waugh spins the narrative of episodes to again and yet again underline how all secular efforts are foredoomed to meet an absurd end.

Frequent reverses at the hands of the irrational and absurd secular world make Adam realize the futility of living by the ethical code of academic scholarship. To match up to the manipulative skills of the dynamic characters peopling the so-called progressive world, he decides to follow suit and play ball measure for measure. Though Adam has been unable to get married to Nina, he buys her with a bad cheque off Ginger to whom she has been married, by now. The episode is suggestive not only of moral disorder but also of Adam's growing conformity to the ways of this disorderly and irrational dynamic world. In his third visit to Doubting All, along with Nina, it is he and not the Colonel who wins. The forgetful Colonel, unable to recognise Adam mistakes him for Ginger, Nina's real husband. The Colonel's confidence, in knowing him as a child, is therefore, rendered amusing and incongruous: "…I used to know your father very well indeed at one time. Used to be a neighbour of mine over at where-was-it. I expect you've forgotten those days. You

[123] Ibid., 6

used to come here to ride with Nina. You can't have been more than ten or eleven...."[124]

The servants, however, recognize him. So does the Rector. What perplexes them is Adam's impersonation as Ginger Littlejohn. The Rector presumes mistakenly that the Colonel's son-in-law also might be suffering from a fickle memory. In this respect, Adam succeeds in throwing dust into the eyes of all those present at Colonel Blount's Doubting All. A ludicrous situation emerges when the Rector sympathises with Adam's supposed handicap. Ignorance of the reality of the situation renders the rector comic and the reader has a hearty laugh at his expense.

"Quite off his head, poor boy. He didn't even remember coming here before. One expects that sort of thing in a man of the Colonel's age, but for a young man like that...a very bad lookout for the next generation...."[125]

If intuition does not provide us with the decisive data to support the existence of the Self , some other way should be found to confirm or deny the intuitive idea. Our past experiences are present in some way in our memory. Yet, Hume remarks, quite rightly, that our experiences or perceptions are different from each other and may exist quite separately, having no need of anything else to support their existence. In fact, we need some kind of permanence and continuity to make the process of understanding possible and when the conditions of permanence are lacking, we experience the comedy of errors. This is precisely the kind of mistake which develops when Adam presents himself as Ginger to the Colonel and the Rector.

The absurdity of secular modern life is perhaps best brought out by the film that Colonel Blount shows to his supposed son-in-law and Nina. The movie picks up pace wherever the action of the movie holds dramatic potential and slows down wherever the action

---

124 Evelyn Waugh, *Vile Bodies, op. cit.*, 204

125 Ibid., 208

is un-dramatic. By not allowing any dramatic situation to develop, the movie becomes dull, drab and uninteresting. By robbing the narrative of the movie of its dramatic element, Waugh makes an oblique comment on the kind of life modern man is living. Waugh compares favourably with Eliot and with the dramatists of The Theatre of the Absurd who too saw no drama in the life of the modern man. The loss of drama highlights the extent of absurdity that the Enlightenment philosophy of secular progress has brought about in the western civilization.

While Adam and Nina are enjoying their Christmas at Doubting All, the war breaks out. The actualization of war lends authenticity to Father Rothschild's penetrating analysis of this world. The news of the war is juxtaposed with the tidings of comfort and joy brought by Christmas. The virtuosity in the act of juxtaposition is significant for only after the destruction of an unstable and irrational secular world can there be a possibility for the establishment of a stable Christian social order, worthy of being called civilisation. Waugh's point is illustrated by his views in one of his essays, "I See Nothing But Boredom… Everywhere".

"…I can see nothing objectionable in the total destruction of the earth, provided it is done, as seems most likely, inadvertently. If it is done in malice someone will have behaved culpably."[126]

It is Waugh's deep discontent with the depravity of the materialistic secular world that prompts him to acquiesce with the total destruction of the world.

At the end of the novel, we find Adam reading a letter from Nina, on the biggest battlefield in the history of the world. By now, Nina is with Adam's child who Ginger thinks mistakenly to be his own. Thus, even Ginger is not spared from comic ridicule. It is during this war that Adam discovers his drunk Major yet again who by now has shot up to the rank of a General. He offers Adam his

---

[126] Evelyn Waugh, "I See Nothing But Boredom Everywhere", *Daily Mail*, 28 December 1959, 4 in ed. Donat Gallagher, *op. cit.*, 45

money which by now has lost much of its value. The receipt of that money makes little difference to Adam's fortunes as it is mere paper now. Waugh here conveys an abstruse fact: not only are the secular actions of man foredoomed to failure but the very standards of measuring secular progress are impermanent and unreliable. There is no hope, therefore, for the modern man in the secular dynamic world. Rebecca West has traced this note of disillusionment from Eliot through Huxley to Waugh most perceptively.

"**Vile Bodies** has, indeed, apart from its success in being really funny, a very considerable value as a further stage in the contemporary literature of disillusionment. That may be said to have started with T.S. Eliot's **The Waste Land.** Although that work had a supreme emotional effect it was not easy to guess what Mr. Aldous Huxley whose contribution... left no doubt whatsoever as to what he was disillusioned with, and why... Now Mr. Evelyn Waugh come along to define this distaste.... Young people, he tells us, are disgusted with the world because it is full of those who drink too much and think too little."[127]

Her analysis, however, fails to bring out the real causes underlying the disillusionment of the youth in Evelyn Waugh's fictive world. She offers a simplistic explanation that ignores the significance of the profound metaphysic concealed in Waugh's comic view of the world. A far more sage analysis comes from L.P. Hartley who attributes the note of disillusionment to the impermanence of the world in which the Bright Young People, ironically called so, live.

"If we read this high-spirited book between the lines, and look its gift-horse, humour, in the mouth, we may find that the ground is not really solid beneath our feet, we are dancing on a volcano, carousing on the edge of a precipice..."[128]

---

127 Rebecca West, *Fortnightly Review*, February 1930, in ed. Martin Stannard, op. cit., 187-188

128 L. P. Hartley, *Saturday Review*, 25 June 1930, 115, in ed. Martin Stannard op. cit., 98

Waugh's artistry needs to be commended for making a seemingly broken plot and apparently descriptive images to sub-serve the thematic line of intention in the novel. The course of Adam's efforts, directed towards marrying Nina, conforms to that of a circle which helps in establishing the analogy between Adam's attempts and those of a person on the wheel of life. The analogy is reinforced by the various circular images suggested in the narrative. The relationship of the 'formal circle' to that of the 'thematic circle'[129] helps in strengthening the feeling of comic helplessness and absurdity of secular change usually found in the lesser comedies of Waugh.

Terry Eagleton, however, deprives Waugh's novels of their legitimate 'universal' quality by including them in the category of the 'upper-class novel' and foisting on them the quality of its restrictive vision: "Both the upper-class and lower middle-class novel confront panic and emptiness, as an 'objective' quality of contemporary experience; yet that sense of uncontrolled collapse is, equally, the quality of a constricted social vision in the novel itself, unable to pass beyond its own specialized social experience to discern and evaluate the total structure of which it is a part."[130]

True, Waugh's novels take their protagonists to the heart of high social life. But that should not be used as a stick to beat the artist with, for

"His knowledge (the author's) of the world is limited by his own experience. It is practically impossible for those who live among poor people to write about the rich, a writer who has never been seriously in love can not make his characters seem so;

[129] Stephen Greenblatt uses these two terms in his book, *Three Modern Satirists* (1965), to arrive at a separate conclusion.

[130] Terry Eagleton, *op. cit.*, 69-70.

upbringing, education, experience of travel, of the war etc., all circumscribe and determine the incidents of a book."[131]

The acid test of a work of art lies not in the choice of its particular incidents, but in the building up of a universal metonymic vision, which **Vile Bodies** surely does. Waugh's novels do pass beyond the particularity of social experiences they describe. This is evident from the comic vision of life that emerges from them. The circuitous path that Adam's fortunes describe, the perpetual nightmarish reality of circuitous motion evident in Agatha's fate and the decline of British social system are ideas that point to the all pervasive idea of the futility of secular change, a vision, which is at once original and profound. **Vile Bodies** thus provides an important step forward in the canon of Waugh literature.

Black Mischief

By the time Waugh came to write **Black Mischief** (1932), at Madresfield, Lord Beauchamp's moated house near Malvern, he had got converted to Roman Catholicism. The change had an impact not only on his personal life but also on his artistry. Though the moral centre of Waugh's irony, the hub of the wheel of life mentioned first in **Decline and Fall** (1928), already displayed Roman Catholic characteristics, it now took on an overtly Catholic significance. Anchored in the Roman Catholic hub of the wheel of life, Waugh now felt himself well-equipped to narrate the Enlightenment story of modernization and development on a larger historical canvas. For this purpose, he chose to narrate the developmental history of a fictive barbaric nation, ruled by an Emperor schooled in the idiom and jargon of Enlightenment thought at Oxford, the Mecca of this philosophy.

The change in the physical setting of this novel has, however, elicited a mixed response from critics. While Gilbert Highet is of

---

131 Evelyn Waugh, "People Who Want to Sue Me", Daily Mail, 31 May 1930, 18 in Donat Gallagher, *op. cit.*, 13

the opinion that this is prompted by the novelist's desire to satirise 'the current idealistic doctrine that all races are brothers under the skin'[132], Lionel Stevenson thinks that it 'gives Waugh equal opportunities for ridiculing Western sophistication and primitive savagery'.[133] Stephen Greenblatt rejects both these opinions and asserts that it is 'a condemnation far more of the cultivated Westerner than of the African'.[134] David Lodge too denies any traces of 'racial snobbery' in the novels dealing with the African situation, when he asserts that in these novels 'if any group survives the author's impartial irony, it is the non-Europeans'.[135] Notwithstanding their appreciation of the change in the physical setting of his novels, Greenblatt and Lodge comprehend the thematic significance of this change inadequately. While the former considers it no more than a means of heightening the ironic force of Waugh's biting scrutiny of his homeland[136], the latter thinks that it merely shows 'the primitivism of Africa... as both a foil to and a portent for a civilization that was itself declining into a new, and less appealing, kind of barbarism'.[137] Insightful though the remark by Lodge is, it stops short of identifying the centrality of the Roman Catholic point of view from which Waugh appraises the Enlightenment discourse of modernization and development. Having localized the hub of the wheel of life in the eternal values of Roman Catholic Church, Waugh highlights the comic futility of a nation's developmental journey on the circular path of secular change. As the circular nature of secular change precludes any measure of development, Waugh equates the natural and unvarnished barbarity of the African nation with the sophisticated barbarity of the so-called developed nations. This double critique

---

132 Gilbert Highet, *The Anatomy of Satire* (New Jersey: Princeton Univ Press, 1962), 204

133 Lionel Stevenson, *The History of the English Novel*, Vol 11 (New York: Barnes & Noble Inc., 1967), 354

134 Stephen J. Greenblatt, op.cit., 19

135 David Lodge, Evelyn Waugh (New York: Columbia Univ. Press, 1971), 23.

136 Stephen J. Greenblatt, op. cit., 19.

137 David Lodge, op. cit., 23.

of Enlightenment historiography lends the lesser comedies of Waugh an incisive edge.

Azania's tryst with the discourse of modernity and development begins with Amurath, the Great, who founded the Azanian Empire, with its capital at Debra Dowa[138]. Inhabited mostly by the savage tribes of Sakuyu and Wanda, Azania was under Arab rule until it passed into the hands of Amurath, a three–fourth Negro. Amurath seeks to transform his nation into a modern state, with respect for all the ideals cherished by the progressive secular historians. So, inflamed by the desire of developing his empire, he unleashes a series of modernizing initiatives. With the new found centre of his incisive irony in Roman Catholicism, Waugh makes these initiatives look ridiculous for their misplaced faith in achieving progress and development through secular efforts. One of the first few steps taken by him is the introduction of a railway line between Matodi and Debra Dowa. Waugh remarks ironically enough: "Reluctantly, step by step, barbarism retreated: the seeds of progress took root and, after years of growth, burst finally into flower in the single, narrow-gauge track of the grand Chemin de Fer Impereal d'Azanie."[139]

---

[138] Despite Waugh's denials, critics have compared Azania to Ethiopia, which Waugh visited in 1930. There are, however, reasons for critics to believe so. A comparison of Black Mischief with Remote People shows a number of similarities in situations and places. For instance, Dierra-Dowa in Remote People becomes Debra Dowa in the novel. Similarly, the King's soldiers are reported to be without shoes in both the books and the access to the British Embassy is reported to be shoddy in both. The preponderance of similarities between the two books has led some to label the novel as a travelogue. But that would be stretching the argument too far. As Waugh once wrote: ' If only the amateurs would get into their heads that novel writing is a highly skilled and laborious trade... One has for one's raw material every single thing one has ever seen or heard or felt, and one has to go over that ...until one finds a few discarded valuables. Then one has to assemble these tarnished and dented fragments, polish them, set them in order, and try to make a coherent and significant arrangement of them. It is not merely a matter of filling up a dustbin haphazard and emptying it out again in another place.' (Evelyn Waugh, "People Who Want to Sue Me", op. cit., 14-15. What distinguishes the novel from its non-fictive counterpart is 'a coherent and significant arrangement' of its incidents.

[139] Evelyn Waugh, *Black Mischief* (Harmondsworth: Penguin, 1938), 11

The mock epic style employed here leaves no room for doubt regarding where the author's sympathies lie. Waugh had no illusions about the extirpation of barbarism with secular change. Barbarism can scarcely be overcome with a change that is incomprehensible to people.

"The first few trains caused numerous deaths among the inhabitants, who for some time did not appreciate the speed or strength of this new thing that had come to their country. Presently they become more cautious and the service less frequent."[140]

Among other changes that he introduces are the abolition of slavery and the declaration of Christianity as the official religion of his country, though the author adds that the former has little impact on the prevalent practice as it is never made known to the real offenders.

"He proclaimed the abolition of slavery and was warmly applauded in the European press; the law was posted up prominently in the capital in English, French and Italian where every foreigner might read it; it was never promulgated in the provinces nor translated into any of the native languages; the ancient system continued unhampered but European intervention had been anticipated."[141]

The appreciative response of the European press, against the backdrop of this eyewash, is not only ludicrous but is also condemnatory of their progressive stance. Again, the declaration of Christianity as the official religion by itself does not lend significance to the progressive designs of Seth as the basis on which they are pursued, is secular: Seth wishes to ward off European intervention.

As a result of these secular changes, Debra Dowa comes up as a modern city with a *gesellschaft* social structure. This is evident

---

[140] Ibid., 11-12

[141] Ibid., 12

from the picture Waugh paints of it. A haphazard jumble of shops, missions, barracks, legations, bungalows and native huts spring up in Debra Dowa. The character of the inhabitants also changes:

"…the main population, however, was always cosmopolitan, and as the country's reputation as a land of opportunity spread through the less successful classes of the outside world Debra Dowa gradually lost all evidence of national character."[142]

The disorder that afflicts a *gesellschaft* social structure also plagues Debra Dowa. Waugh writes: "The ground between and about the buildings was uneven and untidy; stacks of fuel, kitchen refuse, derelict carriages, cannon and ammunition lay in permanent place; sometimes there would be a fly-blown carcase of a donkey or camel, and after the rains pools of stagnant water; gangs of prisoners, chained neck to neck, could often be seen shovelling as though some project were on hand of levelling or draining."[143]

Disarray is a sign not of civilization but of barbarity. Thus, despite the change effected in the Azanian society, it continues to be as it was before. The circular path of secular change deprives human efforts of any significant achievement, a view that is diametrically opposed to that of the Enlightenment and humanist historiographers.

When the action of the novel begins, Amurath and his daughter are already dead, his grandson, Seth is locked in a do-or-die battle with Seyid, the husband of the late Empress, for political control over the country. Oxford-educated, his imagination is fired by the Enlightenment zeal of human progress on the circuitous path of secular change. He is, in this respect, far more dynamic than his grandfather, Amurath. Moreover, Seth has been exposed in his youth to the dynamic life of the western society which has made him conscious of modernity. He, therefore, sees the battle between him and his father as one between progress and barbarity.

---

[142] Ibid., 15

[143] Ibid., 14

"'Fools, what do they know? What can they understand? I am Seth, grandson of Amurath. Defeat is impossible. I have been to Europe. I know. We have the Tank. This is not a war of Seth against Seyid but of progress against Barbarism. And progress must prevail. I have seen the great tattoo of Aldershot, the Paris Exhibition, the Oxford Union. I have read modern books… The whole might of Evolution rides behind me; at my stirrups run woman's suffrage, vaccination and vivisection. I am the New Age. I am the Future'."[144]

Seth's excessive reliance on the tank exhibits his unshakeable faith in the superiority of whatever is modern. In this regard, he is completely hoodwinked by the Western ideas of progress. David Lodge has rightly commented that 'Seth personifies a misplaced faith in Western ideas of progress'[145]. His 'misplaced faith' is comic in so far as it persists in the face of reality. The tank, on which he pins all his hopes, proves to be of no more use in the battle than of serving as a punishment cell. The battle is won, instead, by 'two very ancient weapons – lies and the long spear'[146]. A fitting reply to Seth's notion of modernity comes, though he fails to see the point of the irony, in the manner of Seyid's death: 'They should not have eaten him – after all, he was my father.....It is so..... so barbarous'[147]. In the theme of cannibalism that emerges from the manner of Seyid's death, Waugh shows that the comic misadventures into the territory of modernity can have grave consequences as well. The comic and the tragic get blended quite often in Waugh when the dynamic world is allowed to have its way unhampered. The forces

---

[144] Ibid., 16-17

[145] David Lodge, op. cit., 23

[146] Seth's victory over Seyid is modelled on a real life incident reported by Waugh as a special correspondent in Addis Ababa to *The Times* on 22 December, 1930. Waugh had reported that Lij Yasu, the previous ruler of Ethiopia, had been defeated and deposed by the new Emperor Haile Selassie with the help of a disinformation campaign against him. (Evelyn Waugh, "Ethiopia today: Romance and Reality", The Times, 22 December 1930 in ed. Donat Gallagher, The Essays, Articles and Reviews of Evelyn Waugh, op. cit., 119)

[147] Evelyn Waugh, *Black Mischief, op. cit.*, 43.

of barbarity unleashed in this battle mock at the progressive claims of Seth, and by inference, the Enlightenment and Humanist historiography also. Thus, Seth, as the deity of secular change, becomes the butt of ridicule in this novel. But, Seth fails to see the point. He persists with his infatuation with modernity. He reads in his failure to civilize his people an urgent need for their modernisation:

"I am afraid that as yet the Wanda are totally out of touch with modern thought. They need education. We must start some schools and a university for them when we get things straight."[148]

It may be argued that if education, which is a culture of mind, is not a sure way to civilisation, then what else is. True, education has the noble aim of civilising human society. But the kind of education that Seth chooses for his subjects is the secular education of the West, about which T. S. Eliot has brilliantly written:

"All our knowledge brings us nearer to our ignorance,
All our ignorance brings us nearer to death,
But nearness to death no nearer to GOD."[149]

Moreover, Seth himself, as a product of that system of education, is a figure of fun. The need for modernisation that is accelerated social change in a secular perspective keeps pressing upon his mind. Waiting for the delinquent engine to return, he ponders over the urgency of the need.

"My people are a worthless people. I give orders; there is none to obey me. I am like a great musician without an instrument. A wrecked car broadside across the line of my procession... a royal train without an engine... goats on the platform... I can do nothing with these people. The Metropolitan is drunk. Those land-

---

148 Ibid., 43.

149 T. S. Eliot, *Selected Poems* (London: Faber and Faber, 1976), 107.

owners giggled when the engine broke away; I must find a man of culture, a modern man... a representative of Progress and the New Age."[150]

Modernity, Seth's obsession, has, however, already made an incursion into Azania, in the shape of the Embassies and legations of the so-called civilised West. The co-existence of the decadent West and the barbaric East marks 'a unique stage of the interpenetration of two cultures'[151]. The description of the three Embassies, representatives of the West, shows that the civilisation for which Seth aspires, is no civilisation for its imposed order is unable to contain the forces of impermanence and instability. While the American Ambassador suffers from a false sense of superiority, "... he had chosen that post and had not regretted it, enjoying during the last eight years a popularity and prestige which he would hardly have attained among his own people."[152]

The French Ambassador's excessive suspiciousness verges on the comic. When M. Ballon, the French Ambassador, learns of Bishop Goodchild's visit to the British Legation, he attaches an uncalled for importance to it. He thinks that the British Ambassador keeps himself informed about the town through the Bishop. In other words, he is obsessed with the idea of espionage. The elaborate ritual of his retiring to bed is highly comic as it shows the extent to which he has been taken in by his own imagined fears. Waugh writes:

"M. Ballon ascended the stairs to bed. In his room he first tested the steel shutters, then the lock of the door. Then he went across the bed ... and examined the mosquito curtains ... examined the magazine of his revolver and laid it on the chair at his bedside...

---

150 Evelyn Waugh, *Black Mischief, op. cit.*, 101-102

151 Evelyn Waugh, "A Coronation in 1930", *When the Going was Good* (Harmondsworth: Penguin, 1984), 89

152 Evelyn Waugh, *Black Mischief*, op. cit., 47.

He slipped another revolver under his pillow. He tiptoed to the window and called down softly:

> 'Sergeant.'
> There was a click of heels in the darkness.
> 'Excellence.'
> 'Is all well?'
> 'All well, Excellence.'"[153]

Though M. Ballon looks comical in his adherence to an elaborate security drill, yet underlying this comedy is a deep truth that the world in which he lives is not one of harmonious order but of extreme disorder, with lurking dangers ready to ambush the unwary persons. Waugh makes a subtle point against the Enlightenment historians. For all their meta-narratives of progress and development, the modern world remains as savage and disorderly as the African backwaters of human civilization. A lifetime's association with a disorderly and savage world has made M. Ballon wary of dynamic characters like Margot Beste-Chetwynde and Basil Seal prowling the lanes and by lanes of the civilized world to ambush and debag an unsuspecting character like Paul Pennyfeather. Notwithstanding the high place accorded to reason and rationality by the Enlightenment historiographers, M. Ballon is as superstitious as a savage. Before sinking into the stupor of sleep ('His hand found and grasped a small-curved nut which he kept under his bolster in the belief that it would bring him good luck.'[154]).

If the French Ambassador represents one extreme end of the dynamic world, the Ambassador, Sir Samson Courteney, represents another. Oblivious of the world around him, he is happy in the cocoon of his calm domestic life. If his French counterpart renders himself comic by grossly exaggerating his false fears, he becomes comic by flagrantly belittling the gravity of reality. This has earned him the name of Envoy Extraordinary. Bishop Goodchild's visit,

---

[153] Ibid., 59-61

[154] Ibid., 61

which had made M. Ballon fret so much, reveals on the other hand, Sir Courteney's comic disregard for reality.

"'Everyone is in a great state of alarm in the town,' said the Bishop. 'There are so many rumours. Tell me, Sir Samson, you do not think really, seriously, there is any danger of massacre?'
The Envoy Extraordinary said: 'We seem to have tinned asparagus for luncheon every day... I can't think why... I'm so sorry – you were talking about the massacre. Well, I hardly know. I haven't really thought about it... Yes, I suppose there might be one... Don't do to get worried... I should have thought we could have grown it ourselves."[155]

The Envoy Extraordinary's attitude is that of a man who unconsciously feels himself incapable of restoring order to a disorderly and predatory dynamic world. Having given up all hopes of its redemption, he has chosen to take refuge in the particularities of the daily mundane existence. He, therefore, lets the matters drift without burdening his own mind with the task of changing the direction of its course. As it is a response fathered by a highly unstable world order, there is no distortion of truth in the depiction of Sir Courteney's personality. By being a product of the 'dynamic' world, he is Waugh's indirect and objective indictment of its progressive claims.

Waugh continues to sink the sharp fangs of his irony to unmask the progressive character of these representatives of the so-called civilized world in Azania, when he ridicules the love games of the Envoy's thirteen year old 'silly' daughter, Prudence, and William, the first secretary to the British Legation. Their constant attempts to invent new ways of loving show the superficiality, and consequent insincerity, of their feelings. The impermanence of their love is a sign of decadence in the quality of human relations in the modern world. Given an opportunity, it can easily transfer to another person. Such an occasion arises when the elemental Basil

---

[155] Ibid., 57

Seal arrives on the shores of Azania. Prudence gets so prepossessed with Basil Seal that she forgets William altogether.

The relationship of Prudence with Basil touches the lowest of lows when the theme of cannibalism rears its head in their idle love talk. Basil tells Prudence, "You're a grand girl, Prudence, and I'll like to eat you". To this she replies, "So you shall, my sweet, anything you want". It is gruesomely realised in the denouement when Basil unwittingly consumes his mistress at a cannibal feast. The cannibal instincts portrayed here make mockery of the progressive claims of the Enlightenment and Humanist historiographers as they show a lack of Western cultural superiority over African barbarism. T. S. Eliot, in *Sweeney Agonistes*, points to a similar lack of progress in the secular efforts of human society. Aldous Huxley too, in his fiction, has drawn attention towards the barbaric potential of modern man. In a perceptive piece of critical writing, Stephen Jay Greenblatt rightly remarks: "The abortive attempt to modernize Azania is not a statement of the African nation's inability to share in the glories of civilization but a shy and satiric examination of modernity itself. The struggle which Seth envisages as a mortal combat between barbarism and progress is a miserable sham, for Western culture itself is no longer meaningful."[156]

By having founded itself on the false basis of secularised Christianity, the Western culture, as was seen in the first two novels, has drifted away from the rock of the Roman Catholic hub of the wheel of life and has, thus, exposed itself to the impermanence that keeps on growing as one moves away from the hub. Greenblatt, however, does not interpret the meaninglessness of Western culture in these terms; he does so within the false framework of temporal reality. He writes:

"Those Western ideas which might have given Seth's project real significance have been abandoned. Basil informs Seth: "We

---

[156] Stephen J. Greenblatt, *op. cit.*, 18

have got a much easier job now... If we'd had to modernize a country then it would have meant..."
'What is all that?' asked the Emperor.
'Just a few ideas that have ceased to be modern.'"[157]

The passage on which Greenblatt bases his argument, instead of playing up the meaningful stability of the ideas which would have given Seth's project real significance, exposes the vulnerability of those secular ideas to the change that the modern secular man has been effecting, under the delusion of secular progress. Permanence, according to Waugh, lies only in non-temporal and non-secular values of life, as epitomised for him in Roman Catholicism. Seth, however, lives in blissful ignorance of the reality of the modernised West. He waits for the man who would use the magic wand of accelerated secular change to modernise his nation and thereby, bring it at par with the putative civilisation of the secular West. His choice falls interestingly enough, upon Basil Seal, a person who is the very epitome of instability and change. Upon reading about the trouble in Azania, Basil, who has a natural penchant for rackets, feels an irrepressible urge to go there. He not only deceives his mother who is planning a stable career at the Bar for him, but also robs her of her emerald bracelet when she does not give him any money for his travel expenses. He also has no qualms to beg money of his mistress, to meet his travel expenses. The 'exceptional energy and initiative for an Evelyn Waugh hero'[158]that Spender discovers in him owes to this dynamism of his.

Basil's encounter with Seth is a meeting of two dynamic characters. Seth, by virtue of being placed on the outermost orbit of the wheel of life, is for more dynamic than Basil. Yet, when Seth sees Basil for the first time, he is overcome with the feeling of inferiority ('Seth recognized him in his first grave survey of the restaurant and suddenly, on his triumphal night in his own capital,

---

[157] Ibid., 18

[158] Stephen Spender, op. cit., 167

he was overcome by shyness.'[159]). Seth's shyness springs out of the delusion of Western superiority which Basil represents by his flashy and dashing personality. Waugh clarifies as he writes, 'Basil still stood for him as the personification of all that glittering, intangible Western culture to which he aspired.'[160] Their close association cures Basil of any illusions of scoring over Seth for the latter proves to be far more intractable for him. Seth, however, never learns the truth of Basil's personality. He continues to mistake Basil's disorderliness, a barbaric trait, for his progressiveness. The facade of Western sophistication is too glossy to attract Seth's attention to the barbaric core of Basil's personality. In contrast, the raw and unvarnished barbarity of the Earl of Ngumo, 'pacifically winking at the ladies as they danced past him', does not escape his critical eye.

"'Insupportable barbarians', he thought, 'I am sure that the English lords do not behave in that way before their king. Even my loyalist officers are ruffians and buffoons. If I had *one* man by me whom I could trust... a man of progress and culture.'"[161]

The man of progress and culture that Seth identifies is the mercurial Basil Seal. With the induction of Basil into Seth's service, a string of progressive reforms are introduced at a break-neck and incomprehensible pace. The first progressive reform introduced is the pet project of the Enlightenment philosophers, the project of modernity. The 'Ministry of Modernization' is opened and it is located at the site occupied previously by the old Empress' oratory. The location of the Ministry is an artistic masterstroke on the part of Waugh, who always desisted from making a direct comment in his artistic works. Commenting on the secular nature of the changes contemplated by this Ministry, Greenblatt rightly remarks:
"The attempt to replace the worship of God with the worship of Progress is even more obvious in the site of the Ministry of

---

159 Evelyn Waugh, *Black Mischief, op. cit.*, 112.

160 Ibid., 113.

161 Ibid., 115.

Modernization, which occupies what had formerly been the old Empress' oratory."[162]

One of the first initiatives taken by the newly constituted Ministry is the issue of boots to the bare-footed soldiers of the Azanian Army. On the face of it, it is a great modernizing and civilizing initiative. But underlying this noble initiative is Basil's desire to profit from it. Waugh subtly suggests that the project of modernity is nothing but a deceptive scheme to make money. As a representative of progress and modernity, Basil comes off as a reprehensible character out to satisfy his secret desires. Much before the order is out, he buys boots to be sold later to the army. In this project of self-aggrandisement, he has an accomplice in his deputy, Mr. Youkoumian, an Armenian businessman. He stands to lose when Connolly refuses to buy boots for his army, knowing full well their uselessness for the soldiers who are used to going barefoot. Upon his deputy's request, Basil argues with Seth about the modernity of having booted Guards and cleverly insinuates against Connolly being 'not quite modern' in opposing it. Convinced, Seth issues a royal decree, overruling Connolly's sagacious objections and indirectly furthering Mr. Youkoumian's financial interests. The boots have an ironic end when the soldiers mistake them for extra rations and, therefore, eat them. Hearing their jubilant cries, Basil mistakes them for their extreme satisfaction with being booted. The highly dynamic world of Azanian society is beyond the comprehension of even as dynamic a Western man as Basil Seal. He realises his first defeat when he learns the truth from his own adversary in the venture. Waugh writes:

"'That's one in the eye for Connolly', he said, and next day, meeting the General in the Palace yard, he could not forbear to mention it. 'So the boots went down all right with your men after all, Connolly.'

'They went down'.

'No cases of lameness yet, I hope.'

The General... smiled pleasantly.

---

[162] Stephen J. Greenblatt, op. cit., 21.

'No cases of lameness' he replied. 'One or two of belly ache, though ....You see my adjutant made rather a silly mistake. He hadn't had much truck with boots before and the silly fellow thought they were extra rations. My men ate the whole bag of tricks last night.'"[163]

The comic misadventure of modernity narrated here juxtaposes the raw barbarity of the African country against the sophisticated barbarity of characters like Basil, who seek to profit out of such projects. The comedy of errors enacted here helps Waugh to show how the underdeveloped Africans outwit the developed West in their own game of subterfuge. By making Basil look a fool, Waugh has a hearty laugh at the expense of the progressives' claims to the cultural superiority of the developed West.

The other excursion into modernity, popularisation of birth control measures among the natives, has an equally ironic end. An artist, engaged for the purpose, draws up two posters which distinguish the relative fortunes of a small and a large family. The posters captioned, 'WHICH HOME DO YOU CHOOSE?', are supposed to encourage the natives to have small and contented families. Ironically enough, they encourage the natives to go for larger families. Waugh writes:

"Nowhere was there any doubt about the meaning of the beautiful new pictures. See: On right hand: there is rich man; smoke pipe like big chief; but his wife she no good; sit eating meat: and rich man no good; he only one son.

See: on left hand; poor man; not much to eat, but his wife she very good, work hard in field: man he good too; eleven children; one very mad, very holy.

And in the middle; Emperor's juju. Make you like that good man with eleven children."[164]

---

[163] Evelyn Waugh, *Black Mischief, op. cit.*, 137-138

[164] Ibid., 146-147

The Emperor's juju is mistaken for the promotion of fecundity and the large family concept. Just as the changes effected by his grandfather had had little impact on the transformation of Azanian society, similarly, his secular endeavours also fail in civilising his subjects. According to the Graeco-Roman Humanists, 'whatever happens in history happens as a direct result of human will; that someone is directly responsible for it, to be praised or blamed according as it is a good thing or bad.'[165] They tend to eliminate the role of God and supplant him with 'mere personifications of human agency like the genius of the Emperor.'[166] By showing the miscarriage of all Seth's modernisation plans, Waugh shows the Humanist claims to be exaggerated and false in the realm of secular reality. He thus appears to be in agreement with R. G. Collingwood who opines: "The extent to which people act with a clear idea of their ends, knowing what effects they are aiming at, is easily exaggerated. Most human action is tentative, experimental, direct not by a knowledge of what it will lead to but rather by a desire to know what will come of it."[167]

The indictment of Humanist thought, further robs the secular human endeavours of any meaning they may have had. The dynamic secular world is reduced to the status of a jungle, no matter what its outward form may be.

But Seth refuses to see the limitations of human endeavours, unaided by any divine agency. He pursues his modernisation plans with greater vigour and ardour. The accelerated pace of change introduced by industrialisation is matched fully by his voluble mind. No sooner does his mind ponder over one change in the Azanian social structure than it flits to another. In the less dynamic society of the West, where these ideas have been given time to germinate and sprout, they have at least been understood. The pace of change that Seth introduces in Azania is even greater than that in the western

---

165 R. G. Collingwood, *op. cit.*, 41.

166 Ibid., 42.

167 Ibid., 42.

world. As change has an unsettling effect, the ideas that Seth borrows from the West are not even given time to settle and to be understood in their proper context. They are thus reduced to the level of half-baked concepts. The working of Seth's 'dynamic' mind, thus, tells upon Basil's abilities. Apprehensive about his impulsive love for modernization and development, Mr. Youkoumian cautions Basil: "E's been reading books again, Mr. Seal, that's what it is. You won't get no peace from 'im not till you fix 'im with a woman...'[168]. Even the mercurial Basil, product of the developed West, is no match for Seth's elemental thirst for development. Basil's defeat shows neither him nor Seth in a better light as it is indicative of the victory of one savage over the other. It would not be fair, therefore, to say with Spender that 'Evelyn Waugh's sympathy (lies) with characters like Basil Seal who are not merely sinners but devils.'[169] Basil's arrival in Azania helps to throw into sharp relief the barbarity of the so-called developed West.

The rapid unsettling change introduced by Seth's modernisation plans looms up from the shadows in the form of anarchy and insurrection at the end of the novel. The Church, the army and the crafty French Ambassador, with the aid of the Earl of Ngumo, set up a rival candidate for the throne. On the occasion of the Birth Control Gala Day, there is a rebellion. In the struggle that ensues, Seth loses and has to flee along with Viscount Boaz to the jungles. Debra Dowa's imposed order rips open and the forces of irrationality and barbarity are let loose to have their way in creating chaos and anarchy. Azania returns, after a long circuitous journey of secular change to its original state of barbarity. Seth, the champion of Enlightenment historiography, himself meets with an ironic and grim end in the jungles.

The circular path of Azanian history brings out the absurdity of man's belief in progress through secular change. Seth's position is rendered comic, in so far as he mistakes secular change for progress, and grim, in so far as he has to lose his life for this

---

[168] Evelyn Waugh, *Black Mischief, op. cit.*, 148.

[169] Stephen Spender, op. cit., 169.

mistake. The error of judgement that the tragic hero in Shakespeare falls a victim to, takes a tragi-comic shape here in the fate of Seth, the deity of change in the novel. Eric Linklater shows blatant ignorance of Waugh's attitude to change and progress, when he belittles his achievement in the novel by bringing it down to the plane of Restoration comedy:

"Mr. Waugh is so abominably subversive as to mock the idea of progress, especially in such manifestations as might be expected to promote, by a One Year Plan, the adoption of modern organization and habits of life in the negroid Empire of Azania; but Mr. Waugh, by living rather on the plane of Restoration Comedy, permits his readers, if they prefer it, to take his criticism simply as a good joke."[170]

Linklater fails to appreciate that this novel is a severe indictment of the Enlightenment philosophy of progress through secular change. Waugh once said that there 'is no more agreeable position than that of a dissident from a stable society'[171]which, in his philosophy, implies a Roman Catholic society, for civilisation, which 'has no force of its own beyond what is given it from within,'[172] 'came into being through Christianity, and without it has no significance or power to command allegiance'.[173] The events in the fictional history of Azania testify to Waugh's belief and also reveal the vantage point from which he assesses the secular efforts of human society. Ernest Oldmeadow is caustic in his appraisal of the novel, when he observes: "There may be books in which sordidness of detail does not overwhelm the spirituality of the

---

[170] Erik Linklater in ed. Martin Stannard, op. cit., 129-130

[171] Evelyn Waugh, "Appendix: Conservative Manifesto", *op. cit.*, 162.

[172] Ibid., 161

[173] Jeffrey Heath, *The Picturesque Prison: Evelyn Waugh and His Writing* (London: George Weidenfeld & Nicolson, 1982), 33.

pervading idea, but Mr. Waugh's is not one of them. On his dunghill no lily blooms."[174]

Oldmeadow's review lacks weight in the light of the preceding discussion of the novel from the point of view of the philosophy of change and progress that Waugh espoused. The circular course of Azanian history reinforced by a plot which ends where it began concretises Waugh's comic vision of absurdity against the backdrop of a world that has allowed itself to be deluded by the Enlightenment and Humanist historiographers' claims of achieving progress through secular change. In this respect, **Black Mischief** forms an integral and essential part of the lesser comedies of Evelyn Waugh.

---

[174] Ernest Oldmeadow, "Editorial", *Tablet*, 18 February 1933, in Martin Stannard, op. cit., 135

A Handful of Dust

Inspired by his travel in British Guiana[175], **A Handful of Dust**, Waugh's fourth major novel, had a unique genesis in that its final part had already appeared in the shape of the short story, *The Man Who Liked Dickens*[176]. The novel reveals Waugh's continued preoccupation with debunking the Enlightenment philosophy of progress through secular human efforts. In this sense, the novel bears closer resemblance to **Black Mischief,** where the novelist shows the absurdity of such claims to progress in the tragi-comic fate of Emperor Seth. Having rejected the superiority of the present and the future over the past, Waugh now proceeds to show how the Romanticisation of the past values of life as embedded in the chivalric code of the Gothic Age is equally misleading and absurd. The comic vision of absurdity that develops here is not unlike that in the other lesser comedies of Waugh.

In selecting Tony Last, an out and out feudal character, as his protagonist, Waugh's underlying intention is to show the vulnerability of the secular values of the past to change and the comic fallacy of mistaking them for the eternal values manifest in the Roman Catholic hub of life. Commenting on this attempt in Waugh, David Lodge writes perceptively: "The modern is ridiculed

---

[175] Waugh travelled to Brazil in 1932 and came out with a travelogue, Ninety-two Days, on his experiences there. The novel makes use of many such experiences, particularly the one related to the Amazon forests. Commenting on it, Waugh writes, ' A writer is not really content to leave any experience in the amorphous, haphazard, condition in which life presents it; and putting an experience into shape means, for a writer, putting it into communicable form.' (Evelyn Waugh, "A Journey to Brazil in 1932", *When the Going was Good* (London: Back Bay Books, 1985), 187.)

[176] While all the other novels of Waugh were written from beginning to end, as is the usual manner, this novel, to put it in the words of Waugh, 'began at the end'. Citing the reasons for that Waugh writes, 'I had written a short story about a man trapped in the jungle, ending his days reading Dickens aloud. The idea came naturally from the experience of visiting a lonely settler of that kind and reflecting how easily he could hold me prisoner. Then, after the short story was written and published, the idea kept working in my mind. I wanted to discover how the prisoner got there, and eventually the thing grew into a study of other sorts of savage at home and the civilized man's helpless plight among them.' ('Fanfare', *Life* (International: Chicago), 8 April 1946, in ed. Donat Gallagher, *Evelyn Waugh: A Little Order, op. cit.,* 33.)

by contrast with the traditional, but attempts to maintain or restore the traditional in the face of change are also seen as ridiculous; and in any case the traditional usually turns out to be in some way false or compromised."[177]

As Tony 'attempts to maintain' the traditional values enshrined in the chivalric code of morality, 'in the face of change', he exposes the comic inadequacy of the past values of life. Any charge of romanticisation of the past in Waugh is, therefore, far-fetched and untenable. Tony Last's obstinate refusal to participate in the world of change shows him up as a static character, wishing to shun the dynamic world; a fact that places him in the line of the static heroes of the previous novels. Though critics[178] have been vocal in explaining Tony's pre-occupation with the past in terms of his obsession with his neo-gothic house, Hetton, yet they have been reticent in uncovering its underlying thematic significance. David Lodge comes closest to it when he sees in Tony Last's devotion to Hetton, 'a symptom and a symbol of his innocence and immaturity.'[179] While 'innocence' brings out, at a mental level, his refusal to outgrow the dated values of the past, 'immaturity' brings out, on an emotional plane, his inability to overcome the nightmares of his childhood. Tony Last, in other words, suffers from past-fixation. His entire personality is conditioned by an outlook which prevents him from participating in the process of

---

[177] David Lodge, *Evelyn Waugh* (New York: Columbia Univ. Pr, 1971), 9-10.

[178] A. A. De Vitis says: 'In Tony Last Waugh creates a hero whose nostalgia for the romantic past finds expression in his every action. The rooms of the Victorian Gothic Abbey are appropriately named after the names of the Arthurian Court – Guinevere, Lancelot, Galahad and others (A. A. De Vitis, Roman Holiday: The Catholic Novels of Evelyn Waugh (London: Vision Press Ltd., 1958), 31).' Frank Kermode in "Mr. Waugh's Cities" expresses similar views: 'Tony is a nice dull gentleman who knows vaguely that the defence of Hetton is the defence of everything the past has made valuable (ed. Martin Stannard, *op. cit.*, 283).' Stephen Greenblatt too refers to Waugh evoking ' a whole world, a philosophy, and a way of life as well as an architecture and a landscape' and presenting Hetton as 'a lovely, sentimental, idealized world of the past and of childhood at once silly and charming, hopelessly naive and endearing. (Stephen J. Greenblatt, *op. cit.*, 23)

[179] David Lodge, op. cit., 10.

secular change. His plight is akin to that of a person who takes a seat in the spectators' gallery instead of the one who prefers to jump on the constantly revolving wheel of life. It is this attitude which marks a static character out. David Lodge, however, stops short of calling him so.

In order that Tony's 'static' faith in the secular values of the past may be shown false and inadequate, Waugh employs the familiar 'bed-room farce' as an artistic device. All great artists have shown the tendency to select a familiar plot for the sake of conveying their abstruse themes. While Shakespeare uses in **King Lear**, the story of the betrayal of a father by her power-hungry daughters, T. S. Eliot takes up in **The Cocktail Party**, the seemingly simple story of the break-up of a marriage. Authors have many a times preferred to employ a familiar artistic device for 'unfamiliar' ends. So, the technique of defamiliarization is not a rare practice among authors. Besides, it helps to sustain interest in a new point of view with the help of a familiar artistic tool. By employing the plot of a 'bed-room farce', therefore, Waugh does not show any artistic weakness, as Ernest Oldmeadow[180] makes out. Instead, he reveals his ability to transform an intellectually inert artistic form into a forceful examination not only of 'humanism and modern society'[181]but also of the culpably inadequate values of the past.[182] The fortuitous contriving of the plot mocks at the Humanist tendency of attributing all that happens in history to human agency rather than God or any other unknown factor. It is a matter of chance that Tony should have chosen the dynamic Brenda, a

---

[180] Ernest Oldmeadow, "Editorial", *Tablet*, 3 Sept. 1934, 300 in ed. Martin Stannard, op. cit., 151

[181] Stephen J. Greenblatt, op. cit., 22

[182] Martin Stannard sees an autobiographical element in the theme of infidelity. He writes: 'There was, of course, a strong, if oblique, element of autobiography in it. This was the first time he had explored in detail the delicate subject of a wife's desertion and his pain and disgust at such infidelity springs over from his experience into the novel.' (ed. Martin Stannard, *op. cit.*, 23)

"'nereid' from another domain",[183]for his mate. Her choice of a bed- she 'had insisted on a modern bed'[184]- is quite suggestive of this contrast between her and her husband.

In the 'static' atmosphere of Hetton, her influence is, however, contained. This makes their friends and acquaintances, mistake their shoddy marriage for a successful one. Only Mrs. Beaver, the presiding deity of the dynamic world of London, does not think so. Giving a piece of her mind to her son, she remarks, 'I should say it was time she began to get bored. They've been married five or six years.'[185] What is needed to hasten the breaking up of this marriage is an agent from her dynamic world. Chance intervenes to contrive this. On one of his trips to London, Tony very casually asks John Beaver, the uninteresting son of Mrs. Beaver, to his place. In spite of being aware of the casualness of the invitation- 'Tony asked me in Bratt's the other night. He may have forgotten.'[186]-Beaver resolves upon visiting Tony's place. Acting on his mother's advice, he takes all precautions against Tony trying to prevent that.

With the arrival of Beaver at Hetton, Tony Last's world gets exposed to the buffetings of the dynamic world. Brenda's initial response to him is as cold as that of her husband. But with greater familiarity, she discovers a fellow- dynamic character in him. Distanced for a long time from the hectic merry-go-round of parties in the high society of London, she takes avid interest in Beaver's stories of secular London life. Tony Last, who could never have fully won Brenda's affection, gets supplanted gradually by John Beaver. Commenting on the estrangement of Brenda with Tony, Greenblatt says:

---

[183] Richard Johnstone, op. cit., 24.

[184] Evelyn Waugh, *A Handful of Dust* (Harmondsworth: Penguin, 1985), 16.

[185] Ibid., 9

[186] Ibid., 9

"The lack of communication between Brenda and Tony becomes a clear rift when Brenda tells Beaver that she really detests Hetton. "I shouldn't feel so badly about it if it were really a lively house-like my home for instance…but of course Tony's been brought up here and sees it all differently" (p.34). When on a periodic trip to London, Brenda becomes Beaver's mistress, there is no surprise and practically no explanation."[187]

Greenblatt expects Waugh to explain this, when the novelist has always been a describer and not an explainer. The novelist is not a polemicist. His job is to tell a tale, with suitable guideposts to unravel the deeper sub-textual meanings. Greenblatt, however, attributes the lack of deep psychological examination of the motives behind the breakup of marriage to the satirist's concern with characters 'not as individuals with private lives' but as symbols of societal forces. Greenblatt's contention that Waugh is dealing here with types rather than individuals, is rejected by the novelist himself when he writes, in one of his letters to Katherine Asquith it is 'Very difficult to write because for the first time I am trying to deal with normal people instead of eccentrics. Comic English character parts too easy when one gets to be thirty.'[188] The preoccupation with 'normal people', instead of eccentrics, is a clear indication of Waugh's attempt to portray individual or round characters rather than stylized or highly idiosyncratic typical characters. At yet another place, "Fan Fare", Waugh makes an assertive statement about a novelist's business with individual characters only.

"A lady in Hampstead, N.Y. asks me whether I consider my characters "typical". No, Mrs. Schultz, I do not. It is horrible of you to ask. A novelist has no business with types; they are the property of economists and politicians and advertisers and the

---

187 Stephen J. Greenblatt, op. cit., 24.

188 ed. Mark Amory, *The Letters of Evelyn Waugh* (London: Weidenfeld & Nicolson, 1980), 84.

other professional bores of our period. The artist is interested only in individuals."[189]

As Brenda and Beaver draw nearer, the ramshackle structure of Tony's static world begins to crumble. Tony renders himself comic when he mistakes Brenda's growing interest in Beaver for the gentlemanly code of courtesy towards a guest. Tony fails to see that the *weltanschauung* through which he is appraising Brenda's behaviour is the dated value system of the past, while Brenda belongs to a different world, a world in which success is courted at the altar of all ethical values. This contradiction between what appears to him and what really is leads to the enactment of the comedy of errors. In this respect, it bears resemblance to Restoration comedies like Wycherley's **The Country Wife**, in which Sir Jasper trusts Lady Fidget to Horner's company, presuming Horner to be impotent as reported to him. Yet, a basic disagreement exists between the two situations. Sir Jasper, unlike Tony Last, is very much aware of the moral corruption in London's high society. Besides, his comic deception is a direct result of his ungentlemanly and ribald pleasure in poking fun at the feigned impotence of Horner. His comicality lies, therefore, more in being out-witted than in being a pitiable victim of the designs of the world. Tony Last, in contrast, is a pitiable victim of the ruthless designs of a dynamic world, out to exploit his illusions. The difference sheds light on the genres to which the two works belong. As satire withholds pity from the person satirized, **The Country Wife**, in its unsympathetic attitude towards the characters that people it, is a satire on the follies of the Restoration Age, but **A Handful if Dust**, with its sympathetic attitude towards the deceived hero, is a comedy. By virtue of its tragicomic character, the novel, however, compares favourably with Shakespeare's <u>Othello</u>, in which the central character, Othello elicits our sympathy, like Tony Last, in the act of falling a victim to his illusions. Within the broad parameters of this commonality, there is yet a contradiction between their attitudes to the situation of marital infidelity. While

---

189 Evelyn Waugh, "Fan Fare", *Life,* 8 April 1946, in ed. Donat Gallagher, *Evelyn Waugh: A Little Order, op. cit.*, 32.

Othello, under the artful tutelage of Iago, suspects the virtuous Desdemona and the faithful Michael Cassio of treachery towards him, Tony Last, under the delusive impact of his 'static' beliefs, ignores the infidelity of his wife. Othello, however, is as static as Tony is, in his ignorance of the clever ploys of dynamic Venetians, like Iago. Mistaking Brenda's frequent trips to and long periods of stay in London for her desire to help him with his speeches, when he would stand up for election, Tony applies his static values to an essentially dynamic situation. Brenda is no gentlewoman for she makes discreet enquiries about the 'sex-life' of Beaver from her sister, Marjorie, in London.[190]

Brenda is interested in Beaver not because he fascinates her for he is 'pathetic' to her, but because he is the one man she knows from her native dynamic world. Her affection for him lacks sincerity as does Prudence's in **Black Mischief**. It is purely physical and ephemeral. Modernity has reduced human relationships to the level of ever changing fashion in apparels and/or thoughts. Association with Beaver brings out the elemental dynamic self in Brenda. She uses all her guile to make her gullible husband pay for the flat she hires from Mrs. Beaver for indulging in sexual escapades with Beaver. When Tony is on the brink of discovering her perfidy, she turns the tables on him. In a highly ironic situation, she makes Tony feel not only guilty for his intemperate behaviour but also small for her magnanimous gesture in return.

"Tony went and sat alone in front of the library fire. 'Two men of thirty', he said to himself, 'behaving as if they were up for the night from Sandhurst – getting drunk and ringing people up and dancing with tarts at the Old Hundredth… And it makes it all the worse that Brenda was so nice about it."[191]

The rapier-sharp thrust of the irony shows that static characters like Tony are no match for the dynamic characters, who swear by the virtues of "success' and 'speed' of the modern world.

---

[190] Evelyn Waugh, *A Handful of Dust,* op. cit., 40.

[191] Ibid., 76.

The arrogance and conceit of dynamic characters like Brenda can be gauged from the manner in which she takes her little victory over her 'chivalrous' husband:

"If I know Tony, he'll be tortured with guilt for weeks to come. It was maddening last night but it was worth it. He's put himself so much in the wrong now that he won't dare to feel resentful, let alone say anything, whatever I do…. He had to learn not to make surprise visits."[192]

If Tony is a foil to Seth, Brenda is the foil to Desdemona. Blinded by his static chivalric code to the dynamism of Brenda, he willingly allows himself to be deceived and thus renders himself comic. Tony's commitment to his static ideals is so total that he cannot be made to feel interested in the futile cycle of dynamic life. His wife's attempts to get him interested in some other woman fall flat as Tony does not feel impressed by Princess Jenny Abdul Akbar, an absurd product of modern secular life. Forced upon him by Brenda, he tries his best to get rid of her. When she refuses to comply with his desire, he lets her do what she wants without taking the least interest in her silly gibber.

"'I expect you'd like to see your room', said Tony. 'They'll bring tea soon'. 'No, I'll stay here. I like just to curl up like a cat in front of the fire, and if you're nice to me, I'll purr, and if you're cruel I shall pretend not to notice – just like a cat – shall I purr, Teddy?' 'Er…yes…do, please, if that's what you like doing.'"[193]

Yet, he cannot avoid feeling discomfited by her presumptuous familiarity. Not content with duping Tony, Brenda contrives with Mrs. Beaver's help to tamper with the very symbol of his faith in the past, Hetton. Mrs. Beaver arrives with her workmen to renovate a part of the house, in the modern style. Tony is unable to prevent the desecration of his ideal, as it is insisted upon by his wife. Even when the very symbol of his static faith bows down to

---

192 Ibid., 75

193 Ibid., 85

change, he does not realize the inadequacy and oddity of his static faith in a rapidly changing world.

It is the chance death of John Andrews, their only son, which suddenly brings Tony face to face with the bleak reality of his situation. Viewing the effect of his death on Brenda with the help of his obsolete chivalric code of morality, he anticipates that it would 'hurt' her very much. Jock Grant–Menzies, who is aware of Brenda's dynamic nature, strikes a realistic note by telling Tony that 'You can't ever tell what's going to hurt people'. The events that follow shatter Tony's faith in his wife ('But, you see, I know Brenda so well.'[194]). Unknown to him, Brenda is, in his wife's guise, a *femme fatale* from the dynamic world. Informed about the death of her son, she mistakes it for Beaver's and thus, despite herself, gives out to Jock, the bearer of the news, how much she loves John Beaver. It is only after Jock mentions Hetton that she realises her mistake. Still, her concern for John Beaver's safety overshadows her love for her son.

"She sat down on a hard little Empire chair against the wall, perfectly still with her hand folded in her lap…
She said, 'Tell me what happened. Why do you know about it first?'
'I've been down at Hetton since the week end?'….
She frowned not at once taking in what he was saying. 'John …John Andrew…I…oh, thank God…'
Then she burst into tears."[195]

This is a complete negation of the old moral code. The lover in her triumphs over the mother in her. Despite the seeming ambiguity of her tears, the scene brings out unambiguously Brenda's complete estrangement with the static world of Tony. Waugh deliberately leaves it up to the readers to construct the meaning out of the scene. By choosing ambivalence over clarity, Waugh makes the scene more poignant and our disgust with her behaviour more acute. Graham Martin, however, misses the

---

[194] Ibid., 109.

[195] Ibid., 118.

significance of this authorial withdrawal when he accuses Waugh of 'never… (going) beyond the external accuracy of observation'.[196]

With John Andrew gone, the bond, that held them together, snaps. This paves the way for their physical and legal separation. But, the static character that he is, Tony takes time to realize that. When Brenda breaks the news of her intention to break away from him, Tony shows comic obtuseness in mistaking initially that for their temporary departure from Hetton as a means of mitigating the impact of John Andrew's death.

"'Are you really going?'

'Yes. I can't stay here. You understand that, don't you?'

'Yes, of course. I was thinking we might both go away, abroad somewhere'. Brenda did not answer him but continued in her own line.

'I couldn't stay here. It's all over, don't you see, our life down here'.

'Darling, what *do* you mean?'"[197]

Only after she makes the meaning of her words quite explicit does Tony hear the rumbling of the imminent collapse of his static world. The painful process of Tony's confrontation with his illusions begins with it. The first illusion to be shattered is the compatibility of their two natures. Tony's talk with Jock is quite revelatory, in this regard.

"Tony said to Jock, as they sat alone after dinner, 'I've been trying to understand, and I think I do now. It's not how I feel myself, but Brenda and I are quite different in lots of ways.' "[198]

---

[196] Graham Martin, "Novelists of Society: Evelyn Waugh, Graham Greene, C. P. Snow" in ed. Boris Ford, *The New Pelican History of English Literature*, Vol 7 (Harmondsworth: Penguin, 1984), 123.

[197] Evelyn Waugh, *A Handful of Dust*, op. cit., 123.

[198] Ibid., 124.

Notwithstanding this realisation, he is far from comprehending the culpable inadequacy of his static faith in the secular values of the past. It is in the remarkably comic divorce proceedings, where Waugh inverts the scales of justice, that 'Tony's habits and illusions are systematically destroyed'.[199] In **Decline and Fall**, though Margot had made Paul a sacrificial fool, she had not become a plaintiff pitted against him. Far more dynamic than Margot, Brenda not only grafts her guilt on Tony by making him the accused in the divorce proceedings but also swaps places with him in seeking justice from the court. She succeeds in doing so because of Tony's chivalric generosity towards the weaker sex. Tony is a development over Paul Pennyfeather in that the latter's chivalry does not confront the dynamism of Margot's lot all the time. Paul accepts money from Trumpington, against all the norms of gentlemanly honour, as pointed out by Potts, whereas Tony never acquiesces with the ways of the dynamic world. In contrast, Tony Last becomes a willing scapegoat by virtue of his blind faith in the chivalric code of civility towards women. When Tony sees the point of Brenda's statement, he agrees to grant her divorce. To facilitate that, he agrees to provide evidence against himself and also agrees to pay detectives hired to collect that evidence. Brenda makes Tony agree to being seen in the company of a woman of the town so that she may prove the charge of infidelity against him for getting the divorce. To enable the detectives to collect evidence against him, he goes to the extent of taking two breakfasts and coming out as a balmy character in the eyes of the people.

"'But I want to bathe', said Winnie. 'You said I could bathe if you had two breakfasts.'
The people who had clustered round to witness Tony's discomfort, looked at one another askance.' 'Two breakfasts? Wanting to let the child bathe? The man's balmy.'"[200]

The inversion of the process of justice in this episode shows that the rationality on which the modern world prides itself and

---

[199] Stephen J. Greenblatt, op. cit., 29.

[200] Evelyn Waugh, *A Handful of Dust,* op. cit., 144

Enlightenment historiographers swear by is the first casualty in the run up to success. The world into which Tony has stepped is neither rational nor does it admit any rational interpretation. Johnstone rightly observers, 'The mechanistic modern society cannot be defined by rational means, because it is fundamentally irrational. In Waugh's comic universe, nothing is what it seems.'[201] By drawing attention to the lack of rationality in the dynamic world of modern times, Waugh castigates the Humanist belief in reasoning and that of the Enlightenment historiographers in the progress of the secular world.

Tony's tryst with the dynamic world does not end with that. The filing of divorce petition is only the beginning of this process. Once Tony supplies evidence against himself, the dynamic world plays yet another unholy trick upon him. Brenda refuses to be satisfied with the settlement of five hundred pounds a year, though she had agreed to it earlier orally. The agreement had not been put in writing despite the insistence of his solicitors, as Tony dismissed their advice saying, 'Lady Brenda's word is quite good enough'. Armed with the incriminating evidence against Tony, Lady Brenda changes colour and reneges on her promise. Once again, Waugh shows how the static value system of chivalry by which Tony swears and lives has run out of steam to protect him against the machinations of dynamic characters like Brenda. For the first time in his life, Tony has the intimation of Truth:

"His mind had suddenly become clearer on many points that had puzzled him. A whole Gothic world had come to grief… there was now no armour glittering through the forest glades, no embroidered feet on the green sward; the cream and dappled unicorns had fled."[202]

Tony realises the inadequacy of his static code of chivalry in the modern world; there are no gentlemen, nor any ladies anymore. Only men and women on the prowl to debag characters like him

---

201 Richard Johnstone, *op. cit.*, 91

202 Evelyn Waugh, *A Handful of Dust, op. cit.*, 151.

and Paul Pennyfeather. His static code has led him into a trap out of which there is only escape route: Winnie, the daughter of that lowly woman. So, he decides to stand up for himself with the help of his trump card, Winnie. He tells Reggie, Brenda's brother, that 'If you care to bring the case I shall defend it and win, but I think when you have seen my evidence you will drop it. I am going away for six month or so. When I come back, if she wishes it, I shall divorce Brenda without settlements of any kind. Is that clear?'[203] Tony's firmness stems out of his complete disappointment with Brenda's utter disregard for the chivalric code for morality and justice. So notwithstanding his new found knowledge, Tony's firmness with Brenda is still symptomatic of his static code of morality and justice, which no longer exist in the adventitious reality of the modern world.

The collapse of the static world of Hetton has the effect of orphaning Tony Last. He has two options now. The first option before him is of joining the world of secular change. For this, however, he needs to change his basic character. Being a static character, it is not possible for him to effect such a change. Having sworn by the stable values of the past all through his life, he cannot make himself to accept the morally loose values of success in the modern world at any cost. He finds that repugnant. So, he must look for an alternative world of stability and security. Tony's quest for the lost city shows up his culpable mistake of substituting the City of God[204] with a Gothic one. The elaborate picture he has in his mind about the City is that of another Hetton.

---

[203] Ibid., 152.

[204] In one of his letters to Henry Yorke, Waugh reveals the symbolism of Tony's quest for the City. He writes, 'All that quest for a city seems to me justifiable symbolism.' A. A. De Vitis is of the opinion that Waugh's symbolism is influenced by T. S. Eliot's in *The Wasteland*: 'As Tony dreams of the lost splendours of Hetton, hunting for its replica in the jungles of Brazil, Waugh makes reference to the theme of the city in *The Waste Land* and he implies that the city Tony seeks is the city of God. (A. A. De Vitis, *op. cit.,* 32)

"His mind was occupied with the City, the Shining, the many Watered, the Bright Feathered, the Aromatic Jam. He had a clear picture of it in his mind. It was Gothic in character, all vanes and pinnacles, gargoyles, battlements, groining and tracery, pavilions and terraces, a transfigured Hetton, pennons and banners floating on the sweet breeze, everything luminous and translucent…"[205]

Circumscribed in his vision by the static values of the past, Tony Last cannot think of religious change as a means to transcend the futility of both the static and the dynamic worlds. So, he tends to invest the City of God with the secular values of the past. In the words of David Lodge, his 'real religion is a feudal myth'.[206] The chivalric values that he believes in were never true, not even in their own age. The reference to the story of King Arthur is implicit in the naming of the rooms at Hetton. Despite the valorisation of chivalric code in Malory's **Morte de Arthur**, Guinevere betrays Arthur and Lancelot instead of seeking the Holy Grail as a reward for his chivalry, prefers to seek the hand of Guinevere. The chivalric ideal was as good a sign of static beliefs then as now and Tony Last, the last of the chivalric heroes, falls a prey to the snares of the same dynamic world that his forbear did. His and Arthur's mistake lies in investing secular ideals, that are susceptible to change, with the significance of *sub specie aeternitatis* reality of the hub which is beyond the reach of change and hence true for all times. Helena, on the other hand, guards against such a lapse. Her initial romantic association with the past yields place, as she matures, to the supremacy of the Roman Catholic values of life. When she embarks on a similar journey, she knows that the city she searches has to be a Catholic one. Commenting on Tony's inability to supplant Hetton by the Catholic City, Frank Kermode writes, 'The great houses of England become by an easy transition types of the Catholic City, and in this book the threatened City is Hetton; it will not prove to be continuing city.'[207] Led by the Virgil-figure of Dr.

---

[205] Ibid., 160

[206] David Lodge, op. cit., 27.

[207] Frank Kermode, *Encounter*, Nov. 1960, in ed. Martin Stannard, *op. cit.*, 283

Massinger, Tony Last heads straight into the inferno of the dynamic world of the Amazonian jungles. Tony's childhood nightmares return to him, as a consequence of his mistake of looking for the lost static world in a highly dynamic world. Henry Yorke misses the significance of Tony Last's journey into the Amazonian wilds, when he complained to Waugh that 'you spent far too much time on the trip. You have 348 pages, roughly 100 of these are concerned with Tony running away... my whole mind is clouded by the Amazon.'[208] Waugh replied that 'the Amazon stuff had to be there. The scheme was a Gothic man in the hands of savages – first Mrs. Beaver etc. then the real ones...'[209] It is quite ironic that in flying from the dynamism of British society, Tony should have chosen, in his ignorance, the gasping mouth of demonic dynamism for his static cave of refuge. The nightmarish end of Tony in the Amazonian jungles is anticipated, as Stephen Greenblatt suggests[210], in the symbolic suggestions of Rev. Tendril's comic sermons. Because of his inability to distinguish between the British laity and the troopers serving in India, Rev. Tendril often refers to 'homes and dear ones far away'.[211] Like Lear's madness, Tony's nightmarish state does not lack method. His mind flits from one situation in Britain to that in Brazil. With the help of this technique of juxtaposition, Waugh brings out the similarity of Amazonian life with the British. Tony's nightmarish state, thus, becomes a good objective correlative for Waugh's notion of the futility of secular change. The repeated juxtaposition of a scene in Brazil with a similar one in London suggests in the words of Greenblatt: "The repeated juxtaposition of a scene in Brazil and a similar scene in London makes devastatingly clear Waugh's point that the foul inhuman jungle in which Tony wanders feverishly is London transfigured."[212]

---

[208] Ed. Mark Amory, *op. cit.*, 89.

[209] Ed. Mark Amory, *op. cit.*, 88

[210] Stephen J. Greenblatt, *op. cit.*, 27.

[211] Evelyn Waugh, *A Handful of Dust,* op. cit., 32.

[212] Stephen J. Greenblatt, op. cit., 31.

Tony's nightmares, therefore, become a strong indictment of the claims of the Enlightenment and Humanist historiographers regarding the progressiveness of modernized secular societies. It is in his nightmarish state that Tony perceives the futility of his mistaken search.

"I will tell you that I have learned in the forest, where the time is different. There is no city. Mrs Beaver has covered it with chromium plating and converted it into flats... Very suitable for base love."[213]

He realises that the dynamic world has made inroads into the static world of his beliefs and destroyed it. Despite this realization, he still nurses hopes of finding at least someone who conforms to the chivalric code of morality. He finds this man in Mr. Todd, an embodiment of all that is the worst in both the cultures. There is a glint of lunacy in him, in that he imprisons Tony merely for the sake of hearing the gothic stories of Dickens, and a gleam of guile, in the that he is artful enough in putting the search parties off his scent. Both qualities are signs of an individualism that offends the order of nature. In this respect, he combines the attributes of Captain Grimes and the homicidal carpenter in **Decline and Fall**. Mr. Todd combines with these dynamic traits, the ruthlessness of a savage. In pursuing his objective of holding Tony back, he shows little compassion on his death-in-life existence. It is, therefore, ironic that Tony should have read chivalrous motives in Mr Todd's attempts to restore him to normalcy. By miscalculating Mr Todd's intentions, Tony seals his fate for ever. In order to reciprocate the false chivalry of Mr. Todd, he reads the gothic novels of Dickens to him. It is ironic that the first novel he reads to him should be **Bleak House**, the most gothic of all. Commenting on the contradiction between the values upheld in them and the values rejected in Tony's perpetual imprisonment in the bleak house of Mr. Todd, Greenblatt writes perceptively:

---

[213] Evelyn Waugh, *A Handful of Dust,* op. cit., 207

"Day after day, the readings testify to the ultimate victory of goodness and the sanctity of the personal dream – precisely those values which the hero's life-in-death refutes."[214]
The grotesque end of Tony plays up the tragic-comic consequences of the culpable mistake of investing essentially impermanent secular ideals with the significance of permanent religious values. In this respect, as Bernard Bergonzi rightly maintains, **A Handful of Dust**, looks forward to the Catholic novels of the later period.

"It is the first of his essays in 'serious' fiction, and in its treatment of the doomed Gothic hero – not yet a Catholic hero – it point forward to such ambitious later novels as **Brideshead Revisited** and, in particular, the **Sword of Honour** trilogy where Guy Crouchback, a more complex and developed version of Tony Last in the early novels (both have appropriately suggestive surnames), realises the insufficiency of the gentlemanly ideal and is stripped of his romantic illusions."[215]

The novel, in the serialized from, was also issued with a specially written ending, in *Harper's Bazaar*. It deleted the South American adventure and ended on the happy note of reconciliation. The alternative ending lacks the terrifying force of the culpability of trying to substitute the City of God with the Gothic City. This reduces the novel to the level of a mere bed-room farce from which the South American episode salvages the novel with its original ending. Barnard Bergonzi[216] has, therefore, rightly argued that any interest the novel in its alternative version may have, is more bibliographical than critical.

---

[214] Stephen J. Greenblatt, op. cit., 31.

[215] Bernard Bergonzi, *Blackfriars*, July-Aug. 1964, in ed. Martin Stannard, *op. cit.*, 159.

[216] Ibid., 160.

Notwithstanding the aristocratic lineage of the central character, much played up by Terry Eagleton[217], the novel achieves a unified universal tragic-comic vision in its rejection of both the Romantic and the Humanist tendencies of endowing life with the significance of false secular ideals. The quest for the City, in particular, strikes a Christian anti-humanist and anti-Romantic note. Brigid Brophy[218], an authority on Ronald Firbank – an object of Waugh's admiration – has very rightly drawn attention to the preoccupation of the novel with 'the romantic and eschatological' which Waugh, on his own, associated only with the Catholic novels, beginning with **Brideshead Revisited**.

In condemning Tony to the perpetual fate of reading Dickens' gothic novels one after another in a continuous cyclical motion, Waugh tears down the mask that shields from view the grotesque reality of a dynamic mode of existence. Waugh appears to be saying that all efforts directed towards secular change suck man into the grinding and absurd cyclical motion of the whirl pool of dynamic life. Thus, the comic vision of absurdity revealed in the tragicomic end of Tony Last jolts the readers out of their complacent attitude to secular change.

Scoop

Evelyn Waugh's fifth major novel, **Scoop** (1938), marks a shift in the exploration of the theme of modernity and secular change as the high ways to progress. In the novels prior to this, Waugh's comic vision of lie emerges out of the absurdity inherent in the circuitous

---

217 Terry Eagleton denies the universality of vision in Waugh's novels and accuses them of playing up the obsolete aristocratic values that Waugh adopted in his personal life. Commenting on such charges, Waugh writes, "Nor am I worried at the charge of snobbery. Class consciousness, in England, has been so much inflamed nowadays that to mention a nobleman is like mentioning a prostitute 60 years ago. The new prudes say, No doubt such people do exist but we would sooner not hear about them.' I reserve the right to deal with the kind of people I know best." (Evelyn Waugh, "Fanfare", *op. cit.*, 34.)

218 Brigid Brophy, New Statesman, 25 September 1964, in ed. Martin Stannard, *op. cit.*, 161.

course of secular change. The central characters in these novels invariably return to their original state of existence despite their best efforts to get away from it. In **Scoop**, Waugh digs deeper and unmasks the absurdity arising out of the absence of logic in secular change. The Enlightenment philosophers prided themselves on the superiority of the modern age by virtue of its reliance on human rationality as the agent of change and progress, instead of religious belief and superstition, which characterised the earlier period. By showing the glaring illogicality of events in the narrative of this novel, Waugh not only elicits our ridicule for the project of modernity and secular change as the means of progress, but also shows that the tall claims of the Enlightenment historiographers are tenuous and untenable. The sharp edge of Waugh's stinging irony is almost always directed at those who allow themselves to be deluded by the role of reason in change and progress.

Waugh adopts a gratuitous plot for narrating the incidents in this novel. Unlike the plot of the nineteenth century novel, it has a narrative that appears to have no connecting link other than that of time. This compels a comparison with the eighteenth century novel which too followed a temporal scheme in its narrative. Notwithstanding this similarity, Waugh's use of the gratuitous plot is entirely different from that of the eighteenth century novel. In the case of Waugh, the choice is deliberate. The novelist finds the gratuitous plot convenient for the purpose of exploding the myth of reason as the pillar of change and progress.

It is tempting to draw a comparison between Thomas Hardy and Waugh. Like Waugh, Thomas Hardy also employed the episodic plot for the purpose of focusing attention on the irrationality of change in universal order. Notwithstanding this similarity, there is a basic difference in their respective approaches to life. While Hardy considers both secular and religious changes fortuitous, Waugh does not. The latter does not share Hardy's pessimism with the loss of religion in life. Waugh places religion at the hub of the wheel of life and not at its orbit. Only secular change constitutes in Waugh's comic view of life a sure means to absurdity and disenchantment.

In keeping with the episodic and gratuitous nature of the narrative, Waugh employs the common comic device of mistaken identity to attract attention towards the basic irrationality of secular life. Waugh's use of this literary device, therefore, contrasts sharply with its use by other comic writers like Fielding and Congreve. In none of them is there a suggestion of this kind. It is used only to heighten the comic flavour of their works. Waugh's use of this technique is, therefore, not only appropriate but also innovative. The comic device of mistaken identity impinges the life of two characters in the novel. They are John Boot, a popular novelist and William Boot, an obscure columnist on the staff of the daily, *The Beast*. Waugh adds that both are distant cousins. John Boot wishes to be recruited by Lord Copper, the owner of *The Beast* for covering the outbreak of the civil war in Ishmaelia. He arranges for a high society woman, Mrs. Stitch to drop a hint in this regard to the proprietor of *The Beast*. Made conscious of Boot's strength as a writer by Mrs. Stitch, Lord Copper directs his Foreign News Editor, Mr. Salter, to call up Boot and recruit him for the assignment in Ishmaelia. By a strange quirk of fate, Mr. Salter calls up the wrong Boot. He calls up William Boot, instead of John Boot. Thus, the way is paved for the consequent comedy of mistaken identity. The employment of this artistic device, however, led critics like Rose Macaulay to remark: 'With it Mr. Waugh re-entered his peculiar world; it was a relief to those of us who had begun to fear that we were losing him…'[219]Waugh's own admission in the diary, dated 6 September 1924, should suffice to set off this impression. He writes:

"Rather an amusing incident has happened about the Queen's Dolls' House. One, John Pennell… was allowed… the honour of inserting some small contribution by himself…. This innocent work would have gone quite unnoticed had not Her Majesty decided… to thank all who had contributed to her toy. When it came to Mr. Pennell's turn, it was not unnaturally assumed

---

219 Rose Macaulay, *Horizon*, Dec 1946, in Martin Stannard, *op. cit.*, 202

that J. Pennell must be Joseph Pennell and a letter was accordingly sent to him in America."[220]

Rose Macaulay is one with the Enlightenment historiographers in presuming that the adventitious and fortuitous sequencing of events has to happen only in the wonderland of fantasy and not in terrestrial reality. But the entry in the diary goes to show that Waugh got the idea of the plot of this novel from a real life incident. It is the recurrent pattern of such real incidents that lends an aura of fantasy to Waugh's novels. If Rose Macaulay sees him as an entertainer churning fantasies, Graham Martin accuses Waugh of never transcending the borderline of matter-of-fact reporting, as a result of which his narrative style presents 'a state of affairs which can obstruct 'meaning' quite as effectively as an over-zealous pursuit of it.'[221]One gets the feeling that when it comes to an honest critique of Waugh, criticism has most often gone as crazy as the plots of the lesser comedies.

The comic device of mistaken identity employed in the novel has the consequence of drawing a static character out of his native static world into an alien dynamic world. William's static character is suggested by his attachment with an unchanging country life. William cherishes the insignificant job of contributing a half-column, 'Lush Places', to **The Beast,** as it enables him to stay put in the country-side ('The work was of utmost importance to him: he was paid a guinea a time and it gave him the best possible excuse for remaining uninterruptedly in the country.'[222]). As the project of modernity remains confined to the urban centres of the Western societies, the countryside continues to privilege the feudal and agrarian way of life. So, Waugh presents people living in the countryside as static characters who neither understand the ways of the dynamic characters living in urban centres nor find themselves

---

220 Evelyn Waugh in ed. Michael Davie, *The Diaries of Evelyn Waugh* (London: Weidenfeld & Nicolson, 1976), 177.

221 Graham Martin, "The Novelists of Society", in ed. Boris Ford, *op. cit*, 485.

222 Evelyn Waugh, *Scoop* (Harmondsworth: Penguin, 1985), 26.

capable of matching their wits. The dichotomy between the rural and the urban centres of society needs to be distinguished from that between Europe and Africa. David Lodge appears to have overlooked this distinction when he remarks:

As Europe is to Africa, so the metropolitan world of **The Beast** is to Boot Magna: in both pairings a sophisticated modern barbarism is discomfited by a more intransigent and deeply rooted primitivism.[223]

Though Europe and Africa represent the same side of the coin, Africa and Boot Magna, do not. Both Europe and Africa are dynamic worlds. The lack of progress in secular change removes all distinctions between a supposedly superior secular civilization and a supposedly inferior one. **The Beast** is an essential organ of the dynamic world as it is a product of its quest for secular progress. Boot Magna, William's residence in the countryside, in contrast, is suggestive of the static world's aloofness to change.

William's predilection for country life is, therefore, a sign of his static character. In this regard, he occurs in the long list of static characters we have met so far. Like them, he renders himself comic when he steps into a hostile dynamic world. However, unlike them, he is an enlightened static character. He is very much aware of his static nature and the incompatibility of his nature with the dynamic world of London. William's aversion for urban life and preference for country life flows out of this awareness. William, therefore, escapes the fate of his predecessor – static characters, even though he is caught in the dynamic world for some time.

The comedy of mistaken identity sets into motion once William receives the summons from **The Beast**. In one of his previous contributions, Priscilla had substituted 'the crested grebe' for his 'badger'. This had outraged the veracity of his statement. William suspects that he has, perhaps, been called to give explanation for this lapse. He does not know that the Foreign News Editor, Mr. Salter, is waiting to recruit him as **The Beast**'s special correspondent in war-torn Ishmaelia. Set against the background

---

[223] David Lodge, *op. cit.*, 24-25.

of this reality, William's attempts to discover some means of defence against Lord Copper's admonition look ridiculous and comic. Waugh writes:

"By the time he reached Westbury he had sketched out a little scene for himself, in which he stood resolutely in the board-room defying the doctrinaire zoology of Fleet Street... 'Lord Copper', he was saying, 'no man shall call me a liar unchastised. The great crested grebe does hibernate.'"[224]

If Waugh renders William comic for his ignorance of the irrational working of the dynamic world, he comes down equally well upon Mr. Salter for epitomizing in himself the irrationality of the dynamic world. Describing his irrational attitude to life, Waugh writes:

"If a psychoanalyst testing his associations, had suddenly said to Mr. Salter the word 'farm', the surprising response would have been 'Bang', for he had once been blown up and buried while sheltering in a farm in Flanders. It was his single intimate association with the soil. It had left him with the obstinate though admittedly irrational belief that agriculture was something highly alien and highly dangerous."[225]

The absurdity of Salter's behaviour grows out of his Enlightenment belief in reading rationality into every sequence of events, including those that are purely chronological. Waugh seems to be hitting out at the tendency of the rationalists to stretch rationality even beyond its permissible limits of probability.

In the meeting between Boot and Salter, each confronts his own illusion. Salter has been planning for it since long. He has even collected information about things that may possibly interest a countryman. Each of these things is distasteful to Salter. But as he has to win over William for the assignment in Ishmaelia, he submits

---

[224] Evelyn Waugh, *Scoop, op. cit.*, 23

[225] Ibid., 23.

to the ordeal. Nervousness is writ large on Salter's face when he opens his conversation with him. Waugh writes:

"Mr. Salter planned a frank and disarming opening. 'How are your roots, Boot?' It came out wrong. William glumly awaiting some fulminating rebuke, started and said, 'I beg your pardon?'
'I mean brute', said Mr. Salter.
William gave it up. Mr. Salter gave it up. They sat staring at one another, fascinated helpless."[226]

Waugh renders Salter comic for his irrational and imagined fear of meeting a countryman. It is only after he learns that William has no outlandish tastes and that he is a normal person like him that he feels at ease in his company. The dawning of the truth endows the comic character with a new found confidence, which turns him into a hero. This is the stuff that comedy is made up of and even in the lesser comedies one gets to have a taste of this kind of comedy.

Once Salter feels composed, he proceeds to shatter William's illusion. Salter broaches the matter of reporting the incidents in Ishmaelia for **The Beast**. William sees in it the punishment of 'transportation' for his small mistake. He, therefore, labours to present his defence. It is only after Salter tells him that he would have to work there only for some time and that too for a substantial salary that William feels easy. As the acceptance of the assignment would imply shifting out of Boot Magna, the symbolic representation of his static world, William refuses the offer. His stubborn resistance makes Salter desperate. It is at this moment that William discloses unwittingly his vulnerable point.

"'Is there nothing you want?'
'D' you know, I don't believe there is. Except to keep my job in 'Lush Places' and go on living at home.'"[227]

---

[226] Ibid., 27.

[227] Ibid., 33.

Salter is quick enough to exploit this weakness to his advantage. Accordingly, he uses this information as a weapon against William.

"'Oh, but Lord Copper expects his staff to work wherever the best interests of the paper call them. I don't think he would employ anyone of whose loyalties he was doubtful, *in any capacity.*'

'You mean if I don't go to Ishmaelia I get the sack?'

'Yes', said Mr. Salter."[228]

William surrenders to Mr. Salter in the extreme fear of losing his job. Should he defy Lord Copper's wishes, he would be deprived of writing for **The Beast**. Without it, William would lose the opportunity of staying uninterruptedly in his static world of Boot Manga. Ironically enough, William's job not only helps William to stay on in his native world, it also makes him vulnerable to the irrationality of the dynamic world. Thus, despite his awareness of his true identity, William is drawn into the vortex of dynamic life.

William's elevation to the rank of a special correspondent is a superb act of comedy. The honour that should have been done to John Boot goes to William Boot. More than that, the comedy is enhanced by their contrasting attitudes also. While John Boot is much too eager to have it, William wants somehow to get rid of it. The cardinal principle of logic stands outraged here. So, when the reader laughs at this comic situation, he also ridicules the Enlightenment and Humanist historiographers who see reason and logic as the guiding forces of change in the secular world. Waugh, however, does not allow our ridicule to fade into satiric condemnation as he constantly engages our sympathy for William and Salter.

Having seen for ourselves the irrational working of the dynamic world, we may now turn our attention to the extent of absurdity implicit in the illogical nature of the Ishmaelite strife. Ishmaelia presents a picture of raw decadence in that successive missionary groups have failed in civilizing its barbaric inhabitants.

---

[228] Ibid., 34.

Out of their inability to root out barbarism from the Ishmaelite society, the advanced 'European Powers' have written it off their maps. In Waugh's view of life, such a society occupies a place farthest from the hub of the wheel of life and is, as a consequence, most dynamic. It is pertinent to recall here that the degree of instability is felt the most on the outermost orbit of the revolving wheel of life. Ishmaelia presents an unabashed portrait of dynamism compared to the dynamic societies of the West which hide it beneath the veneer of civilization.

Left to itself, Ishmaelia has formed into a republic. The lack of any 'tie of language, history, habit or belief' has left it with no other alternative. The republic of Ishmaelia has been ruled by the Jacksons who have enacted every year the farce of elections to weather any resistance to their rule from the people. The people of this African state continue to remain as savage as they were before. The disorder within the social fabric of this state assumes international dimensions when one of the Jacksons, Mr. Smiles Soumes, rebels against the family. Only one quarter Jackson and three quarters Ishmaelite, he presents himself as a champion of the Ishmaelite cause. In order to obtain the support of the Western powers, he concocts a ridiculous racial theory in favour of his claim for the control of the Ishmaelite government. He declares that though the savage Ishmaelite were originally white, yet owing to constant exposure to the sun, they had grown red. In comparison, he makes out the Jacksons to be Negroes. Accordingly, he starts a White Shirt movement against their so-called Negro-government. Traces of Jonathan Swift's in **Gulliver's Travels** are discernible here. Like Swift, Waugh is ridiculing here the idea of democratic politics. However, more than that, he is exposing the inadequacy of logic itself. Waugh is drawing attention here to the idea that logic is a double edged sword which may be used to cut its own self. The excessive faith of Enlightenment and Humanist historiographers in its civilizing force is ridiculed through the subversive logic given in the narrative of the racial theory. An avowed Roman Catholic, Waugh veered to the Roman Catholic thesis of reason being an unreliable instrument of verifying the veracity of a fact. Unaided by divine grace, it leads one astray. Thus, the rejection of the role of reason is not at all a sign of valuelessness in Waugh. As secular change rests on the edifice of human reason, Waugh only wishes to draw attention towards the absurdity of achieving progress through secular change.

Aboard the ship, bound for Ishmaelia, William acquires his first tips about the absurdity inherent in the dynamic world of journalism from his follow-journalist, Corker. William gets to know how Wenlock Jakes demonstrated the power of the press in the modern world with his false reports. Corker tells William how Wenlock Jakes was instrumental in starting an armed conflict with his false reportage. Despite the lack of any real basis for Jake's stories, the faith of the governments of the world and that of the people in the validity of press reports was so great that "Government stocks dropped, financial panic, state of emergency declared, army mobilized, famine, mutiny and in less than a week there was an honest to god revolution under way, just as Jakes said. There's the power of the press for you."[229]

The chain of these irrational incidents does not end here. It continues and concludes most illogically in the award of Nobel Peace Prize to Jake for his role in starting the war.

The succeeding narrative of William's metamorphosis from a non-descript half column writer in **The Beast** to a celebrated professional investigative journalist, a variation on Wenlock Jake's rise to international fame, is a stinging indictment of the lack of logic and rationality in the affairs of a world that has hitched itself to the bandwagon of the Enlightenment project of modernity and secular change. Waugh goes on to narrate at length as to how every scoop of Boot is a testimony of his incompetence as a professional journalist and yet celebrated by the world and his peers as a sign of his maturity as a seasoned journalist. Waugh's persistent preoccupation with the narration of logically inconsistent events resembles to some extent that of Franz Kafka in novels such as **The Trial** and **The Castle**. In **The Trial,** Joseph K. in spite of having

[229] Ibid., 67.

committed no offence is arrested one morning. Upon his persistence with trying to know the causes thereof, he is warned that it shall make his case more complicated and stern. He must, therefore, concern himself only with defending himself. However, while it is difficult even to divine the cause hidden behind the irrational pattern of events in the narrative in Kafka, it is not so in Waugh.

The story of William's success as a journalist begins with his chance meetings with Bannister, Vice Consul at the British Legation and with Katchen, a woman of uncertain nationality, putting up at Frau Dressler's pension. When most of his fellow journalists have been making frantic efforts to reach Laku where they believe Smiles Saum, the leader of the rebellion, to be, he stumbles upon a real scoop, due to no personal or professional merit of his. When the other journalists head Laku-wards for their cherished scoop, only William does not. William gets to know from Bannister that though the Ishmaelite word, Laku, appears on the maps of Ishmaelia, it does not indicate any real place as it means, 'I don't know'. In other words, the place simply does not exist and that the journalists have been befooled. Waugh shows how reality cannot be taken at its face value in the secular world and one who does so, runs the risk of becoming the butt of comic ridicule like these journalists. By having stumbled on this piece of information, William stays on in Jacksonburg, the locale of future anarchy and reaps profit out of it as a journalist. That chance not personal merit secures William the fame of a good investigative journalist becomes clear from his inability to follow the hints supplied by Bannister who asks him to watch out for a Russian agent and to keep an eye on Dr. Benito, the man who insists on William's departure for Laku. William does neither. Instead, he whiles away his time in the company of Katchen. He even fails to look up his mail which has been growing insistent. When Bannister tells him that his paper is worried about his safety and silence, he replies most irresponsibly:

"PLEASE DON'T WORRY QUITE SAFE AND WELL IN FACT RATHER ENJOYING THINGS WEATHER

IMPROVING WILL CABLE AGAIN IF THERE IS ANY NEWS YOURS BOOT."[230]

Obviously enough, his cable has the effect of driving Salter mad. When he has been waiting for some breaking news from him, all he gets from him is news about his welfare and his enjoying his stay in Ishmaelia, as if he has gone there as a tourist. To add salt to the injury, all that he further reports from Ishmaelia is about weather improving there ('Weather improving', said Mr. Salter. '*Weather improving.* He's been in Jacksonburg ten days, all he can tell us is that the weather is improving.'[231]). Salter's impatience arises out of his knowledge that William was as unsuited to the job as the trick cyclist, appointed by Lord Copper, was to that of a Sports Editor. The irrational course of events reduces his plight to that of comic helplessness. Waugh shows here that the dynamic characters themselves at time become victims of the irrationality of their world. In **Black Mischief,** he had already shown how Seth was victimized ruthlessly by the instability he himself created.

Lest Salter should derive satisfaction out of having been wise enough to gauge William's true abilities, Waugh introduces a chance breakthrough in the latter's journalistic career. Katchen, the woman to whom William has become attracted, brings news of the President's house arrest by 'Doctor Benito and the Russian and the black secretaries who came from America'. William's incompetence as a journalist is accentuated by his inability to understand its significance. He dispatches the information to his paper only to assuage their demand for some news. Bringing out the illogical imposition of a value of momentous importance on this act, Waugh writes:

"No one observing that sluggish and hesitant composition could have guessed that this was a moment of history… held up as a model to aspiring pupils of Correspondence Schools of Profitable

---

[230] Ibid., 138.

[231] Ibid., 138.

Writing, perennially fresh in the jaded memories of a hundred editors; the moment when Boot began to make good."[232]

Far from being a model worthy of citing, William's first scoop is the saga of incompetence and indifference to duty. He realizes little the value of the news he is dispatching to his paper. Besides, he has made no effort to obtain it. He has merely stumbled upon it. William's accidental success is an indication of the illogical nature of the process of secular change, for those who really deserve it are deprived of it. Waugh, therefore, conveys unequivocally the absurdity of attributing progress in the secular world to any logical cause.

William's second scoop is again indicative of his incompetence as a professional journalist. As the political unrest in Ishmaelia grows, Katchen is arrested and some men approach William for taking possession of the stones he had bought from her. He refuses to part with them and the men have to go back empty-handed despite their best efforts to gain their possession. For the sake of keeping them in safe custody, he takes them to Bannister's place where William stumbles upon the true worth of those stones. He learns that what he had been mistaking for stones are in fact gold. Believing William to have been sacked by **The Beast,** Bannister updates Boot unhesitatingly with not only the role of gold but also with that of Russia in the political turmoil of Ishmaelia. Bannister tells William:

"It's been between smiles and Benito now and it looks to me as if Benito had won hands down.... We stand to lose quite a lot if they start a Soviet state here ... Now you've stopped being a journalist I can tell you these things."[233]

William's response to this discovery is characteristically like that of a static person. While a dynamic character would have thought of exploiting it to his own personal advantage, he does not.

---

[232] Ibid., 146.

[233] Ibid., 154.

He thinks of his country and his lady-love, Katchen (Love, patriotism, zeal for justice, and personal spite flamed within him as he sat at his typewriter and began his message. One finger was not enough: ne used both hands.'[234]). Loyalty to one's nation and rendering help to a woman in distress constitute two essential features of the outdated and ideal chivalric code of feudal life. Even the money that he gives to the clerk at the wireless station is not an act of his dynamism but one of static nature as it is rooted in William's chivalrous concerns. His action, therefore, is not unlike that of Tony Last in A Handful of Dust, when he refuses to play ball with his deceitful wife. When Tony's wife tries to act smart with him by using the evidence willingly given by him to her against him for extracting a huge maintenance from him, Tony's chivalric sense is so deeply offended that he turns the tables against her by threatening to blow her evidence away and denying her divorce too. Similarly, seeing the ramifications of the happenings in Ishmaelia for his native country, Boot is transformed into a crusader of sorts, ready to use any trick to protect his country's interests.

When William's dispatch reaches Salter's office, it confounds his confidence in his ability of judging. Waugh draws comic blood, when he makes Salter confess his inability to judge people.

"'He's all right. Lord Copper knew best.' … 'You know', he said meditatively, 'it's a great experience to work for a man like lord Copper. Again and again I' ve thought he was losing grip. But always it turns out he knew best. What made him spot Boot? It's a sixth sense… real genius."[235]

Salter's new-found confidence in Lord Copper's genius is equally ridiculous for it ignores the reality behind William's second scoop. He thus looks comic, in the Platonic sense of the word. Yet, it would be too much to say that he has been satirized for satire evokes moral indignation; Salter in his comic plight evokes our sympathy over his ridiculous ignorance of truth. So, the irrational

---

[234] Ibid.,155.

[235] Ibid., 157.

nature of secular change lends a comic glow to the novel. We do not find this in Thomas Hardy where the increased role of chance only gives a gloomy and melancholy air to the situations described.

While the professional journalists going 'Lakuward' warm their pates in the African sun for nothing, William, the novice journalist, is an accidental witness to yet another series of cataclysmic incidents, which provide him material for his third scoop, The brief spell of superimposed order in the state of Ishmaelia is over. The barbaric forces held in the leash so far, burst forth with the complicity of the dynamic world of the economically developed nations, which have an eye on its natural resources. A revolution is hatched by them in alliance with the anti-civilizational forces. The thin veneer of civilization that the Jacksons had given to this Africa state is torn down. Ishmaelia returns to its original state of barbarity and anarchy. Waugh conveys the futility of secular change as a means to progress in the circular history of Ishmaelia. Seeing the shape of things to come, William instinctively sings Uncle Theodore's pet refrain in the manner of a character in a Greek chorus ('Change and decay in all around I see', he sang softly, almost unctuously. It was the favourite tune of his uncle Theodore.[236]). The revolution is short-lived, for Baldwin, the man who arrives on the chaotic scene of Ishmaelia like a *deus ex machina*, engineers a counter-revolution in a way that mocks at the ideological considerations often attributed to such movements. Eric Olafsen in a drunken state, contrived by Baldwin, goes to the stage from where Dr. Benito is issuing his revolutionary orders. When he lifts the chair against Benito, the latter jumps down from the balcony to his death on the ground for 'the traditional ineradicable awe of the white man' frighten him too much. With the dethroning of Dr. Benito, the crowd begins chanting the counter-revolutionary slogan of 'Jackson. Jackson, Jackson'.

William profits from his accidental proximity with Baldwin, in composing his third important dispatch. Baldwin is no other than

[236] Ibid., 165-166.

the man who William had helped by granting permission to board the plane which was to carry him on his journalistic mission. "'No', said a gentleman behind him. 'If you would not resent my cooperation, I think I can compose a dispatch more likely to please my good friend Copper'.

Mr. Baldwin sat at William's table and drew the typewriter towards himself. He inserted a new sheet of paper… and began to write with immense speed:

MYSTERY FINDNCIER RECALLED EXPOITS RHODES LAWRENCE TODAY SECURING VAST EAST AFRICAN CONCESSION…"[237]

Not only does Baldwin offer William the scoop of his life but he also writes it out for him. When the news of Boot's success in sending breaking news from Ishmaelia reaches Lord Copper's ears, he thinks himself fortunate for having listened to Mrs. Stitch's advice. Poor Lord Copper does not know that the Boot reporting from Ishmaelia is different from the Boot recommended by Mrs. Stitch. As if this were not enough, Waugh gives the story another twist whereby the two Boots once again exchange places. Lord Copper plans to host a banquet in Boot's honour. He also requests the Prime Minister to recommend Boot for knighthood by the Queen of England. Lord Copper's recommendation is mistaken in the Prime Minister's office for John Boot's knighthood, instead of William Boot's. So, his name, instead of William's, appears in the list of persons to be honoured by Her Majesty, the Queen of England. The mistake is discovered too late to be rectified. Consequently, John Boot steps into the shoes of William Boot, completing the circle of the game of mistaken identities. The preponderance of chance in the swapping of places between the two Boots highlights the gratuitous nature of secular change, hitting out at the Enlightenment historians' faith in the sovereignty of reason in effecting secular change and progress. The illogical course of secular change revealed here also drives home the comic

[237] Ibid., 177.

absurdity of seeking the improvement of one's lot through secular change. William is, however, immune to this conspiracy of fate as he has already taken a decision against any more truck with the dynamic world of journalism and London. It is evident from his merciless response to the handsome offers of employment in big newspaper establishment.

"William released them, one by one as he read them, at the open window. The rush of air whirled them across the charred embankment to the fields of stubble and stacked corn beyond."[238]

William's refusal to be seduced not only by the blandishments of "wealth and elegance" but also by that of the 'power' of press does not, however, imply a step towards real progress as they do in the case of Charles Ryder and Guy Crouchback for he re-enters the sheltered cocoon of his static world at Boot Magna, after his disenchantment with the dynamic world. The Evelyn Waugh hero has not by now realized the significance of the cloister in getting away from the dynamic world and forging ahead on the path of progress.[239] It is left to his successors to comprehend that vision and carry it out. A.A. De Vitis has rightly pointed out this inadequacy in William Boot thus:
"William is incapable of coping with the force he has come to understand. To invade the world he would need a banner, and the banner that flies over Boot Magna is in tatters. It is left to Guy Crouchback to invade the world under a banner still whole enough to demand the allegiance of the many."[240]

---

[238] Ibid., 186.

[239] Commenting on the significance of the cloister in the modern age, Evelyn Waugh writes in the "Foreword" to *Elected Silence* by Thomas Merton: 'In the natural order the modern world is rapidly being made uninhabitable by the scientists and politicians. We are back in the age of Gregory, Augustine and Boniface and in compensation the Devil is being disarmed of many of his former enchantments. Power is all he can offer now; the temptation of wealth and elegance no longer assail us. As in the Dark Ages the cloister offers the sanest and the most civilized way of life.' (Evelyn Waugh, in ed. Donat Gallagher, *The Essays, Articles and Reviews of Evelyn Waugh, op. cit.*, 369.)

[240] A. A. De Vitis, *op. cit.*, 36.

The comic vision of life that grows out of this novel is shaped and structured by the absurdity implicit in the logical inconsistency of secular change. The successive scoops of William indicate that a person need not deserve what he gets. Chance and accident rule the roost in the anarchic dynamic world. Waugh shows that the immense faith reposed in the role of reason in effecting a transformation of human society is comically unjustified. Without divine grace, reason is an inadequate guide to reality, and hence, an ineffective means of achieving real progress. But the Enlightenment and Humanist historiographers refuse to see this. So, their point of view is ridiculed.

Brigid Brophy, whose other remarks on Waugh have been quite illuminating, gives evidence of less than adequate comprehension of the comic vision of absurdity implicit in the illogical process of secular change when she argues:

"**Scoop** has always struck me as a mere, though entertaining, after-flutter of the fine imaginative flight which had produced **Black Mischief**; it is a **Black Mischief** without the great Seal set on it, and starting from a spring-board of mistaken identity which is not quite bouncy enough to get the invention into the air."[241]

Like her, Christopher Hollis also shows incomprehension of the abstruse comic vision in this novel, when he argues that '**Scoop** is concerned with how Europeans, who know nothing of their culture except its superficial patter, make use of Africans for their absurd purposes.'[242] In contrast, Martin Stannard shows an appreciable grasp of the novel's thematic line of intention. He observes:

"The underlying notion of the absurdity of the rationalist viewpoint… is another rendering of a continuous theme in

---

[241] Brigid Brophy, *New Statesman*, 23 Sept 1964, 450, in ed. Martin Stannard, op. cit., 161

[242] Christopher Hollis, *Evelyn Waugh* (London: Longmans, Green & Co., 1954), 14.

Waugh's fiction. The world is not, he suggests, as Lucas Dockery or Seth would suppose, a composite of discernible facts; without the dimension of 'spiritual' experience, human behaviour is seen to be unreasonable."[243]

The examination of the incidents in the novel reveals an underlying circular pattern in the plot of the novel. A mistake had thrust William, at the beginning of the novel, into the inimical world of dynamic London and Ishmaelia. A similar mistake, at the end of the novel, redeems him from its absurdity. The circular nature of the plot of the novel calls up the central image of the wheel of life. The relentless circular motion of the wheel of life brings one to the original point despite all efforts to progress. The circular nature of secular change leaves no room for progress as it brings one back to one's original place. Thus, Waugh conveys that life lived at the secular plane does not hold out the promise of progress. It displays a sheer temporal movement. Logical movement is conspicuous by its absence for the circular nature of secular change is scarcely amenable to logical evaluation. Thus, the comic vision of life rooted in the logically inconsistent movement of secular change is underlined by the circular plot of the novel. The unique combination of form and content in the novel speaks of Waugh's artistic brilliance even in the early years of his artistic career.

Put Out More Flags

Waugh's sixth major novel, **Put Out More Flags** (1942) also remains preoccupied with debunking the idea of progress as publicised in the discourse of modernity by showing the comic ridiculousness of the Humanist and Enlightenment historiographers' claims of progress through secular change. Set against the background of World War II, the novel depicts a world, in which the forces of disruption and deceit roam without impunity to ambush and 'debag' static characters, who still continue to live in

---

243 Ed. Martin Stannard, "Introduction", *Evelyn Waugh: The Critical Heritage, op. cit.*, 30-31.

the Elysium of their make-believe world of chivalric values. Unaware of the extent of craft and guile in the dynamic characters, the static characters are rendered comic in the act of trusting them. Thus, Waugh exposes the ridiculous insufficiency of the static mode of life to take on the challenge of the valueless dynamic world. Appreciation for the dynamic world is, however, withheld as its triumphs are a sign not of progress but of valuelessness and barbarity.

The turbulent time of war serves as an appropriate temporal setting to the expression of this idea. The outbreak of war symbolizes, in Waugh, a return to the state of barbarity. In the imagery of the wheel of life, it is comparable to the extreme degree of instability felt on its outermost orbit. Attention may here be invited to the points of similarity and distinction between Nietzsche and Evelyn Waugh. Nietzsche too sees history as a story of decadence, a falling away from the great into the trivial and finally, into nihilism. But, he differs from Waugh in so far as he believes that Christianity has played an important role in this process of decadence and debility. Waugh's decadent world is the dynamic world which has snapped its ties with religion in favour of its tryst with secular change as the Holy Grail of progress.

As the comic element in this novel grows largely out of the deception played on the ignorant static characters by the knowing dynamic characters, is is not unexpected that Waugh should have chosen the mercurial Basil Seal, the most dynamic of all his characters, as the chief protagonist of this novel. So, Christopher Hollis misses the point when he complains against the suitability of Basil Seal to the world of this novel, in the following words:

"The trouble with Basil Seal is that, if we consider him as a real character, he is too odious to be funny. Had he been content to remain a character in one of Mr. Waugh's earlier novels ... we could have laughed at him as a mere formula of villainy without any attempt to pass a moral judgment on a person. We can tolerate him even in Azania. But in a real world, alongside real and suffering people at a great crisis of our history, he is too horrible."[244]

Even when he admits that the 'bulk of the novel is concerned with Basil Seal's attempt to extract profit and amusement out of the war',[245] he does not see the point of his suitability. An attempt has been made in this direction by Alan Pryce-Jones and Lionel Stevenson. Alan Pryce-Jones feels that the 'English world is neatly, and to some extent justly, divided into those who get away with it and those who don't by a judge who has a weakness for the former'.[246] By classifying the English society thus, he comes very near the division of the world of Waugh's fiction into dynamic and static characters. But, when he attributes the victory of the former over the latter to Waugh's sympathy for the former, he appears to disregard the purpose of such a division in this work. Lionel Stevenson does not agree with Alan Pryce-Jones. He maintains that Waugh's attitude towards the former group is by no means that of connivance. Rather, the group is indicted for its lack of sincerity towards friends and mercilessness towards the harmless rural residents.

"...while in charge of prisoners of war on a troopship, Waugh was able to write **Put out More Flags**, an angry *expose* of civilians who were profiting by the war. Appropriately, the central character is the ineffable Basil Seal, now insidiously reporting innocent friends to the authorities as Nazi plotters and blackmailing rural residents by threatening to billet a detestable family of slum evacuees in their houses."[247]

---

[244] Christopher Hollis, op. cit., 19.

[245] Ibid., 18.

[246] Alan Pryce-Jones, *New Statesman*, 11 April 1942, in ed. Martin Stannard, *op. cit.*, 216.

[247] Lionel Stevenson, *The History of the English Novel*, Vol. 11, (New York: Barnes & Noble Inc., 1967), 357.

Lionel Stevenson's defence, howsoever favourable, suffers from taking a period-interest in the novel and Waugh has been accused of it by Martin Standard too.

"Few would now agree with those who considered it Waugh's finest achievement of the period 1928-42. Although still entertaining, the specific contemporary relevance perhaps leaves it with the flavour of a periodic piece relying for its maximum effect upon a detailed knowledge of events beyond the text."[248]

Both the critics adopt an attitude similar to what we can find in Christopher Hollis, as they deny the anti-Humanist significance of the incidents concerning Basil Seal. They overlook the fact that the conflict between the dynamic and static characters brings out the inconsequence of secular life, whether dynamic or static, an attitude that stems out of Waugh's Christian anti-humanism.

It is Sonia, who anticipates Basil's comic adventures during the period of war: 'I expect Basil will have the most tremendous adventures. He always did in peace time. Goodness knows what he will do in war'.[249] Implicit in this comment is Sonia's recognition of Basil's innate tendency to unleash disruptive forces. True to his sister's expectations, Basil has the best of time during the war. Not for him the military discipline of a recruit, but the license to harass peace-loving rural folks and an opportunity to fatten his purse out of their discomfiture.

Basil wages his first war against the peace-loving static people of Malfrey. He goes there to avoid his mother who is bent upon seeing him recruited as a subaltern. His sister, Barbara, who lives in Malfrey, has been made the billeting officer for her district. When he visits his sister, she is wrestling with an intractable problem. She cannot find a family who would accept the Connolly children. No family in the village is ready to accept them as they have earned notoriety for their destructive potential. Indeed, they

---

248 Ed. Martin Stannard, *op. cit.*, 33.

249 Evelyn Waugh, *Put Out More Flags* (Harmondsworth: Penguin, 1985), 38.

epitomise the forces of anarchy, disorder and irrationality, which have been let loose by the outbreak of war in the dynamic world. In the war between the unscrupulous and unpredictable dynamic characters, on the one hand, and the unsuspecting peace loving people of Malfrey, the former win hands down. The static people of Malfrey are no match for the unpredictably destructive Connolly children. Their inability to gauge the extent to which the Connolly children can go renders them comic. Plato[250] regards ignorance as one of the primary reasons for rendering a person comic. The static people of Malfrey exhibit ignorance in no small measure even as they become the butt of our comic ridicule.

One of the first families to fall a prey to these agents of the destructive dynamic world is Mr. Mudge's. Seeing Mr. Mudge kill a goose one day, Michy, the second Connolly child kills all six of them and also, the old cat. As for the others, Marlene, the third child goes about soiling every place in the house, while Doris, the eldest, tries to seduce not only young Willie but even Mr. Mudge. Mr. Mudge's old woman shuts herself up and refuses to come down until they have been despatched from their home. Such is the terror struck in her mind. Appalled with their unimaginably unbecoming conduct, Mr. Mudge returns them to Barbara, with the complaint:

"If you ask me, mum, she's [Doris] the worst of the lot .... Soft about the men she is, mum. Why she even comes making up to me and I'm getting on to be her grandfer. She won't leave our Willie alone not for a minute, and he's a bashful boy our Willie and he can't get on with the work, her always coming after him."[251]

Only a person as dynamic as they themselves are can control them. Such a person arrives at Malfrey in the person of Basil Seal. Unlike the peace-loving static people of Malfrey, Basil does not find them a disturbing encumbrance. Like any dynamic person, he senses in the situation an opportunity of making quick money. The kind of contribution that he makes to the war is not unlike the Nazi

---

250 Plato, *Philebus* (Harmondsworth: Penguin, 1982), 1-83

251 Evelyn Waugh, *Put Out More Flags*, *op. cit.*, 82.

diplomacy of push, appeasement, agitation and blackmail ('Like Nazi diplomacy it postulated for success a peace-loving, orderly and honourable world in which to operate.[252]). The world of Malfrey is of exactly that kind. It is the static world, still clinging to the old world charm of gentlemanly ethics and honour that modernity has steamrolled over with its Enlightenment agenda. So, in his first war-effort, Basil employs the Connolly children as grenades against unwary static characters such as Mr. Harkness. In the war of wits between the dynamic Basil Seal and the static Mr. Harkness, Basil scores over the latter by virtue of the comic inadequacy of the gentlemanly ethics of the bygone age. Waugh highlights the static predisposition of Mr. Harkness in the following words:

"...his years of waiting had been haunted by only one fear; that he would return to find the place 'developed'.... But modernity spared North Grappling; he returned to find the place just as he had first come upon it, on a walking tour, late in the evening..."[253]

Mr. Harkness' response to change is indicative of the outlook shared by all static characters. But, poor Mr. Harkness is not aware that the dynamic world has already made inroads into the static world of Malfrey in the guise of Basil Seal and the Connolly children. So, when Basil presents himself as the billeting officer charged with the responsibility of housing 'evacuees' at Mr. Harkness' place, the poor man misunderstands the word, 'evacuees' to connote simply townsfolk in search of sanctuary. Like any gentleman, he is quick to cooperate and to accept the rent, quoted by Basil in the local paper.

"'May I ask what *are* your friends?'
'Well, I suppose you might call them evacuees.'
Mr. and Mrs. Harkness laughed pleasantly at the little joke.
'Townsfolk in search of sanctuary, eh?'
'Exactly.'

---

[252] Ibid., 49.

[253] Ibid., 91.

'Well, they will find it here, eh, Agnes?'''[254]
In the war between the knowing Basil and the ignorant Harknesses, the couple's innocuous laughter at the 'little joke' soon turns into a nightmare when they get to know the real identity of the 'townsfolk' and Basil Seal. Their 'little joke' becomes a trap out of which there is no easy escape.

"'Eight shillings and six pence?' said Mr. Harkness.
'I 'm afraid there's been some misunderstanding.'
Five, Six, *Seven.* Here it comes. Bang!
'Perhaps I should have told you at once. I am the billeting officer. I have three children for you in the car outside.' It was magnificent. It was war."[255]

Basil is enacting here, on a small scale, the war waged by Nazi forces against the other unsuspecting European powers. While Hitler is annexing countries, Basil is busy fleecing the unwary static residents of Malfrey. The Harknesses are able to rid themselves of the Connolly children only after they have disgorged thirty pounds to Basil as a price for that. More victims follow and his earnings from the war keep on swelling. The problem-children become means of profit in his hands. The repeated victories of Basil over the static people of Malfrey show how the outbreak of war unleashes unscrupulous dynamic characters like predatory animals out to profit from the deception they practise on static characters. To be static, therefore, is a particular disadvantage in such a chaotic world. Waugh exposes the comic inadequacy of the static ideals of honesty and honour from the standpoint of the ground reality of the valuelessness of the dynamic modern world. At the same time, as his comedy is tinged with sympathy for the befooled static characters, he comes down equally heavily upon the valueless dynamic world from the standpoint of Christian Humanism. Thus, the success of the dynamic character, by no means, implies upholding of the lack of principles and values that dynamic stands

---

[254] Ibid., 94.

[255] Ibid., 95

for. As Waugh himself once said, it is better to be static than dynamic.

"It is better to be narrow-minded than to have no mind, to hold limited and rigid principles than none at all… to put up with what is wasteful and harmful with the excuse that there is "good in everything" ... means an inability to distinguish between good and bad."[256]

What Waugh is hitting out at here is the promiscuity of thought fathered by the individualism of Enlightenment thought. Individualism leading to atomization and self-seeking creates a heady brew which befuddles people, making them resort to deceit and chicanery in pursuit of their petty personal goals. Such is the effect generated by the pursuit of progress through secular change. Waugh is clearly adopting a post-modernist stance, while consciously shunning the post-modernist narrative style. In the incidents surrounding the Connolly children, Waugh is as much critical of Basil Seal as he is of the tendency to look for permanence in the old order of things. By making us sympathise with the static characters victimised by Basil, Waugh shows where his sympathies lie. Christopher Hollis completely misses the significance of these incidents in the narrative scheme of the novel, when he considers them 'though ingenious', but not, 'to tell the truth, especially amusing.'[257]

The second string of Basil's comic adventures begins in London with his success in befooling Colonel Plum to whom he sells the tale of a lunatic carrying a bomb. The Colonel does not know that it is Basil himself who has brought the lunatic inside, despite the heavy security at the gate. Made a Second Lieutenant for this war-effort, the Colonel promises to fulfil his aspirations for a higher post provided he catches a fascist for him: 'Not for watching communities. Catch a fascist for me and I'll think about making you

---

[256] Evelyn Waugh, "Tolerance", *John Bull*, 2 April 1932, 7, in ed. Donat Gallagher, *A Little Order, op. cit.*, 26.

[257] Christopher Hollis, op. cit., 19.

a captain of Marines.'[258] The incident brings out the lack of rationality in the concatenation of events in secular life. Reward does not necessarily follow one's personal merit: a view that Waugh explored deeply in **Scoop**. Waugh's post-modernist antipathy to Humanist and Enlightenment emphasis on the role of reason in the modern world is made clear in this episode.

Egged by Colonel Plum to find a fascist for him, Basil looks out for the man he could frame as one. The man Basil chooses to be his 'fascist' prey is Ambrose Silk, his old acquaintance. Ambrose occurs in the long line of static academic characters beginning with Paul Pennyfeather and continuing with Adam, William Boot and Tony Last. That Waugh associates the scholarly profession with the static mode of life is clear from Basil's habit of taking to writing whenever he feels exhausted and tired of keeping pace with the world of change; though such periods of hibernation are very short-lived, owing to his resilient dynamic spirit. As Waugh Writes:

"For year now, whenever things were very bad with Basil, he had begun writing a book. It was as near surrender as he ever came and the fact that these books – two novels, a book of travel, … never got beyond the first ten thousand words was testimony to the resilience of his character."[259]

Apart from being scholarly, Ambrose is also attached to the chivalric values of the past, like Tony Last. Waugh describes him as a person '[b]orn after his time, in an age which made a type of him, a figure of farce'.[260] Like any static character, he is perturbed by any threat to his nation. When the war breaks out, he puts on his crusading armour to fight the enemies of his country. He volunteers himself for the Ministry of Information as a writer.

---

258 Evelyn Waugh, Put Out More Flags, op. cit., 150.

259 Ibid., 76.

260 Ibid., 42.

By taking this decision, he unknowingly pitchforks himself into the dynamic world of the war-time England. Unlike Boot, Ambrose willingly gives up the privileged position of an objective spectator to take part in the anarchic action of the changing world. Like Paul and Tony before him, he is not aware that the times have changed and that the days of chivalric honour and patriotism have long since been replaced with those of deceit and profit. His ignorance makes him vulnerable to the dynamic persons prowling in the jungle of modern world. Besides, he has imposed upon himself the role of a dynamic character, which runs counter to his real static personality. This imposition, just as in the case of Paul Pennyfeather, robs him of his real identity; he has become a 'shadow' character. It is on account of this contradiction within him that he suffers from persecution-mania, both from the fascists and the public. Waugh writes:

"…There were only a few restaurants, now which he could frequent without fear of ridicule and there he was surrounded, as though by distorting mirrors, with gross reflections and caricatures of himself."[261]

Even his voice has lost its seriousness, because of the diminution of his real personality to the state of a shadow ('Mine is the brazen voice of Apuleius' ass, turning its own words to ridicule.'[262]). Basil's fears come home to roost when Basil frames him as a fascist. Basil gets started on this trail by Poppet Green's causal reference to Ambrose as a fascist.

"'Did you say "fascist"?'"

'Didn't you know? He's gone to the Ministry of Information and he's bringing out a fascist paper next month.' 'This is very interesting', said Basil.

'Tell me some more.'"[263]

---

[261] Ibid., 41.

[262] Ibid., 61.

[263] Ibid., 174.

The paper that Ambrose is planning to publish is actually a literary journal entitled *Ivory Tower,* a name that also suggests Ambrose's state of mind. As Ambrose's attitude to art rejects the idea of art for art's sake, the paper begins with an enunciation of its aims. In doing so, he sows the seeds of controversy in it which do not escape the notice of even his publisher, Mr. Bentley.

"'It's all very controversial', said Mr. Bentley sadly. 'When you first told me about it, I though you meant it to be a purely artistic paper.'

'We must show people where we stand,' said Ambrose. 'Art will follow – anyway there's 'Monument to a Spartan'. 'Yes', said Mr. Bentley. 'There's that'. 'It covers fifty pages, my dear. All pure art.'"[264]

The essay that Ambrose considers an example of pure art is everything but that. It talks about his old friend Hans who in the first flush of youth was taken in by Nazi ideals but later on discovered their fatuity. It thus purports to show the hollowness of Nazism. Ambrose's assessment of his own committed writing as pure art is an error of judgment, arising out of his inability to sift truth from fiction. Basil pounces on this vulnerable trait. The essay, 'Monument to a Spartan', needs only a slight modification to turn into a truly fascist article. Chance helps Basil in doing so. Basil happens to drop into Ambrose's room when he is not present there. To his supreme relish, he discovers the galley-proofs of the essay. Stealing it away, he pores over its contents to choose his points of devious alteration. When he meets Ambrose, he convinces the latter that the second part which deals with Hans' awakening robs the story of its value as pure art and lends it instead an air of propaganda. He suggests to him that the essay should end 'with

---

[264] Ibid., 186.

Hans still full of his illusions, marching into Poland'.[265] What Ambrose fails to see is that an ending like this would make the readers mistake Hans' illusions for Ambrose's political position. His inability to see the point renders him comic.

If Ambrose by his association with the past is the opposite of Basil, Angela Lyne, by her true contemporaneity with him, parallels him in more ways than one. Her dynamism is reflected not only in her American appearance and general deportment but also in her descent: she is the daughter of a Glasgow millionaire who rose to heights from the 'life in a street gang'. 'Angela', Waugh says 'is a decadent modern woman'. In other worlds, she is thoroughly steeped in the decadent spirit of the constantly changing modern secular world. The impact of mechanization, is writ large on her face ('But the face was mute. It might have been covered in jade, it was so smooth and cool and conventionally removed from the human.'[266]). The narcissism manifest in Basil and Barbara ('Narcissus greeted Narcissus from the watery depth as Basil kissed her.'[267]), can be detected in her too ('For seven years she had been on a desert island; her appearance had become a hobby and distraction, a pursuit entirely self-regarding and self rewarding'[268]).

---

[265] The Ambrose Silk episode has an autobiographical undertone. Like Ambrose, Waugh was accused of being a fascist by the popular press and even his reviewers alluded to his qualified support for fascism in the "Spanish Civil War", though that was far from the truth. Waugh had in fact shown his antipathy to fascism in it when he wrote: 'As an Englishman I am not in the predicament of choosing between two evils. I am not a Fascist nor shall I become one unless it were the only alternative to Marxism. It is mischievous to suggest that such a choice is imminent.' His comparative preference for Fascism over Marxism was rooted in the belief that ' for something that has not developed may reach the right end, while something that has fully developed wrongly cannot...the disillusioned Marxist becomes a Fascist; the disillusioned anarchist a Christian.' (Evelyn Waugh, "Art from Anarchy", ed. Donat Gallagher, *The Essays, Articles and Reviews of Evelyn Waugh, op. cit.*, 205.)

[266] Evelyn Waugh, *Put Out More Flags, op. cit.*, 25.

[267] Ibid., 25

[268] Ibid., 26

She owes her proximity with Basil not to any sensual reason but to the 'other bonds' of their common dynamic nature. In Basil's absence, when she shuts herself in, she falls sick and suffers from insomnia. Her sickness results from her decision to impose a static self upon her essentially dynamic self. It is only after Basil's arrival and in his company that she gradually recovers. It is, therefore, quite expected that she should get married to him after her husband, Cedric's death. In Waugh, marriage in the dynamic world has lost the permanence and sanctity bestowed on it by its sacramental value; it is only a social arrangement.

"'What's the sense of marrying with things as they are? I don't know what there is to marriage, if it isn't looking forward to a comfortable old age.' The only thing in war-time is not to think ahead. It's like walking in the blackout with a shaded torch. You can just see as far as the step you're taking."[269]

Angela leaves no room for doubt as to how even a sacramental institution like marriage has degenerated into a temporary arrangement in the modern world, especially so in the times of the World War II. War, as has been said earlier represents the worst state of the dynamic world, a world in which all disruptive forces have been let loose.

Basil's decision to join the war towards the end of the novel has, however, been interpreted by some critics as a sign of hope, a sort of regeneration of the decadent aristocracy. Lionel Stevenson sees in the breaking out of the war, a 'succumb[ing] to a delusive hope that it might bring regeneration to the effete aristocracy.'[270] He disregards the cues available throughout the Waugh cannon in regard to the significance of war. Our preceding discussion has shown that the outbreak of war in the dynamic world implies the unleashing of the forces of destabilisation which push human society to an extreme form of dynamism like what we can find in the barbaric circles of humanity. In the terminology of **Decline &**

---

[269] Ibid., 26.

[270] Lionel Stevenson, *op. cit.*, 357

Fall, it implies a rapid movement away from the hub of the wheel of life. The war cannot, therefore, offer the hope that Lionel Stevenson speaks of. **The Sword of Honour** trilogy, written much later, further presents the evils of war and its inability to provide any such hope. Its chief protagonist, Guy Crouchback, sees in the war an expression of the unholy desire of killing each other to satisfy one's manhood. Basil Seal too joins the war not with any holy intention or for that matter for the sake of any ideal; he joins it only to satisfy his irrepressible desire of putting to sword hordes of Germans. Christopher Hollis too appears to have ignored the sadistic motives which work in Basil's mind before he joins the war when he writes of his reformation in the war-torn world.

"We are indeed left at the end of **Put More Flags**_with a vague impression that in the new atmosphere of the Churchillian Renaissance even Basil Seal is going to behave decently."[271]

The character who really reforms himself in this novel is Alastair Digby-Vane-Trumpington. He does so, however, by joining the war in order to express his penance for his unruly and wasteful past. A.A. De Vitis has rightly perceived the future artistic potential of Waugh on the basis of this change in Alastair.

"Here is Waugh tenuously moving into the penance prescribed by the Catholic Church, although his outlook in **Put Out More Flags** is specifically secular. But the introduction of the religious note indicates more strongly than ever before the direction he will take in **Brideshead Revisited**."[272]

In spite of it, A.A. De Vitis sees in Waugh a rejection of war when he observes, 'Yet war is no solution, and Waugh is conscious of the fact.'[273]

---

[271] Christopher Hollis, *op. cit.*, 29.

[272] A. A. De Vitis, *op. cit.*, 38.

[273] Ibid., 39.

Apart from these episodes which indicate a general trend away from the hub and towards greater chaos and consequent instability on the periphery of the wheel of life, the novel also brings out the absurdity of change in the secular world by resorting to the use of the circular image in the search for the right man at the Ministry of Information. They keep moving from one office to another until they end up in the same office from where they had begun their search for the person who will attend to them. They have the same feeling that a person standing or running on a rotating wheel has when he keeps coming back to the point from where he started. The 'new spirit' that sir Joseph sees 'on every side' has no foundation in the grim prospect that dynamic life holds out. Whatever comic fun we find in the novel owes not to the regeneration of life but to the sense of absurdity of secular human actions, in the way Ionesco defines this term:

"Absurd is that which is devoid of purpose… Cut off from his religious, metaphysical and transcendental roots, man is lost; all his actions become senseless, absurd, useless."[274]

Basil's comic adventures may please but they also reveal the vacuity of his purpose in life. The aim that he discovers at the end is nothing more than a satisfaction of irrational and senseless desire of killing, a wish that brings him closer to his barbaric forbears.

Conceived on board a troopship carrying prisoners of war, the novel, in the words of Waugh, is 'a minor work dashed off to occupy a tedious voyage'[275] Critics appear to have taken a cue from it to appraise it unsympathetically. Alan Pryce-Jones, Waugh's friend and reviewer, considers the plot of the novel too fragile to act as a controlling agent of the incidents described in it.

"The plot does not matter; it imposes a vague pattern on selected instances of incompetence, lying, theft, graft, fornication,

---

[274] Eugene Ionesco, in Martin Esslin, *The Theatre of the Absurd* (Harmondsworth: Penguin, 1972), 23.

[275] Ed. Mark Amory, *op. cit.*, 158.

unkindness, ineptitude, snobbery, cowardice, drink and unnatural vice during the first year of the war."[276]
Even David Lodge sees signs of structural and thematic disunity in the novel.

"Though **Put Out More Flags** (1942) certainly has its moment... the novel has neither structural nor thematic unity... But one should not judge **Put Out More Flags** too harshly for it was written on a troopship, partly to relieve the author's own boredom."[277]

The criticism is, however, tempered with an extenuating reference to its peculiar mode of composition.
Notwithstanding Waugh's own unsympathetic assessment of his sixth major novel, the theme of inverse relationship between secular change and progress does recur in it as a unifying bond of apparently disparate episodes which lends the novel an aesthetic wholeness. Just like his previous novels, **Put Out More Flags** follows the basic structural pattern of a circle, as suggested in the motif of the wheel of life. The action of the novel unfolds in 'Autumn' with three rich women thinking of Basil in terms of his suitability for the war. Barbara Sothill, Basil's sister, thinks that '... Basil *needed* a war**.** He's not meant for peace'.[278] Angela Lyne, his mistress, and Lady Cynthia, his mother, too picture him as a subaltern leading an action. Basil, however, eludes their attempts to get him recruited. It does not, by any means, falsify the assessments of these three rich women for the reasons that make him do so, are in no way pacific. It is the discipline that the armed forces demand which repels him. As he is a true dynamic character, he wishes to have a taste of impartial killing from the war ('Conscription has rather taken the gilt off that particular gingerbread' said Basil. 'Besides, this ain't going to be a soldier's war.'[279]). The desires of the

---

[276] Alan Pryce-Jones, *op. cit.*, 216.

[277] David Lodge, *op. cit.*, 29.

[278] Evelyn Waugh, *Put Out More Flags, op. cit.*, 16.

[279] Ibid., 38.

three women close to him materialize only towards the end of the novel because by now, in his own words, 'There's only one serous occupation for a chap now, that's killing Germans. I have an idea I shall rather enjoy it.'[280] His anticipation of the relish in killing the Germans is comparable to the homicidal carpenter's relish in exterminating heathens like Prendergast in **Decline and Fall**. While the resemblance with the homicidal carpenter emphasizes the common bond of dynamism, the contrast with Guy Crouchback reveals the dynamism of Basil against the backdrop of Guy Crouchback's static life. Basil's entry into the war thus completes the framework of the novel and lends it a circular nature by bringing the action to the point from where it began. Even movement of time in the novel reinforces this impression, for the operation of seasons, within which the action is contained, is itself cyclical.

By manifesting a concern with the absurdity of secular change, the novel falls in line with the other lesser comedies that Waugh wrote. In our analytical study of the next novel, we shall see the same the trend depicted with a firmer grasp of manners and material.

The Loved One

In **Decline and Fall**, the critique of civilization unfolded itself against the backdrop of modern Britain. In **The Loved One** (1948)[281], notwithstanding the change in setting from Britain to America, the same theme finds a vigorous expression once again. The change in setting is, however, significant for America compared to Britain is a far more 'dynamic' society. In the words of Waugh himself:

---

280 Ibid., 221.

281 Waugh began writing this novel on Friday, 21 May 1947, as per his own admission in his diary. (ed. Michael Davie, *op. cit.*, 379.)

"She is the child of late eighteenth-century 'Enlightenment' and the liberalism of her founders has persisted through all the changes of her history and penetrated into every part of her life."[282]

Enlightenment and liberalism have been the cornerstones of progressive American society and culture. Together, the two philosophies have injected a pace of change so stupendous that what was at one time a mere colony of Britain has come to occupy a position more powerful than its erstwhile rulers. Waugh's anti-Enlightenment attitude does not allow him to celebrate this change. Instead, like the post-modernists, he finds this change comically macabre. As the edifice of American development rests on the shoulders of breakneck technological change, it is not dissimilar to the state of an individual standing on the outermost orbit of a rotating wheel. As the rapidity of movement felt on the outermost orbit of the wheel robs the individual standing there of any feeling of stability, so does the rapid pace of technological change rob the American society of any semblance of stability. In the world view of Waugh, the degree of stability increases as one approaches the transcendent hub of the wheel and decreases as one moves away from it. It is significant that Waugh measures progress not in terms of the cyclical motion of a society on the wheel of life but in terms of its distance from the Roman Catholic hub of the wheel of life. As Waugh puts it in his very first novel, **Decline and Fall,** 'You see, the nearer you can get to the hub of the wheel the slower it is moving and the easier it is to stay on.'[283] Britain, by virtue of its conservatism in comparison with liberal America, is closer to the hub of the wheel of life than America. In consequence, an interaction between the two cultures exposes America, in all its vulnerability, to the buffetings of Britain. In the "Commentary for **The Private Man**", Waugh remarks:

"The more uprooted they are from their essential loyalties, the more the control of their own lives and families and the pride in

---

282 Evelyn Waugh, "The American Epoch in the Catholic Church", in ed. Donat Gallagher, *The Essays, Articles and Reviews of Evelyn Waugh, op. cit.*, 379.

283 Evelyn Waugh, *Decline and Fall, op. cit.*, 208.

their possessions are taken from them so much the more readily will they fall victim to attack from nations which have not been so enervated."[284]

The defeat of America at the hands of a British intruder also helps to highlight the American illusion of progress as comically false and delusive. The novel stops short of being a satirical attack on American society as the shattering of this illusion elicits our sympathy and admittedly, it is one of the cathartic emotions created by comedy. However, the **Times Literary Supplement** chooses to ignore this when it observes:

"It is as an Old Testament prophet exposing our festering sores, as a flayer of society that he excels. **The Loved One** perhaps indicates that he has finally accepted his métier. At any rate, he has given us a satire, witty and macabre, ominous and polished, which strikes straight at the heart of the contemporary problem."[285]

Waugh's choice of Hollywood as the backdrop to the action of this novel is not without reason. The home of cinema in English, Hollywood is to Waugh the very epitome of futile secular change. In "Why Hollywood is a term of Disparagement", he remarks, 'As far as the home of a living art is concerned, Hollywood has no importance. It may be a useful laboratory for technical experiment.'[286] By distinguishing between 'living art' and 'technical experiment', Waugh tries to draw a line between quintessential and superficial change. While the first is of a religious kind, the second is of a secular kind. Hollywood represents a secular world in flux. Accordingly, it is a very appropriate background for showing the absurdity of secular change. In Waugh's philosophical terminology, we may, therefore, call it the dynamic centre of a dynamic society.

---

284 Evelyn Waugh, "Commentary" for T. A. Mc Iverney's *The Private Man,* in ed. Donat Gallagher, *Evelyn Waugh: A Little Order, op. cit.,* 145.

285 Unsigned Review, *Times Literary Supplement*, 20 Nov 1948, 652, in ed. Martin Stannard, op. cit., 307.

286 Evelyn Waugh, "Why Hollywood is a Term of Disparagement", *Daily Telegraph*, 30 April 1947, 4, in ed. Donat Gallagher, *Evelyn Waugh: A Little Order, op. cit.*, 41.

Two categories of artists are shown to be converging on this dynamic heart of America. The first is comprised of those who have allowed art to give up its quest for the aesthetic expression of permanent values of life. The second is comprised of those who have been true to their artistic calling. Waugh's anguish and pain for the first type of artists is neatly formulated in these words:

> "The great danger is that the European climate is becoming inclement for artists; they are notoriously comfort-loving people. The allurements of the modest luxury of Hollywood are strong. Will they be seduced there to their own extinction?"[287]

The answer to this question is implied in the downward sloping curve of sir Francis Hinsley's artistic career. He has joined initially as a chief script-writer in Megalopolitian pictures, after his arrival in Hollywood. By the fag-end of his career there, he has come down to the Publicity Department where his job is to endow actors and actresses with saleable identities. Change in the dynamic world is so rampant that even the tastes of the people keep on changing. Sir Hinsley's job is to fashion and refashion the identities of the actors and actresses with a view to catering to these changing tastes. Waugh's art thus imitates life in his respect as in so many other. Assuredly, his novelistic writing is not marred by the impression that he has created the character of sir Hinsley on dishonest scales. The final impression depends not on whether the novelist explicitly passes judgment but on whether the judgment he passes seems defendable in the light of the dramatized facts associated with the fashioning and refashioning of the identities of the actors and actresses with a view to catering to these changing tastes.

By making art serve the ends of the dynamic world, Sir Hinsley has not only reduced himself to the rank of an apostate artist but also exposed himself to the possibility of 'extinction' of which Waugh is never tried of writing. The Megalopolitan Pictures retrench him as they find his approach outdated. The fact of his

[287] Ibid., 41.

retrenchment, however, escapes his notice as the company does not even inform him. When it does come to his notice, he refuses to accept the reality, for he cannot believe that he has finally fallen a victim to the denigration and debasement of his trade. The illusion concerning the supremacy of impure and corrupt art in a way renders his position comic, though he does not fail to draw the sympathy of the sensitive readers.

"I've just found a Mr. Medici in my office,'
'Why, yes, Frank. Only he says it "Medissy", like that, how you said sounds kinda like a wop and Mr. Medici is a very fine young man with a very, very fine and wonderful record, Frank, who I'd be proud to have you meet.'
'Then where do I work?'
'Well, now see here, Frank that's a thing I want very much to talk about but I haven't the time right now. I haven't the time, have I dear?'
'No, Mr. Baumbein,' said one of the secretaries. 'You certainly haven't the time.'"[288]

It is only after Sir Erikson tells Sir Hinsley in blunt Nordic terms about his retrenchment that he realizes that he has been added to the long list of 'has beens' in the ever changing world of Megalopolitan Pictures.

"He had seen the rooms filled and refilled, the name-plates change on the doors. He had seen arrivals and departures, Mr. Erikson and Mr. Baumbein coming, others whose names now escaped him, going."[289]

As he leaves the building of Megalopolitan Pictures, the girl at the reception desk asks him, 'Did you find who you were looking for?'[290] Significantly enough, he leaves her question unanswered. Sir

---

[288] Evelyn Waugh, *The Loved One* (Harmondsworth: Penguin, 1984), 27-28.

[289] Ibid., 29.

[290] Ibid., 29.

Hinsley has found out his own real self and the fact of its discovery stares him in the face now. Waugh presents a just and lively image of human nature by playing up the passions and humours of the characters depicted, and also by representing the changes of fortune to which men are subject. If Hamlet's father had not been murdered by his uncle and his mother had not married the same uncle, Hamlet would never have been driven to exhibit the true image of human nature and thus hold the mirror up to nature. The wisdom with which Sir Hinsley recognizes the reality of the situation following his retrenchment provides the acid test that illuminates his character. A grim note is added to the comic situation that obtains in Sir Hinsley's retrenchment by his death which imparts particularity to one of his own comments on life in America:

"Did you see the photograph… of a dog's head severed from its body which the Russians are keeping alive … by pumping blood into it from a bottle? It dribbles at the tongue when it smells a cat. That's what all of us are, you know, out here. The studios keep us going with a pump. We are still just capable of a few crude reactions – nothing more. If we ever get disconnected from our bottle, we should simply crumble."[291]

Despite his awareness of the nature of life found in America, yet Sir Francis Hinsley is unable to escape this fate. His death illustrates the tragic potential of a comic situation, that Northrop Frye[292] refers to in his easy on comedy.

There is another set of artists too who have descended on Hollywood in search of fame and pelf. Dennis Barlow is representative of such artists. Despite going 'Native', he always maintains an intellectual detachment from the dynamic world of America. We get flashes of it in his alert artistic sense which refuses

[291] Ibid., 15.

[292] Northrop Frye is of the view that 'comedy contains a potential tragedy within itself.' (Northrop Frye, "The Argument of Comedy", in ed. D. J. Palmer, *Comedy: Developments in Criticism* (Houndmills: Macmillan Education, 1984), 79.

to stoop the way Sir Hinsley did. Having won fame with his book of poems published during the last war, he comes to Hollywood to write the life of Shelley for the Megalopolitan Pictures. Three months of his stay there convince him of the decadent nature of secular art encouraged there. He, therefore, prefers the job of an assistant at the Happier Hunting Ground after the expiry of his period of contract. This introduces him to the ultimate stage of decadence, death, that the dynamic world is prone to. Besides, it saves him from the ordeal of sub-serving his artistic perception to the ends of a decedent dynamic world. Barlow's work as an assistant at the Happier Hunting Ground decides Sir Ambrose's choice for the person who can look after the funeral preparation of Sir Hinsley at Whispering Glades; an opportunity that brings him into contact with the most vulnerable area of the dynamic world of America. Being a person nearer to the hub, by virtue of his inner stability reflected in his artistic rectitude, he becomes a good medium for expositing the American notion of progress as comic and false.

Waugh's art of novelistic writing may rightly be regarded as our storehouse of recorded values in so far as they spring from and perpetuate hours in the lives of exceptional people. In depicting the character of Dennis Barlow, the author underlines the varying possibilities of existence and the discriminating reader can easily understand that the habitual narrowness of interests in his acts and activities are replaced by an intricately wrought composure because he is endowed with an artistic rectitude. In the "Conservative Manifesto" to **Robbery Under Law** Waugh clarifies this point beyond doubt, when he writes:

"There is no more agreeable position than that of a dissident from a stable society. Theirs are all the solid advantages of other people's creation and preservation, and all the fun of detecting hypocrisies and inconsistencies. There are times when dissidents are not only enviable but valuable."[293]

---

293 Evelyn Waugh, "Appendix: Conservative Manifesto", *op. cit.*, 162.

Barlow fulfils the requirements of a 'dissident' far better than Paul Pennyfeather or for that matter Adam Fenwick Symes or William Boot. He neither suffers from the bewilderment of a static character nor from the pointless dynamism of a dynamic character like Basil Seal whose deep sense of participation in the world of change prevents him from viewing his world with a detached wisdom that Barlow brings to bear on the follies of the dynamic world. Barlow may, therefore, be said to occupy a place near the hub of the wheel of life.

The Enlightenment and Humanist historiographers judged, as a matter of general rule, the progress of human civilization by the pace of secular change. Men upholding such a view show a culpable disregard for the mortality of man and the transience of his achievements. The insignificance of man's achievement in the face of death compelled Marlowe's Doctor Faustus to abandon the study of subjects that would not alter his condition of 'but Faustus and a man'. While he evaded a suitable answer to this problem by succumbing to the delusive charms of evil necromancy, the dynamic society of America has gone a step further. With a view to preventing death from undoing its quest for secular progress, it has launched a frontal attack on the very significance of death as on eye-opener of the insignificance of secular human efforts. Referring to this tendency, Waugh records his conviction in "Death in Hollywood" in these words:

"They are gently spinning the cocoon which will cover their final transition. Death is the only event which can disturb them, and priests of countless preposterous cults have gathered round to shade off that change until it becomes imperceptible."[294]

Thus, the America society has burrowed itself deeper into the comic delusion of investing mortal life with the permanent values of spirituality. This contradiction manifests itself in the comic unreality of Whispering Glades, a cemetery of great repute for the Americans. Nothing here is what it seems to be. Like Iago's

---

[294] Evelyn Waugh, "Death in Hollywood", *Life,* 29 Sept 1947, 83.

famous line in **Othello**, 'I am not what I am', here there is a tacit understanding of inversion of reality. The unreality of the place is accentuated in its being the product of a dream. The dream-like quality can be found around most of the objects of art installed here. Here are the Kaiser's stoneless peaches, the buzzing sound of non-existent honey bees, three-dimensional houses that look artificial and two-dimensional facades that look natural. Besides, most objects of classical art and architecture here are debased replicas of their originals found elsewhere. Waugh did not have to strain his imagination much for creating the fantastic environs of whispering Glades. The preceding description may look exaggerated and a deliberate attempt to distort reality on Waugh's part. That it is not so is clear from Waugh's tour of California. While on this tour to discuss the filming of **Brideshead Revisited**, Waugh came across the apotheosis of Whispering Glades in the Forest Lawn cemetery. In his diary for this period, he says, 'I found a deep mine of literary gold in the cemetery of Forest Lawn.'[295] Obviously, not only the cemetery in the novel, but the very idea of this novel was inspired by this American enterprise of inversion and perversion of values in the nature of services provided by the Forest Lawn cemetery. It seemed to Waugh a brazen attempt to invest the temporal and the transient with the spiritual values of permanence. Waugh was so deeply impacted by his visit to the cemetery that we find hardly any change in the description of the place in the novel, as compared to its original description in "Half in Love with Easeful Death".[296] The letter to Cyril Connolly, written on 2 January 1948, also leaves no room for doubt about the impact of this experience on his fecund imagination: 'The ideas I had in mind in writing were: 1st & quite predominantly overexcitement with the scene of Forest Lawn....'[297]

---

[295] Ed. Michael Davie, *op. cit.*, 675.

[296] Evelyn Waugh, "Half in Love with Easeful Death", *Tablet,* 18 Oct 1947, 246-248, in ed. Donat Gallagher, *Evelyn Waugh: A Little Order*, *op. cit.*, 155-157.

[297] Ed. Mark Amory, *op. cit.*, 265.

The contradiction that renders the physical façade of Whispering Glades comic does not stop here: it extends event to the practices adopted. The dead bodies brought for burial here are called the loved ones. Large scale operations are undertaken, in case of injury, to bring them back to their original beauty and appearance. Only after that are the corpses sent to their respective burial spots. Even then, no effort is spared to avoid the body getting mixed up with earth and decaying. The burial place of Whispering Glade thus tries to arrogate to itself the spirit of blissful eternity that is the foundation of Heaven according to the Christian conception of life. Commenting on a similar inversion of values in Forest Lawn, Waugh writes perceptively in "Half in Love with Easeful Death" thus:

"We are very far here from the traditional conception of an adult soul naked at the judgment seat and a body turning to corruption … In those realistic times Hell waited for the wicked and a long purgation for all but the saints, but Heaven, if at last attained, was a place of perfect knowledge. In Forest Lawn, as the builder claims these values are reversed. The body does not decay; it lives on, more chic in death than ever before... the soul goes straight from Slumber Room to Paradise, where it enjoys an endless infancy…"[298]

The travesty of Christian truth in Whispering Glades in well illustrated by Evelyn Waugh in these words about its apotheosis:

"Forest Lawn has consciously turned its back on the old customs of death, the grim traditional alternatives of Heaven and Hell and promises eternal happiness for all its inmates. Dr. Eaton [the founder] is the first man to offer eternal salvation at an inclusive charge as part of his undertaking service."[299]

The eternal salvation sold at Whispering Glades contravenes the Catholic stand that Waugh takes in "The American Epoch in

---

298 Evelyn Waugh, "Half in Love with Easeful Death", *op. cit.*, 159-160.

299 Ibid., 159.

the Catholic Church": 'The Christian believes that he [man] was created to know, love and serve God in this world and to be happy with him in the next. That is the sole reason for his existence.'[300] Lionel Stevenson[301] rightly remarks that this novel conveys abhorrence for the blasphemous parody of religion practised in the modern materialistic world. However, Edmund Wilson, who had reacted to the overt expression of Catholicism in **Brideshead Revisited,** finds fault with the novel for its Catholic viewpoint in the ironic presentation of American attitude to death:

"To the non-religious reader... the patrons and proprietors of Whispering Glades (the cemetery in the book) seem more sensible and less absurd than the priest-guided Evelyn Waugh. What the former are trying to do is, after all merely to gloss over physical death with smooth lawns and soothing rites; but, for the Catholic, the fact of death is not to be faced at all: he is solaced with the fantasy of another world."[302]

John Farrelly of *Scrutiny*, however, finds Wilson's approach rather 'depressing'. He remarks, 'If Mr. Wilson finds the attitude to life implicit in Whispering Glades more congenial than that explicit in the traditional 'Christian myth, that should prove' disturbing; as I said above... Rather, 'depressing', would be the more sympathetic term.'[303] What Edmund Wilson failed to notice while criticising the Catholic vision of the book may be summed up best in the words of Desmond McCarthy who observes, 'The book is a ruthless exposure of a silly optimistic trend in modern civilization which takes for granted that the consolation of religion can be enjoyed without belief in them...'[304]

---

300 Evelyn Waugh, "The American Epoch in the Catholic Church", *op. cit.*, 388.

301 Lionel Stevenson, *op. cit.*, 359.

302 Edmund Wilson, in John Farrelly, *Scrutiny*, XIII, Winter, 1951-52, 233, in ed. Martin Stannard, *op. cit.*, 316.

303 John Farrelly, *op. cit.*, 317.

304 Desmond McCarthy, *Sunday Times*, 21 Nov 1948, 3, in ed. Martin Stannard, *op. cit.*, 308.

The comic fun that Waugh arouses here emerges from the incongruity between the real value of death, as defined by Roman Catholicism, and the false one superimposed on it by the secular American notion of progress. The latter is held up to ridicule for its delusive attempt to assert the supremacy of man by trying to conquer even death. In his book Evelyn Waugh, A.A. De Vitis has, therefore, rightly pointed out: "Waugh lamented the fact that the traditional concepts of the soul standing naked at the judgment seat, of the mystery and enormity of death … were minimized and replaced by an infantile and imbecile idea of the permanence and beauty of life.[305]

Yet, the imbecility of the American attitude to life and death also make us sympathise with them. So, when De Vitis calls the novel a 'caustic condemnation of the American way of life'[306]and when Cyril Connolly calls it a Swiftean satire on the burial customs of Southern Califonria',[307] they overlook the significance of sympathy in the creation of the comic world.

Observing the self-delusion evident in the American attitude to death with his alert 'literary sense', Barlow feels an urge within him to translate this into a work of art. Waugh writes evocatively about it: 'In that zone of insecurity in the mind where none but the artist dare trespass, the tribes were mustering. Dennis the frontiersman could read the signs.'[308] But as his experience of the depravity and illusions of American life is not yet complete and as he has still a duty toward his deceased host to perform, Barlow lets the impulse lie low. He engages himself, instead, in writing an elegy on Sir Hinsley. The poem suggests Barlow's disenchantment with the American no holds-barred notion of progress.

"They told me, Francis Hinsley, they told me you were hung

---

305 A. A. De Vitis, *op. cit.*, 55.

306 Ibid., 54

307 Cyril Connolly, *Horizon*, Feb 1948, in ed. Martin Stannard, *op. cit.*, 299.

308 Evelyn Waugh, *The Loved One, op. cit.*, 64.

With red protruding eye-balls and black-protruding tongue;
I wept as I remembered how often you and I
Had laughed about Los Angeles and now 'tis here you'll lie;
Here pickled in formaldehyde and painted like a whore,
Shrimp-pink incorruptible, not lost nor gone before."[309]

The two kinds of women that Barlow meets at Whispering Glades are indicative of the degradation that human life has undergone in the highly dynamic atmosphere of America. Those who belong to the first kind are no more than the standardized product of a factory. Waugh writes poignantly:

"A man could leave such a girl in delicatessen shop in New York, fly three thousand miles and find her again in the cigar hall at San Francisco, just as he would find his favourite comic strip in the local paper; and she would croon the same words to him in moments of endearment and express the same views and preferences in moments of social discourse."[310]

The sameness that permeates them is a sign of their servility to the mechanical order of things that they themselves have given precedence over all else under the false impression that it would lead them ahead on the path of secular progress. In the "Commentary" for **The Private Man,** Waugh says: 'Men are not naturally equal and can only be so when enslaved.'[311] The servility to a mechanical order of things is here conveyed through the act of denaturing life. In Hard Times, when Charles Dickens wanted to highlight the absurdity of a similar travesty of life, he endowed Thomas Gradgrind not just with a mechanistic description of personality but also a mechanical and cold name.

We recall here that Waugh made oblique criticism concerning individuality in **Decline and Fall,** and considered it

---

309 Ibid., 69.

310 Ibid., 45.

311 Evelyn Waugh, "Commentary" for T. A. McIverney's *The Private Man, op. cit.*, 142

the root cause of the disorder prevalent in the dynamic world, and hence the critical account of sameness in human life presented here may be construed as a departure from views originally held. In his book **The Picturesque Prison**[312]**,** Jeffrey Heath analyses this problem at length. He argues that Waugh believes, with St. Augustine, that every individual nature is god-given and good so long as it keeps man 'in the place assigned by the order of nature'. It is only when man relinquishes his ordained place that his nature assumes barbaric potential and threatens the stability of human society. The presentation of events in which the essential humanity of man is denied is, therefore, only an apparent contradiction in Waugh. The comic laughter that Waugh elicits over this self contrived situation is saved from being satiric by the element of sympathy which pervades all along, for the folly committed by the dynamic characters is an unconscious one and is rooted in the delusive faith in the notion of secular progress.

The second category of women that one comes across in America is of those whose individuality has a streak of barbarity. They occur in the long line of dynamic characters beginning with Captain Grimes and Prendergast in **Decline and Fall.** Dennis Barlow discovers such a kind of woman in Aimee Thenatogenos. Describing her impact on Barlow, Waugh writes: 'But the girl who now entered was unique. Not indefinably; the appropriate distinguishing epithet leapt to Dennis' mind the moment he saw her; sole Eve in a bustling hygienic Eden, this girl was a decadent.'[313] Her uniqueness, as Dennis detects, lies in her decadent nature and is, therefore not a sign of her superiority. The parallel drawn with Eve underlines this fact. The 'rich glint of lunacy' he discovers in her plays up the wildness of her individuality. Like in the case of Prendergast, it is ever ready to upset the established order of things. Her heathen parental lineage also reinforces the idea of this dangerous quality in her. As a student, she had wished to take up art as her first major subject. But

---

[312] Jeffrey Heath, *The Picturesque Prison* (London: George Weidenfeld & Nicolson, 1982), 7

[313] Evelyn Waugh, *The Loved One, op. cit., 46.*

because her father had lost money in religion, another sign of perversity in American life, she was forced to give that up and learn beauty-craft instead. The choice is guided by monetary considerations than any high ideals and the alternative chosen is accordingly one which lacks the permanent values of the fine arts. Aimee's choice, therefore, sheds light on her growing conformity to the dynamic world where the quest for secular progress robs all things of a permanent value. She suffers another fall when she willingly opts for working on dead corpses as a cosmetician. This makes her sub-serve her false art to the pseudo-religion of Whispering Glades. This is clearly indicative of the travesty of truth found in the dynamic world. Dennis wins her admiration not by reciting his own poems which she does not like but by reading out the poems of Keats. This is illustrative of the fact that Aimee who prefers the heathen values celebrated in the poems of Keats rather than the Christian ones in Dennis' poems is an out and out dynamic creature. Wishing to gain greater insight into this decadent world, Dennis keeps up her interest in him by making her believe that he is the author of those heathen poems. Unlike the apostate artists, Aimee and Sir Hinsley, Barlow cannot make his art stoop to the level of self-deception practiced in the dynamic world. So, he prefers instead to borrow others' poems and pass them off as his own. Describing his mental state, Waugh writes:

"That was not what the Muse wanted. There was a very long, complicated, and important message she was trying to convey to him. It was about Whispering Glades, but it was not, except quite indirectly, about Aimee. Sooner or later, the Muse would have to be placated. She comes first. Meanwhile, Aimee must draw from the barn-tub of the anthologies."[314]

Aimee contrasts the transience of her work (the paint she applies on the dead faces flakes off after some time) with the permanence of the Hellenic poetry supposedly written by Dennis and thereby, begins to feel for him in a way she has never felt for Mr. Joyboy, the chief Mortician at Whispering Glades. His arrival

[314] Ibid., 84.

minimises the impressiveness of Mr. Joyboy who till now has reigned in her mind as the epitome of artistic excellence. The courtship of Mr. Joyboy in the sombre setting of the mortuary is not only an inversion but also a perversion of all sacred values of life. Death which is a grim reminder of the transience of human joys and life is itself used as a love-broker to further and celebrate the impermanent pleasures of life implicit in human love. Mr. Joyboy expresses his admiration and love for Aimee through the smiles that he imparts to the dead faces under his care. The contradiction between what should be and what is makes the entre process of courtship look repulsive and ridiculous.

"'It's true, Miss Thenatogenos. It seems I am just powerless to prevent it. When I am working for you there's something inside me says "He's on his way to Miss Thenatogenos" and my fingers just seem to take control. Haven't you noticed it?' 'Well, Mr. Jyoboy, I did remark it only last week. "All the Loved Ones that come from Mr. Joyboy lately", I said, "have the most beautiful smiles." 'All for you Miss Thenatogenos.'"[315]

Aimee confides the vicissitudes of her love-life in a fake spiritual guide, Guru Brahmin, who is not one but two persons. In the dynamic world of America where religion has been robbed of its eternal significance and made to come to terms with secularism on a dubious note, there is no dearth of 'preposterous cults' and commercialized religiosity'. We find instances of these developments in other novels. In **Decline and Fall,** Mr. Prendergast sets himself up as a Modern Churchman and in **Vile Bodies,** Mrs. Melrose Ape uses religion for personal aggrandizement. Wishing to take up a respectable job, Dennis asks Mr. Bartholomew how he can become a non-sectarian clergyman. He expects that some bishop may be responsible for ordaining such priests. Mr. Bartholomew, however, disagrees with him. He discounts the need of a bishop as anyone "who has received the Call has no need for human intervention'. The dangers of such an attitude to religion have already been referred to in **Decline and**

---

[315] Ibid., 56.

Fall where the homicidal carpenter becomes a potential source of menace to the social order by virtue of the call he supposedly receives from the angels of God. Waugh re-emphasizes here the dangers of an individualistic approach to religion and suggests his preference for the collective approach manifest in the concept of Church as a body of believers in Christ. By pointing out the absurdity of an individualistic approach to religion, Waugh ridicules the impermanence associated with its essentially humanistic and temporal outlook. Waugh's religious attitude is appreciable in the light of Freud's discoveries. Sigmund Freud clearly demonstrated in his theory of mind that the so-called rational decisions of man were basically cast in the mould of his hidden emotional desires. The power of the unconscious revealed by him put a big question mark on the objective validity of man's rational decisions. The kind of religious change advocated by Evelyn Waugh steers clear from this dubiousness as Roman Catholic Church hinges on the decisions taken by the collective group of the College of Bishops. Waugh's emphasis on Roman Catholic Church is therefore, not a simplistic one.

The spiritual life of America is dominated not only by the pseudo-Christian cults but also by non-Christian faiths. The Guru Brahimin and the Hindu love-song are cases in point. As the dynamic world in founded on a secular approach to life, the exponents of progressive ideology here take pride in their atheism. They do not realise that by depriving the wheel of life of its religious hub, they are exposing themselves to the Sisiphean absurdity of an endless and meaningless circular motion. Aimee admittedly is a representative figure of this type. Upon having been informed by Dennis of his desire of being a priest, she writes to Guru Brahmin, her confidante.

"He says he is going to be a pastor. Well as I told you I am progressive and therefore have no religion but I do not think religion is a thing to be cynical about because it makes some people very happy and all cannot be progressive at this stage of Evolution…"[316]

Waugh is ostensibly referring to this erosion of religious stability in the dynamic world in his essay, 'Tolerance' where he prefers narrow-mindedness to mindlessness, rigidity to senseless elasticity of opinion.[317] Dennis exploits this false progressiveness in Aimee. When she learns the truth about the real authorship of the poems he has addressed to her till now, she tries to get away from him and get married, instead, to Mr. Joyboy. Dennis who knows the extent of her foolish faith in the inverted secular ideals of Whispering Glades, wins her back by reminding her of the oath of living together they had taken in the Lovers' Nook at Whispering Glades.

"It may be that by the Dreamer's standards there are defects in my character…So what? You loved me and swore to love me eternally with the most sacred oath in the religion of Whispering Glades ….sanctity is indivisible. If it isn't sacred to kiss me through the heart of Burns or Bruce, it isn't sacred to go to bed with old Joyboy."[318]

The false religion of Whispering Glade has so overpowering a hold on her mind that she can hardly ignore its demand for obedience. She, therefore, comes down to requesting Dennis to release her from that oath. As Dennis has discovered its effectiveness, he is unwilling to do so for fear of losing her to his rival, Mr. Joyboy. The episode heightens the comic contrast between Dennis and Aimee. The former with his awareness of the fallacy of the secular ideal renders the secular ideals followed by Aimee ridiculous and preposterous. At the same time, Aimee's ignorance of the retrogressive character of Whispering Glades' secular ideals deserves our sympathy. Thus, the Anglo-American

---

316 Ibid., 101.

317 Evelyn Waugh, "Tolerance", op. cit., 26.

318 Evelyn Waugh, *The Loved One, op. cit.*, 111

encounter in this novel is essentially of a comic character rather than being satiric.

In her bewildered condition, Aimee turns for guidance to none but the fake Guru Brahmin. The situation that develops out of this decision may be best explicated in Waugh's own words: 'A people who have forfeited their privacy will easily succumb to rogues and charlatans who promise a change of condition.'[319] The advice that Aimee receives seals her fate for ever. The man who has till now been replying to her letters is in a drunken condition as he himself is in a quandary after his retrenchment from the paper for which he wrote as Guru Brahmin. Irritated by Aimee's phone call, he thoughtlessly asks her to jump off a building. Aimee takes his advice seriously. She repairs to the mortuary at Whispering Glades where she takes her life in Mr. Joyboy's room. The 'rich glint of lunacy' that Dennis had noticed in her suddenly gains complete control over her and consumes her in her own destructive passion. The heathen gods she had abandoned get her at the end. Waugh writes appropriately:

"Her mind was quite free from anxiety. Somehow, somewhere in the blank black hours she had found counsel; she had communed perhaps with the spirits of her ancestors, the impious and haunted race who had deserted the altars of the old Gods, had taken ship and wandered, driven by what pursuing furies through what mean streets and among what barbarous tongues!"[320]

Apart from highlighting the tragic end of the dynamic world's false sense of progress in abjuring fixity of opinion, the incident sheds light on the incompatibility of British and American cultures. At this point, it is worthwhile to remember that Waugh's novel under discussion is not seriously flawed by careless intrusions. In fact, he strikes a happy balance between artful showing and inartistic telling. Indeed, his fruitful ideas associated with the false sense of progress in the dynamic world grow effortlessly out of this

---

319 Evelyn Waugh, "Commentary" for T. A. McIverney's *The Private Man, op. cit.*, 143.

320 Evelyn Waugh, *The Loved One, op. cit.*, 116.

happy balance and provide a valuable yardstick in interpreting his novels. Waugh referred to this incompatibility in his letter to Cyril Connolly: 'The tale should not be read as a satire on morticians but as a study of the Anglo-American cultural impasse with the mortuary as a jolly setting.'[321]

This statement of Waugh and the tragedy of Aimee connote that a culture which lacks stability because of having pushed itself to the fringes of the wheel of life cannot withstand the incursion of a more stable culture which is found nearer the hub of the wheel of life. In other words, secular change introduced through greater industrialisation may increase the acquisitions of man but so far as achieving real progress is concerned, it has a marginal impact. A really progressive culture should be able to withstand and resist all attempts aimed at its destruction. The victory of a more stable culture indicates that progress can be achieved not through liberalism and Enlightenment Thought but through greater acceptance of a religious attitude to life. A.A. De Vitis has rightly stressed the significance of this point of view for a proper understanding of the novel.

"**The Loved One** is interesting, too, because it shows clearly the position from which Waugh criticizes the world ... In **The Loved One** the Christian context from out of which Waugh creates his people and devises his situations is so completely conveyed by the indignant tone that his fundamental humanity is apparent. The beliefs of Christianity so pervade the novel that unless they are appreciated the novel cannot be understood."[322]

Through John Bayley does not like the Christian predisposition of Evelyn Waugh, he does not overlook the Christian standpoint either. In his own words: 'Both Evelyn Waugh and Graham Greene are writers who use their Catholicism as a weapon and a probe; they explore vice and anarchy from a definite

---

[321] Ed. Mark Amory, *op. cit.*, 259.

[322] A. A. De Vitis, *op. cit.*, 57-58.

standpoint.'[323] The assertion of the Christian standpoint in this novel owes not only to the travesty of truth Waugh saw in the construction of Forest Lawn but also in the conscious artistry Waugh adopted for the first time in composition. The record of his diary entry of 2 June 1947 illustrates this method well.

"I have decided to try a new method of work. When I began writing I worked straight on into the void, curious to see what would happen to my characters, with no preconceived plan for them, and few technical corrections. Now I waste hours going back and over my work. I intend trying in **The Loved One** to push straight ahead with a rough draft, have it typed and then work over it once, with the conclusion firmly in my mind when I come to give definite form to the beginning."[324]

The 'conclusion' that Waugh evidently had in mind while ridiculing the achievements of the American society, is quite clear: true progress can be achieved only by striving for the permanence implicit in the Roman Catholic hub of an otherwise absurd wheel-like life. Mrs. R.D. Smith appears to have overlooked this thrust in the thematic pattern of events narrated in the novel when she faults the novel for its seemingly hackneyed themes.

"Hollywood, funeral hypocrisy and the adman's domain of nutbergers, Jungle Venom perfume, and peaches without stones are themes that have been well worked over before, more effectively indeed, by Mr. Aldous Huxley, Mr. Sinclair Lewis, and by various hands in the 'New Yorker', notably Mr. S.J. Perelman."[325]

She also criticises the novel for 'the contradiction between what Mr. Waugh intends us to understand are his values, and what the feel and texture of his writing reveal'.[326] The inability of most

---

323 John Bayley, *National Review*, Feb 1949, in ed. Martin Stannard, *op. cit.*, 312.

324 Ed. Michael Davie, *op. cit.*, 680.

325 R. D. Smith, New Statesman, 11 Dec 1948, in ed. Martin Stannard, *op. cit.*, 310.

326 Ibid., 312.

reviewers in perceiving the underlying 'thematic line of intention' in the novel owes partly to Waugh's own sense of pleasure in keeping his critics always guessing. His letter to Nancy Mitford is quite revealing in this regard. He writes there: '**Loved One** is being well received in intellectual circles. They think my heart is in the right place after all. I will show them.'[327]

Waugh's comic vision thus develops out of the tendency to mistake the apparently progressive secular change for the truly progressive religious change. Concepts concerning change and progress are thus the recurrent themes in a Waugh novel; admittedly the author achieves his effects by the kind of silence he maintains and also by the manner in which he leaves his characters to work out their own destinies to tell their own stories. We realize it also for certain that Waugh could not have brought out his preoccupation with ideas of alternation and advance in life and living if he had tried to become a reliable spokesman, speaking directly and authoritatively to us. When at the end of the novel, Dennis leaves with his artist's load of experiences for England, Waugh seems to be dramatizing the concept of comedy signified in regeneration which he has portrayed brilliantly in the character of Charles Ryder in **Brideshead Revisited**. Still, the absurd vision implicit in the inverted ideals of the dynamic American society retains a dominate impression.

The Ordeal of Gilbert Pinfold

In **The Ordeal of Gilbert Pinfold** (1957), Waugh's persona, Pinfold, is of the opinion that 'most men harbour the germs of one or two books only; all else is professional trickery of which the most demonic of the masters-Dickens and Balzac even-were flagrantly guilty.'[328] This is Waugh spilling the beans of his artistic craft, though in a characteristically oblique manner. Occurring at the eighth slot in the series of the Lesser Comedies, the novel continues to remain preoccupied with the theme that has been seen to shape

[327] Ed. Mark Amory, *op. cit.*, 273.

[328] Evelyn Waugh, *The Ordeal of Gilbert Pinfold* (Harmondsworth: Penguin, 1984), 10.

and structure the other seven lesser comedies written before it. In the earlier novels, Waugh had either debunked the myth of the permanence of the chivalric code or had come down with his biting comic fun on the inadequacy of the modernist project of development. In **The Ordeal of Gilbert Pinfold** (1957), Waugh again comes down upon both ways of life while psychoanalyzing its central character, Gilbert Pinfold.

But before any analysis of the comedy obtaining in this novel may be undertaken, attention must surely be invited to its 'confessedly autobiographical' quality[329]. In his diary entry during this period, Waugh remarks, 'I have worked hard and easily, seldom writing less than a thousand words a day. The book is too personal for me to be able to judge it.'[330] Again, in the letter of 2 October, 1956 to Daphne Fielding, Waugh writes, 'I say, talking of mad, I am fully in the middle of writing an account of my going off my rocker.'[331] However, it is the letter of 15 August, 1957, addressed to Robert Henrique that elaborates the similarity.

"Mr. Pinfold's experiences were almost exactly my own. In turning them into a novel I had to summarize them. I heard 'voices' such as I describe almost continuously night and day for three weeks. They were tediously repetitive and sometimes obscene and blasphemous. I have given the gist of them."[332]

In order to see how far Pinfold's experiences' almost exactly' resemble Waugh's own, we have to rely on the letters as the diary for this period is completely silent. Michael Davie, who has collected and edited the diaries, says, 'In the second half of January 1954 Waugh left England on the voyage to Ceylon that produced the hallucinations described in **The Ordeal of Gilbert**

---

329 Evelyn Waugh, "Anything Wrong with Priestley?, *Spectator*, 13 Sept 1957, in ed. Donat Gallagher, Evelyn Waugh: A Little Order, op. cit., 136.

330 Ed., Michael Davie, *op. cit.*, 769.

331 Ed. Mark Amory, *op. cit.*, 475.

332 Ibid., 493-494.

Pinfold.... The existing MS has no entry between January 1954 and June 1955.'[333]

One of the instances narrated in the novel that finds an echo in the letters concerns the copper tap. In the novel, Pinfold is highly agitated over the conspicuous absence of 'a prominent, highly ornamental, copper tap in the centre' of 'a wash-hand stand of the greatest elaboration' which has been sent to him by a friend in London who shares his taste in furniture. Only after his friend, James Lance, informs him that he had never given him any such tap does Mr. Pinfold realize that his memory has played a trick on him. Waugh was a victim of a similar capricious working of his memory. In one of his letters to John Betjeman, dated 29 Dec. 1953, Waugh writes, 'As I remember the G.B. there was an ornamental bronze pipe which led from the dragon's mouth to the bowl below ... Did I dream this or did it exist.'[334] The other similarity concerns the B.B.C. Radio programme that Pinfold seems to hear on board the ship, *S.S. Caliban*. Pinfold thinks mistakenly that he is listening to a BBC radio programme on his artistic merits and also some noise which he attributes to faulty wiring. The incident finds a parallel in the letter dated 3 Feb (1954), in which Evelyn Waugh writes to Laura Waugh:

"The chief trouble is the noise of my cabin. All the pipes and air shafts in the ship seem to run through them. To add to my balminess there are intermittent bits of 3rd Programme talks played in private cabin and two mentioned me very faintly and my p.m. (Persecution mania) took it for other passengers whispering about me."[335]

Yet again, Pinfold's imputation of his hallucinations to telepathy and the Box at Upper Mewling figures in another letter of Waugh, dated 8 February, 1954 to Laura.

---

333 Ed. Mark Davie, *op. cit.*, 724

334 Ed. Mark Amory, *op. cit.*, 417.

335 Ibid., 418.

"I must have been more poisoned than I knew. Then when I was beginning to rally round myself the 'victim' of an experiment in telepathy which made me think I really was going crazy. I will tell you when I get home. It has made me more credulous about Tanker's box."[336]

The voices that haunt Pinfold even after he has disembarked abruptly at Port Said and reached Colombo by air, persecuted Waugh too. In the letter of 12 February, 1954, addressed to his wife, Luara, he writes:
"It is rather difficult to write to you because everything I say or think or read is read aloud by the group of psychologists whom I met in the ship. I hoped that they would lose their art after I went ashore but the artful creatures can communicate from many hundreds of miles away. Please don't think this is balmy, I should certainly have thought so three weeks ago, but it is a fact & therefore doesn't worry me particularly.... But it is a huge relief to realize that I am merely the victim of the malice of others, not mad myself as I really feared for a few days."[337]

Pinfold also thinks in a similar vein and accordingly counsels his wife not to be perturbed by his madness.
The parallels indicated above create an impression that the novel holds no more than an autobiographical interest. But that is not so. Such an impression is misleading as it detracts attention from the artistic significance of the novel. Gustave Flaubert, the noted nineteenth century French novelist, says in a letter to Mlle Leroyer de Chantepie, 'It is one of my principles that a writer should not be his own theme. An artist must be in his work like God in creation, invisible and all-powerful; he should be everywhere felt, but nowhere seen.'[338] Waugh's persona, Gilbert Pinfold, also holds

---

336 Ibid., 418.

337 Ibid., 419-420.

338 Gustave Flaubert, in Francis Stegmuller (tr.), Selected Letters (London: Farrar Strauss & Co. and Hamish Hamilton, 1954), in ed. Richard Ellmann and Charles Fiedelson, Jr., *Modern Tradition* (New York: OUP, 1965), 132.

similar views: 'He regarded his books as objects which he had made, things quite external to himself to be used and judged by others.'[339] Waugh himself once said, 'I am not interested in myself, it is these works I make that interest me.'[340] It is obvious from these statements that Waugh falls in the line of those artists who have upheld the impersonality of art. Though the materials with which Waugh has composed this novel were such as had occurred in his own life, yet they contained within them elements that were amenable to an artistic rendering of the attitude to change and progress. Waugh saw in his madness, after his recovery, the conflict between a natural and inherent static character, on the one hand and a superimposed dynamic façade of personality, on the other. By grafting his madness on his artistic creation, Pinfold, Waugh sought to expose the ridiculous inadequacy of both attitudes to life in comparison with the religious one. It goes to the credit of Waugh that he could detach himself from so personal experiences as these to transmute them into an artistic work.

We have seen that in Waugh's comic vision of life a static attitude of life implies withdrawal from the absurd action of the world of change, and a dynamic attitude, participation in change under the delusive impression that secular change fathers progress. Very early in his life, Waugh showed a static tendency in himself. Waugh's preference, as a child, for the things of the past clearly demonstrates it. In his own words: "This cellar and this wilderness I took as my special province, thus early falling victim to the common English confusion of the antiquated with the sublime, which has remained with me; all my life I have sought dark and musty seclusions, like an animal preparing to whelp."[341]

This brutal self-confession shows the artist's ability to turn his artistic gaze even on his own weaknesses. The confusion of the antiquated with the sublime is a typical static trait that Waugh

---

339 Evelyn Waugh, The Ordeal of Gilbert Pinfold, op. cit., 9.

340 Evelyn Waugh, "Personal Call", BBC Radio, 16 Nov 1953.

341 Evelyn Waugh, *A Little Learning* (Harmondsworth: Penguin, 1984), 44.

himself explored in the tragi-comic end of Tony Last. The confusion, therefore, sheds light on Waugh's dual attitude to life. Though, at the emotional level, he chose to withdraw from the high action of a world in flux, yet, at the intellectual level, he realised his folly in mistaking the placidity of a withdrawn static life for the stability of the transcendental hub-reality of Roman Catholicism. It is the latter that shapes his artistic work and in consequence, he is able to transcend his personal limitation as well. In work after work, Waugh rejects both the static and the dynamic ways of existence, while keeping himself firmly anchored in the *sub-specie aeternitatis* vision of the hub of life. Interestingly enough, while he is able to transcend his static nature in the creative process of art, it is precisely because of his artistic calling that he is also able to suckle his static character. What is being attempted here is a differentiation between the artist and his art, one that Pinfold and Waugh themselves admit. The trade of an artist, being more of an observant and retiring nature than an active one, the artist can easily slip into the life of a recluse. Not unexpectedly, therefore, Waugh took to a sort of semi-feudal life towards his middle age when he shifted to the country side. Jeffery Heath has rightly said that 'Essentially, Waugh's love of the artistic life was a love of solitude…'[342] Unfortunately, critics who mistake the artist for his art have criticized him for being a conservative reactionary in trying to glorify and play up redundant value of the past. They overlook that in Waugh's fiction it is these very values which are shown obsolete and culpably inadequate. When Waugh ridicules his static characters who are invariably men of letters, he is in a way condemning his own personal prejudices, Dennis Barlow is the one exception who like Carl Van is the 'one man of letters who is also a man of the world'.[343]

While writing **The Ordeal of Gilbert Pinfold** (1957), Waugh grafted his static nature on Pinfold, a middle-aged novelist, passing his 'long, lonely, tranquil days at Lychpole, a secluded

---

[342] Jeffrey Heath, *op. cit.*, 40.

[343] Ed. Michael Davie, *op. cit.*, 317.

village some hundred miles from London'.[344] In this respect, Pinfold is the precise replica of his creator. A little ahead, Waugh elaborates the reasons for his staying away from London at a remote place and he attributes them to his concern for privacy; 'since the end of the war his life had been strictly private.'[345] In his static concern for privacy, Pinfold fully resembles his creator who too shunned public life on account of his static character. Lest Mr. Pinfold's seclusion should be mistaken for mere friendlessness, Waugh says, 'But Mr. Pinfold was far from friendless and he set great store by his friends.'[346] Pinfold thus occurs in the long line of static-artistic characters and is a sign of Waugh's growing artistic genius which could now turn inwards.

Paradoxically enough, the trade of an artist not only helped Waugh's static personality to flourish but also exposed it to the dangers of the dynamic world of his audience. In the words of Waugh, 'There is no art or of profession, except possibly higher mathematics, which one can practice without exposing oneself to amateur criticism and interference.'[347] In the essay, 'People who want to sue me', he goes on to elaborate how his readers have many a time tried to drag him into public controversies by imputing motives of caricaturing real-life persons in the depiction of his characters. Some would go to extent of suggesting to him about the people he could put into his books. To one such proposer, Waugh retorted that he did not put real-life people into books, instead they 'take themselves out'.[348] To checkmate the incursion of the dynamic world into his static world, not only did he not allow visitors but also assumed the persona of a snobbish and arrogant man. As Martin Standard has rightly observed, 'The real Mr. Waugh, however, would never stand up before the microphone or camera. There was

---

344 Evelyn Waugh, The Ordeal of Gilbert Pinfold, *op. cit.*, 10.

345 Ibid., 10.

346 Ibid., 13.

347 Evelyn Waugh, "People Who Want to Sue Me", Daily Mail, 31 May 1930, 10, in ed. Donat Gallagher, Evelyn Waugh: A Little Order, op. cit., 13.

348 Ibid., 14.

always a melodramatic disguise, a parodied prejudice, to defend his privacy.'[349] By behaving thus, Waugh was in effect employing the dynamic world's own weapons against it. Jeffrey Health who has analyzed this split between the static and the dynamic in Waugh's personal self says:

"At Heath Mount School Waugh was both aggressive and artistic. The same divided temperament is apparent in Waugh at Lancing College, which he attended on 17 May 1977. Waugh's diaries for the period (they do not begin until 1919) are the product of a public self concerned with advancement and prestige, but there is at the same time a persistent preoccupation with art and the need for privacy."[350]

As Heath's analysis also shows, Waugh's preoccupation with the furtherance of his public self was a means to protecting his own insecure and retiring self from the unjust censure of a dynamic world.
Just as Waugh transferred his static character to Pinfold, so did he his dynamic façade. Pinfold too has imposed on his static self, a dynamic front which has lent him a dual personality. Outlining the nature of this superimposition in his personality, Waugh writes:

"He was neither a scholar nor a regular soldier; the part for which he cast himself was a combination of eccentric don and testy colonel and he acted it strenuously, before his children at Lychpole and his cronies in London, until it come to dominate his whole outward personality."[351]

Managing these two irreconcilable attitudes is not always easy. It finally takes its toll on Pinfold as it did on Waugh, when it manifests in a schizophrenic divide. Thus, like Shakespeare in King Lear, Waugh makes Pinfold-Waugh's madness a metaphor of the

---

349 Ed. Martin Stannard, *op. cit.*, xxiii.

350 Jeffrey Heath, op. cit., 13.

351 Evelyn Waugh, *The Ordeal of Gilbert Pinfold, op. cit.*, 15.

incongruity between the two approaches to change and progress. Waugh illustrates the division within Pinfold's personality in these words: 'When he ceased to be alone, when he swung into his club or stumped up the nursery stairs, he left half of himself behind, and the other half swelled to fill its place.'[352] Waugh uses this metaphor to come down upon both the approaches to change and progress with his characteristic wit and comic pungency.

In **Put out More Flags,** Angela Lyne's insomnia, an anticipatory symptom of madness, resulted from the superimposition of a static facade on an essentially dynamic self. In the case of Pinfold, Waugh reverses the process. Pinfold's insomnia and later madness arise from the superimposition of a dynamic front on a quintessentially static personality. The hallucinations that Pinfold has are not mere nothings but an outward projection of his own superimposed dynamic self. In being pitted against them, he is fighting his own superimposed dynamic self. His madness thus becomes an analogical device that creditably externalizes the psychological conflict between the static and the dynamic halves of his personality. Lionel Stevenson[353] has rightly pointed out the uniqueness of this 'excursion into psycho-analysis' in this novel. Even when Priestley accepts the psychological nature of the conflict in the novel, he fails to apprehend the true nature of the divide in Pinfold's personality. He maintains wrongly enough: "He is not a Catholic landed gentleman pretending to be an author. He is an author pretending to be a Catholic landed gentleman. But why, you may ask, should he not be both? Because they are not compatible. And this is not merely my opinion. It is really Pinfold's opinion too."[354]

Priestley appears to have overlooked the fact that the roles of an author and of a Catholic country gentleman, far from differing

---

[352] Ibid., 15.

[353] Lionel Stevenson, *op. cit.,* 362.

[354] J. B. Priestley, "What was wrong with Pinfold?", New Statesman, 31 August 1957, 224, in ed. Martin Stannard, *op. cit.*, 389.

with one another, aid one another as both roles are symptomatic of a static attitude to life. Waugh was therefore quick to retaliate to this interpretation, in his famous essay 'Anything Wrong with Priestley? In this essay, Waugh imputed Priestley's harsh criticism to his socialist aversion for the aristocracy. Waugh writes, 'No, what gets Mr. Priestley's goat (supposing he allows such a deleterious animal in his lush pastures) is my attempt to behave like a gentleman.'[355] David Lodge is nearer the truth when he maintains that Pinfold's hallucinations are the displaced and distorted projections of Mr. Pinfold-Waugh's public and private life.

"What is fascinating about the hallucinations is that they are "displaced" and distorted projections of Mr. Pinfold-Waugh's public and private life….The "ordeal" is therefore a kind of identity crisis and the writing up of the experience a therapeutic exercise in self analysis."[356]

Having seen how elements within Waugh's own harrowing experience of madness were amenable to an artistically objective treatment, we may now safely consider the novel, in its own right. A dual narrative scheme helps Waugh to unfold his unique comic vision of life. Within the circular narrative framework of the novel, is inset an allegorical narrative. The circular narrative begins with the description of the split-personality of Pinfold, his falling sick, voyaging to Ceylon to recuperate his failing health and recovering only after his return from Colombo. The allegorical narrative framework narrates the confrontation of the static self of Pinfold with his superimposed dynamic self, in which the former suffers ridicule and torture initially but triumphs in the long run over his dynamic adversary.

As the chief protagonist of this novel, Gilbert Pinfold, is a static character, he prefers the placid and unchanging life of the village of Lychpole. In keeping with his nature, he has set up his

---

355 Evelyn Waugh, "Anything Wrong with Priestley?", *Spectator*, 13 Sept 1957, in ed. Donat Gallagher, *Evelyn Waugh: A Little Order, op. cit.*, 137.

356 David Lodge, *op. cit.*, 38.

house here in the manner of feudal lords. In this sense, he is close to the other static characters like Paul Pennyfeather and Tony Last. Like his predecessors, he endangers his peace of mind when he takes the decision of leaving the safe environs of the static world of Lychpole to travel to Ceylon. The life on board the ship, bound for Ceylon, is unlike that of Lychpole. Waugh suggests the dynamism of the public world aboard the ship, by naming it after one of Shakespeare's most mercurial character, Caliban. He is neither a complete man nor a complete monster. He, therefore, combines in himself the qualities of man and the barbarity of beasts. By naming the ship after him, Waugh gives us an idea of the deep-rooted dynamism in modern secular society in a most artistic and non-committal way. Pinfold shall have to battle, like Tony Last, against such a barbaric world.

Once on board the ship, the first narrative pauses to make way for the second one. The second narrative begins with Pinfold going off his mind on board the ship. Pinfold's mind externalizes his superimposed dynamic self in the shape of hallucinations and thus begins the hilarious comedy of static Pinfold's conflict with his superimposed dynamic self. Pinfold's hallucinations people the world of the ship, S. S. Caliban, with the most unabashed and brutal persons and the atmosphere of the ship soon acquires the nature of its apotheosis in Shakespeare's **The Tempest.** Pinfold, however, does not realize that the supposed monstrous characters stalking on board the ship are a manifestation of his own snobbish and arrogant persona. Ignorance of the true character of this battle and his own personality renders him ridiculous and Waugh draws much fun at his expense. The allegorical conflict between the real self which is static and the false self, which is dynamic, becomes, therefore, a perfect objective correlative for Waugh's idea of the rejection of both the static and the dynamic worlds. The rejection is cast in a comic mould for while the static man is ridiculed for his helplessness in combating the dynamic world, the latter itself does not escape comic censure for its caddishness. The two narratives, however, are not disjoint. While the second narrative unfolds itself, the first narrative does not cease altogether. It continues to hang about like the halo of a saint, manifesting itself in the split-personality – Pinfold's comically abortive attempts at knowing the truth about his hallucinations.

In the state of hallucination, the static Pinfold overhears some Bright Young People playing jazz and raising a lot of din. Later, he overhears about a Lascar crew member getting hurt at work and the Captain coming down upon him for that. Still later, he overhears a conversation full of recriminations against a man who appears to have seduced the woman who Pinfold names Goneril. The Captain of the ship beats him so much so that he dies and is consequently thrown overboard. The static Pinfold is horrified by the frightening barbarity of the people on board the ship. The first narrative intrudes here when Pinfold tries to verify what he had overheard. When Pinfold enquires from other passengers on board the ship about these events, he learns to his utter dismay that they have neither seen nor heard anything of the sort. Obviously, it raises a question about the veracity of what he had overheard. Not ready yet to admit the reality of his madness, he circumvents the truth by attributing these bizarre happenings to defective wiring in the ship. Persisting with this illusion deprives Pinfold of the ability to realize that he was not mentally well and renders him comic in the eyes of the readers.

The microcosmic conflict between the static Pinfold and the dynamic world of his hallucinations acquires a threatening proportion when the supposed hooligans, acting out plays near his cabin, warn him of a physical assault. When Pinfold comes out of his cabin to confront them, he finds no one outside. He returns disappointed to his cabin. Immediately afterwards, the girls in this group rob Pinfold of his peace of mind with a loud bawdy song. The situation is not different from the one at the beginning of Kafka's **Trial**. The central protagonist in Kafka's novel is confronted with a similar problem when he is summoned to the court one morning. He finds the table of the jury covered with obscene photographs and one man in the court-room trying to seduce a woman. The world that baffles Kafka's hero also perplexes Waugh's protagonist. In both cases, however, this world is in actuality that part of the hero's own self which is being denied.

Waugh makes Pinfold look comic as does Kafka, for his inability to tear down the veil of ignorance and see the reality clearly. While this illusion lasts, the microcosmic struggle of the static Pinfold continues.

The static Pinfold now finds himself in a world deprived of order, a trait that likens it to the highly dynamic world of savagery and barbarity. He can neither rid himself of these hooligans nor seek remedy against them as the even Captain of the ship is no more upright than they are. However, he exonerates the Captain once he overhears a BBC Programme that heaps unjustified censure and personal vendetta against him. Infuriated, he comes round to the inference that the episode involving the Captain, Goneril and the murdered man must have been a part of a BBC play.

"Now it was apparent that many of the sounds in his cabin emanated from the Broadcasting House, he became certain that what he had overheard was part of a play. The similarity of June's was part of a play. The similarity of June's voice and Goneril's seemed to confirm it."[357]

Pinfold's cocksureness in having lighted upon the reality of the conversation involving the captain renders him comic for it is no nearer the reality than his previous conclusion. Fortified with this self-derived inference, he sees an ally in the Captain in his war against the dynamic world of the hooligans.

The next episode that brings out the conflict between the static Pinfold and the dynamic world is titled the International Incident. He overhears a plot involving the forcible substitution of a dark little old man with him when the Spanish officials come on board the ship in search of that man. He gets to hear that the dark old man is on 'HMG's secret service' and how important it is to prevent his capture by the Spanish officials. Patriotism comes naturally to Pinfold as he is a static character. Like most static

---

[357] Evelyn Waugh, *The Ordeal of Gilbert Pinfold, op. cit.*, 83-84.

characters, he is patriotic an ideal that has become obsolete in the age of mercenaries. He would, therefore, have gladly agreed to perform this arduous task, if consulted and taken into confidence. What infuriates Pinfold is that the Captain intends to force him into doing it without trying to seek his cooperation even once. The concern for his country, however, prevails upon his rage and Pinfold resolves that he would perform this substitute role willingly but that only after making his adversaries aware of his willingness to doing so. When the time arrives, Pinfold saunters out to carry out his resolve. At this point, the first narrative pauses to let the second one take over. The split-personality Pinfold is thoroughly disappointed to find the deck deserted and no Spanish official holding the ship captive. For the first time, he fears that he may be going mad. His piteous outburst makes him a person deserving of our sympathy despite being the butt of our ridicule till now.

"He had been dauntless a minute before in the face of his enemies. Now he was struck with real fear, something totally different from the superficial alarms he had once or twice known in moments of danger, something he had quite often read about and dismissed as over-writing. He was possessed from outside himself with atavistic pain: 'O let me not be mad, not mad sweet heaven', he cried."[358]

The peals of Goneril's laughter that he overhears convince him wrongly that it must have been a trick played by the hooligans to persecute him. However, unpalatable this idea may be, Pinfold finds it still soothing as it means that he has not gone mad: 'He might be unpopular; he might be ridiculous; but he was not mad.'[359] Once again Pinfold fails in comprehending the real nature of his hallucinations which alone can redeem him from the ordeal of persecution.

Upon approaching the Captain with the complaint against the young men and women, supposedly belonging to one family,

---

358 Ibid., 98.

359 Ibid., 98.

that have continuously been harassing him, he learns that no family travelling by the ship matches his specifications. Instead, there is a quiet family of Angels. Upon hearing the name, Angel, Pinfold is reminded of the Angel who had once come to interview him for the B.B.C. and soon concludes that his family must include that man from the B.B. C. Having made himself believe that the static self of Pinfold finds itself facing an inquisition which is staffed by Angel, Goneril and the other hooligans. His cross-examination resembles that of Joseph K. in Kafka's **The Trial** where the jury that sits in judgement upon the hero is itself culpable of moral offences. With a view to escaping from his persecutors, Pinfold disembarks from the ship, makes for Cairo from where he flies to Colombo. But despite that, he gets no respite from his persecutors. It is only when Pinfold is on his way back home that these persecutors soften and even betray a plaintive note in their speech. They plead that he should not divulge their identity to any one in England. The static Pinfold refuses to oblige them for he neither trusts their world nor wishes to shield them from censure and just punishment. Angel's threat, 'All right, Gilbert. You'll pay for this', lacks strength as the static Pinfold has at last asserted his supremacy over the imposed dynamic self whose projections these persecuting hallucinations are.

With the successful resolution of the micro-cosmic conflict between the static and the dynamic selves of Pinfold, the path becomes clear for him to tread back to normalcy. Upon learning from his wife that Angels had all along been in England only, he begins to understand the true nature of the hallucinations. When therefore Doctor Drake, his medical attendant, considers his hallucinations as a 'simple case of poisoning', Mr. Pinfold's reaction is different from his wife's.

"That's a relief', said Mrs. Pinfold, but Mr. Pinfold accepted this diagnosis less eagerly. He knew, and the others did not know – not even his wife, least of all his medical adviser – that he had endured a great ordeal, and unaided, had emerged the victor."[360]

---

[360] Ibid., 156.

Priestley appears to have overlooked the significance of this passage, apart from distorting the nature of the psychological conflict in the novel, when he says, 'Let Pinfold take warning. He will break down again, and next time may never find a way back to his study. The central self he is trying to deny...will crack if it is walled up again within a false style of life.'[361] In fact, Pinfold is very much aware that the pills were not to blame so much as the false self he had superimposed on himself. Fortified with this knowledge, Pinfold feels the urge of transmuting his harrowing experience into a work of art; an action that echoes Waugh's own. The novel, therefore, ends on a note of self-discovery. John Raymond appears to have overlooked the neat culmination of Pinfold's identity-crisis in his self-discovery at the end, while coming down unjustly upon it for lacking 'a satisfactory denouement'[362]. But what Northrop Frye in his 'The Argument of Comedy' (1949) calls epiphany is not effected here for the simple reason that though the protagonist discovers his true self and thereby gets reborn, his rebirth lacks significance as it does not lead him ahead towards the nerve-centre of the wheel of life which along can guarantee real progress. Pinfold's journey of self discovery ends up in his burrowing into his familiar static habitat. Jeffrey Heath appears to have ignored the thematic thrust of this novel while considering all novels after **Brideshead Revisited** to be displaying the acceptance of the correct refuge from the dynamic world.

"In the novels before **Brideshead Revisited** Waugh's protagonists typically find solitary refuges which are false... while in the fiction of later date they discover the correct refuge which has been adumbrated by the false ones: The Household of the Faith."[363]

---

[361] J. B. Priestley, "What Was Wrong with Pinfold?", New Statesman, 31 August 1957, 224, in ed. Martin Stannard, *op. cit.*, 391.

[362] John Raymond, *New Statesman*, 20 July 1957, 88, in ed. Martin Stannard, *op. cit.*, 385-386

[363] Jeffrey Heath, *op. cit.*, 2.

What Heath enunciates here applies more aptly to the **Sword of Honour Trilogy** and **Helena,** the only books that show this thematic pattern after **Brideshead Revisited.**

The thematic pattern of this novel is well reinforced by its unique structure. Waugh conveys the absurdity of the world into which Pinfold thrusts himself by the circular pattern of the narrative concerning his voyage. Pinfold's return to Lychpole, after his circular trip, is suggestive of the return of a spectator to the spectator's gallery after jumping off a circular wheel. The step is regressive rather than progressive for Pinfold does not pierce through the absurd circular notion of the wheel to its transcendental hub. Waugh's comic vision of life thus unfolds itself with the subtle and implied use of the symbolic imagery of the wheel of life both at the thematic and structural level. The artistic coherence that Waugh has lent to his own experiences while transmuting them into an artistic work speaks of Waugh's mature artistry in handling a theme so intractable by reason of its personal character. What Waugh said of Firbank may very rightly be applied to him as well.

"His introduction of his own name in **The Flower beneath the Foot** and **Prancing Nigger** is intolerable *vieux jeu*; perhaps Firbank's sense of humour had reached a degree of sophistication when it could turn on itself and find the best fun of all in the doubly banal; if so it was a development where few will be able to follow him."[364]

Philip Toynbee[365] too concedes that Waugh showed maturity in handling so personal a theme, when he says that Waugh has begun to explore depths of experience which were previously beyond his reach or at least beyond his desire. However, the **Times Literary Supplement** wrote, 'He is a light weight who has suffered from being bracketed with completely different writers like

---

364 Evelyn Waugh, "Ronald Firbank", in ed. Donat Gallagher, Evelyn Waugh: A Little Order, *op. cit.*, 77.

365 Philip Toynbee, *Observer*, 21 July 1937, 13, in ed. Martin Stannard, *op. cit.*, 387.

Mr. Graham Greene.'[366] Similarly, Donat O' Donnell had little praise for the novel.

"... he has chosen to make 'a light novel' out of material fundamentally unsuited to such treatment. It may be said that the comic treatment of the grimmest themes... is precisely where Mr. Waugh excels. That is true when as a satirist he allows himself a free hand... but not when he is treating sacred subjects such as himself."[367]

Both betray insensitivity to the thematic pattern underlying the novel while mistaking the comic element in it for a sign of its lightness. In fact, the comic mould of Waugh's novel is a measure of his superior artistic ability in rendering a profound vision of life in an artistically agreeable manner.

---

366 Unsigned Review, Times Literary Supplement, 19 July 1957, 437, in ed. Martin Stannard, *op. cit.*, 383.

367 Donat O' Donnell, Spectator, 19 July 1957, 112, in ed. Martin Stannard, *op. cit.*, 381.

Chapter 3

The Greater Comedies

The greater comedies present a *weltanschauung* diametrically opposed to that in the lesser comedies. While the lesser comedies foregrounded the absurdity of secular change and progress, the greater comedies present the fulfilment of life lived according to religious principles. In the lesser comedies, Waugh was preoccupied with showing the absurdity of claims of progress made by the Enlightenment philosophy. In the greater comedies, Waugh narrates the story of the gradual emancipation of the central character from the shackles of error and illusion associated with the static and the dynamic modes of existence to the realm of wisdom and truth associated with the ever-stable Roman Catholic hub of the wheel of life.

The image of the wheel of life captures comprehensively the dual character of Waugh's comic art and vision. While the circular motion of the wheel negates all possibilities of progress, the linear motion towards its ever-stable and transcendental hub opens up the possibility of progress. The lesser comedies liken secular change to the circular motion of the wheel, while the greater comedies portray religious change as a linear movement towards the ever-stable hub of the wheel of life. Waugh associates the hub of the wheel of life with Roman Catholic Church, the Church which he joined as a conscious and deliberate act of faith. So, any change which encourages (wo)man to embrace Roman Catholicism in letter and spirit constitutes in Waugh a linear journey towards the Roman Catholic hub of the wheel of life. As the conscious decision to accept the Saviour and His Church saves (wo)man from sin and damnation, such a change is redemptive. Also, as the acceptance of the values of Roman Catholicism is seen as an act of resurrection, it constitutes true progress. The characters, who successfully complete this odyssey, evoke not comic ridicule but our wonder and admiration. In contrast with the static and dynamic characters we met in the lesser comedies, they are the spiritual elites. By adding this dimension to his comic oeuvre, Waugh takes comedy from its lowest levels of slapstick and buffoonery to its grandest level of the sublime.

Brideshead Revisited

Brideshead Revisited (1945)[368] marks a transition in Waugh's comic art and vision. As a novel of transition, it displays characteristics of both the lesser comedies and the greater comedies. The lesser comic vision of absurdity is still there in the circular plot and the circular journeys of the characters who engage in the pursuit of progress through secular change. But, as a greater comedy, the novel for the first time presents the grand spectacle of the central characters describing a linear path in their spiritual resurrection through religious change. That is why, the warning on the dust-jacket of the first edition reads:

> "...**Brideshead Revisited** is not meant to be funny. There are passages of buffoonery, but the general theme is at once romantic and eschatological. It is ambitious...nothing less than an attempt to trace the workings of the divine purpose in a pagan world, in the lives of an English Catholic family, half paganised themselves, in the world of 1923-1939."[369]

---

368 While convalescing from an injury in his leg during World War II, Waugh conceived the idea of this book. In one of his letters dated 25 January 1944 to Laura Waugh, he wrote, 'I have written to Col. Fergusson asking for three months' leave to write a book & am going to the Ministry of Information this afternoon to try & enlist their support. It will be an enormous boon if it is granted.' (ed. Mark Amory, The Letters of Evelyn Waugh (London: Weidenfeld & Nicolson, 1980), 176. Waugh retired to Chagford to write this book. In the diary entry of 31 January 1944, he wrote, 'Today, Monday, I came to Chagford with the intention of starting on an ambitious novel tomorrow morning. I still have a cold and am low in spirits but I feel full of literary power which only this evening gives place to qualms of impotence.' (ed. Michael Davie, The Diaries of Evelyn Waugh (London: Weidenfeld & Nicolson, 1976), 557-558. As per this entry, Waugh should have begun the novel on February 1, 1944. But in his letter of February 1, 1944, to Laura Waugh, he claims to have already 'done 2,387 (words) in 1 ½ days'. For four successive months, Waugh lived the life of a recluse to complete writing the novel on 16 June, 1944.

369 The 'warning' appeared on the inside flap of the dust jacket of the novel.

Mark the co-existence of words like 'buffoonery' with 'romantic' and 'pagan' with 'divine'. Also worth noting is the word, 'ambitious'. What Waugh attempted till now was the use of the popular comic forms for conveying the absurdity of human existence, when it strips itself of all religious trappings. That was familiar ground and the artist in Waugh could easily skip and gallop in it. What Waugh attempts now is a foray into an area that very few artists feel comfortable with. Milton failed when he attempted it in Paradise Lost and Regained. Not because he was a lesser artist but because the canvas of the story he set to out relate was beyond his personal vision. So, Satan in his epical work emerges as a far more powerful character than the Saviour. Not surprisingly, Waugh refers to this attempt as 'ambitious'. The warning that appeared on the dust jacket of the first edition of the novel sets at rest any intention on the part of the novelist to locate a utopia of progress and civilization on the continuum of time.

"... (to) those who look to the future with black forebodings and need more solid comfort than rosy memories... I have given my hero, and them, if they will allow me, a hope, not, indeed, that anything but disaster lies ahead, but that the human spirit, redeemed, can survive all disasters."[370]

The comic art that Waugh deploys in this work is one that takes the comic hero from the region of dark despair to the starry skies of hope and sublimity. It is in this sense of the resurrection and redemption of human life that **Brideshead Revisited** lays claim to the appellation of comedy. Such an approach is fully supported by F.M. Cornford's 'The Ritual Origins of Comedy'

---

[370] Evelyn Waugh, Brideshead Revisited: The Sacred & Profane Memories of Captain Charles Ryder (London: Chapman & Hall, 1945)

(1914) and by Northrop Fry's 'The Argument of Comedy' (1949)[371]. As the characters here trace their movement from an 'absurd' and vegetative state of existence to a higher and meaningful one, the comedy enacted in the novel may be termed a divine one, after the manner of Dante's **Divine Comedy.**

The novel is concerned primarily with the change that Charles Ryder, the narrator of the story of the Flytes, undergoes. It goes to the credit of Waugh's artistic genius that he should make his point clear by externalizing the process of Charles Ryder's spiritual progress through the shifts in his association with the different members of the Flyte family. One is reminded of Shakespeare's **King Lear** where the process of Lear's madness and consequent recovery is allegorically conveyed in the extent of his nearness to each of his three daughters. The dramatization of Charles Ryder's religious change and progress through his proximity to the different members of the Flyte family helps Waugh to retain his classical poise of objectivity without sacrificing at the same time the thematic value of his work. Bernard Bergonzi misses this point when he argues: 'Certainly the story suffers from being filtered through the consciousness of Ryder; the events can scarcely transcend the personality of their narrator.'[372]

In order that the graph of Charles Ryder's gradual religious change be plotted, it is essential to have a look at the members of the Flyte family. In the account that Waugh submitted to the directors of MGM Film Company, he wanted that the 'Flytes should be represented as one of the English noble families which retained their religion throughout the reformation period'. But in

---

[371] F. M. Cornford in 'The Ritual Origins of Comedy', **The Origin of the Attic Comedy** (London: CUP, 1914), argues the association of Comedy with the theme of triumphant renewal of life, celebrated in various forms of ancient games and rituals. Northrop Frye's well-known essay 'The Argument of Comedy', in English Institute Essays, 1948 (New York, 1949) brought the ritual pattern of death and resurrection in different forms. Their view of comedy has redeemed comedy from the straightjacket of the ludicrous and endowed it with grandeur, that was earlier reserved for only tragedy.

[372] Bernard Bergonzi, The Situation of the Novel (London: Macmillan, 1979), 111.

the novel, it is only Lady Marchmain's side of the family which is 'old Catholic', Lord Marchmain's side of the family having given up Roman Catholicism long ago and become Anglican, a form of neo-paganism that suited the 'dynamic' sprit of the times. It is the marriage with Lady Marchmain that restores the family to the faith of its forefathers. The children born of this wedlock embody this schism. While the neo-pagan spirit is inherited by Sebastian and Julia, the Catholic spirit is imbibed by Brideshead and Cordelia. The Flyte family, therefore, presents a divided house. The schism within this family takes its toll soon: Lord Marchmain deserts his wife, runs away to Italy and seeks the protection, not love, of his mistress, Cara, against his wife. Sebastian and Julia follow suit, impelled by their wild neo-pagan spirit. The errant members of the Flyte family harbour in themselves the seeds of dynamic life that sucks them in and thus prevents their progress towards the transcendental hub of the wheel of life.

Like other static characters before him, Charles Ryder is fascinated by the dynamic members of the Flyte family. But by virtue of his closeness to the dynamic characters, he also comes aCross the spiritually inclined ones like Cordelia, Brideshead and Lady Marchmain. As at this moment, he is far from realizing the value of religious change as a means to progress, he is unable to comprehend their attitude to life. Speaking about the inability of the secular-minded people to comprehend the religious approach to life, Harry Blamires has observed, 'The religious view of life differs so fundamentally and comprehensively from the secular view of life that it seems scarcely possible for the Christian to communicate intelligibly with the modern secularist.'[373] Nancy Mitford failed to see this point, when in one of her letters to Waugh she complained, 'I can't explain why but he seemed to me a tiny bit dim.'[374] Understandably enough, Waugh replied, 'Yes I know what you mean; he *is* dim, but then he is telling the story and it is not his

---

[373] Harry Blamires, The Christian Mind (London: SPCK, 1963), 67.

[374] Ed. Mark Amory, The Letters of Evelyn Waugh (London: Weidenfeld & Nicolson, 1982), 196

story'[375]. V.C. Clinton-Baddeley commends Waugh for making a non-Catholic character like Charles Ryder tell the tale of a Catholic family's reaffirmation of its old faith, when he writes, 'The story he has to tell is that of a Catholic family's apostasies and repentances, and it is a brilliant stroke of Mr. Waugh's to tell that story through the mind of a non-Catholic.'[376]

Doubts concerning Charles Ryder's capability as a narrator emerge out of a critical approach that overlooks the primacy of the narrative related to his conversion to the narrative of the return of the Flyte family to its old Catholic fold. As the two narratives unfold, we realize that the narrative of the Flyte family is only an allegorical representation of the narrative pertaining to Charles Ryder's conversion. Ryder's increasing familiarity with this family not only helps him to overcome his incomprehension of the Catholic view of life but also convinces him of the need of accepting such a standpoint. Charles Ryder's conversion, however, is not smooth. The pagan spirit of the world of change restrains him at every step. Jeffery Heath has rightly said, 'It would be wrong to say that Ryder struggles toward his vocation; in fact he struggles violently against it, repeatedly refusing to conform to the plan God has made for him.'[377] The struggle in his case follows a violent course because he is a pagan through and through while Sebastian and Julia are not; they are only 'half-heathen'. His redemption must therefore follow that of the errant members rather than precede it.

The first of the Flyte family children who Charles Ryder meets is Sebastian. The meeting has so overpowering an impact that Charles sheds all his old friends and is drawn into the vortex of the Flyte family's fortunes by Sebastian's charm. Unwittingly, he is drawn into a plan that affects both him and the Flyte family. He,

---

375 Ibid., 196.

376 V. C. Clinton-Baddeley, Spectator, 8 June 1945, 532, in ed. Martin Stannard, Evelyn Waugh: The Critical Heritage (London: Routledge & Kegan Paul, 1984), 237

377 Jeffrey Heath, The Picturesque Fiction (London: George Weidenfeld & Nicolson, 1982), 161.

however, is struck more by Sebastian's queer habit of carrying a teddy-bear, Aloysius, than by his conspicuous beauty. One other thing that strikes strange to Charles is Sebastian's behaviour during their first joint visit to Brideshead. While Sebastian feels free in introducing Charles to his nanny, Hawkins, he is circumspect against his meeting any other member of his family. Ryder notices that the 'farther [they] drove from Brideshead, the more he seemed to cast off his uneasiness – the almost furtive restlessness and irritability that [had] possessed him.'[378] Also, Sebastian shows an unusual indifference towards his family residence. Pointing towards Brideshead House, he says, it's where my family live'. Sebastian's attachment with the teddy-bear and nanny, Hawkins, shows his deliberate refusal to outgrow the fancies of childhood. They also provide him with a protective shield against the Catholicism of his family. As signs of his regressive growth, they take Sebastian not nearer but farther from the hub of the wheel of life. He is not unaware of this fall as he fully believes in the truth propounded by Roman Catholicism. The only obstacle in his trying to achieve that is the heathen part of his own self which has gained complete authority over his actions. The heathen part of his self makes him drink hard. As most of the members of his family observe, he is not happy when he takes to drink. It is, for him, a means of psychological escape from the domineering personality of his mother, Lady Marchmain who he hates with all his strength, for she epitomizes the Roman Catholic values not only is his eye but in the eyes of others as well.

Excessive drinking turns out to be hazardous for his stay at Oxford twice. Each time Lady Marchmain manages to dissuade the authorities from rusticating him. Her attempts to reform him prove futile. Rather, they goad Sebastian to take to his inordinate life with greater vigour and zest. Drink also makes him deceitful so that when he is sent with Mr. Samgrass to the continent for a change, he escapes from the tutelage of his guardianship. Again, when Rex Mottram his brother-in-law, takes him to the continent for a cure, he not only loses track of Sebastian but also his money which the

[378] Evelyn Waugh, Brideshead Revisited (Harmondsworth: Penguin 1968), 41.

latter steals from him. The life of depravity culminates in Sebastian's eventual departure from Brideshead for good. Following the example of his errant father who he likes very much, he heads for the Continent to stay there forever, far away from the interference of his mother. Sebastian's decision symbolises man's misuse of free will and the consequent fall from grace.

The story of Sebastian's fall follows a course similar to that of his father. Both choose drinking as an escape route from the overbearing Catholicism of Lady Marchmain, who they both detest with all fervour. Like his father, he suspects anyone who is close to his mother. When Ryder's meetings become much too frequent, Sebastian first grows wary of his friend and then accuses him of teaming up with his mother to conspire against him. Sebastian and his father have even personal resemblance. The two have similar voice.

The second member of the Flyte family to enter Ryder's life is Julia Flyte. With her entry, Sebastian who dominates the earlier portion of the book drops out of the narrative. Critics have been unhappy over this sudden shift in the novelist's interest in the creation of his characters. David Lodge in his remarkable book on Evelyn Waugh considers the treatment of Sebastian artistically faulty as he is given disproportionate attention in the first and the second parts of the book.

"The book is quite unbalanced by the long and leisurely treatment of Sebastian, who then drops almost entirely out of the picture. Rather clumsy second hand reports of his progress to an unorthodox kind of sanctity, and the attempt to identity him as the "forerunner" of Charles' passion for Julia, do not solve this problem."[379]

A.E. Dyson echoes David Lodge, when he writes, '**Brideshead Revisited**, which begins like a masterpiece, ends

---

379 David Lodge, Evelyn Waugh (New York: Columbia University Press, 1971), 33.

with the most explicit of Waugh's evasions.'[380] V.C. Clinton-Baddeley, Waugh's reviewer, however, differs on this issue. In his opinion, Julia's supersession of Sebastian is justifiable as the story of the novel 'is not the story of Sebastian, but the reclamation of the whole family, whose most important member is Julia. Her story is told to perfection.'[381] While there is some segment of truth in what V./C. Clinton-Baddeley has written, but the remark does not contain the whole truth. The novel is much more than a story of Flyte family. It is the story of Charles Ryder's gradual progress towards comprehending the hub –like value of Roman Catholicism and subsequent conversion. The supersession of Sebastian by Julia should thus be viewed in the light of this thematic intention. Sebastian represents that adolescent phase of Ryder's life which the former has imposed on himself and the latter has never lived fully because of an inimical and unsympathetic father. Not surprisingly, after Ryder quits Brideshead House and Sebastian's company for good, he is undecided about what he has felt behind: 'I had left behind me – what? Youth? Adolescence? Romance?'[382] Notwithstanding his personal inability to single out the phase he has outgrown, it is decidedly adolescence that he has left behind. Having matured, Ryder must surely taste the life of youthfulness before he may be in a position to distinguish between human and divine love. It is therefore natural that Julia should now enter Ryder's life to fulfil this need and so overshadow Sebastian. Ryder gives voice to this transition in his life, when he confesses, 'as Sebastian in his sharp decline seemed daily to fade and crumble, so much the more did Julia stand out clear and firm.'[383]

As one who succeeds her brother in Ryder's interest in the Flyte family, she resembles her brother so closely that sitting beside her Ryder feels 'confused by the double illusion of familiarity and

[380] A. E. Dyson, "Evelyn Waugh and the Mysteriously Disappearing Hero", The Crazy Fabric (London: Macmillan, 1966), 194.

[381] V. C. Clinton-Baddeley, op. cit., 238.

[382] Evelyn Waugh, Brideshead Revisited, op. cit., 163.

[383] Ibid., 172.

strangeness'. Not only does she possess her brother's charm but his voice and manner of speech also. Like Sebastian, she is aware of her 'waywardness and wilfulness'. But unlike him, she does not hate her mother and is also not so close to her father; Sebastian is the only member of the family who maintains close contact with Lord Marchmain. The pious aspect of Julia's self is thus not as meek and submissive as that of her brother. But in the conflict that ensues between the sacred impulse towards the Roman Catholic hub of life, which means progress and the profane impulse towards the wheel- like dynamic life, which signifies decline, the latter appears to be victorious in the beginning.

Her downward Journey begins with her search for a husband outside the Roman Catholic community. For some time past, she has been dreaming of having a fashionable husband whom she has not been able to find in her own community. Such a man looms up in her life in the person of the flashy and hollow Rex Mottram. She steps out of the sacred confines of her Church when she drifts into a pre-marital sexual relationship with him, despite the Church forbidding that.

"'Surely, Father, it can't be wrong to commit a small sin myself in order to keep him from a much worse one? But the gentle old Jesuit was unyielding. She barely listened to him: he was refusing her what she wanted, that was all she wanted to know.
When he had finished he said, 'Now you had better make your confession'.
'No, thank you', she said...
From that moment she shut her mind against her religion."[384]

As she drifts away from the Roman Catholic hub of the wheel of life, she is thrown into the meaningless circular motion of secular life. The fact that her marriage with Rex is not going to last long is clear from the very beginning. Rex is too brazenly worldly and unethical. Before they are to get married, it comes to light that he is a divorcee. The Roman Catholic Church prohibits marriage

---

384 Ibid., 182.

with such a person. Annulment of the previous marriage, the only way out, is a lengthy and uncertain process. So, she has to step out of her Church by renouncing it in favour of the Protestant Church, which alone permits such a marriage. Waugh shows that Julia can go to any length to fulfil her desires and passions, thereby equating her with the other dynamic characters in his other novels. There is an autobiographical element in this turn of the narrative. Placed in similar circumstances, Waugh had waited for the annulment of his first marriage, before he remarried.

The lady most affected by these desertions, Lady Marchmain, represents to a great extent the Roman Catholic hub of life in the novel. Unable to prevent the fall of her husband, son and daughter, she gets bed-ridden and dies eventually. Her death, however, makes her more potent. The heathen spirit of the errant members of her family may have killed her in body but in sprit, she continues to goad them to their true and eternal refuge, the Roman Catholic hub of life. Her death is followed by the return of all the errant members of her family to the Church of their forefathers. As the lost sheep return to their original fold, Charles Ryder begins to comprehend the Roman Catholic values of life and also get converted. Lady Marchmain's death may, therefore, be said to have acted like the 'invisible line' and 'unseen hook' of Father Brown. Julia compares her death to that of Christ and she believes that like Christ her mother died on the Cross of their sins that they might be redeemed. Just as the martyrdom of a saint opens the eyes of the sinful, she awakens her sinful children and husband to the life of sin they lead and makes them return to their true and eternal home, the Roman Catholic Church. The comedy of their lives must be viewed in this context and the profundity of Waugh's comic vision and art should be appreciated form this viewpoint.

Sebastian is the first person to feel the pangs of remorse and as repentance washes sins, he is the first of the errant children to be redeemed. Waugh narrates the story of his redemption through a series of changes in him, first of these being outgrowing his self-imposed adolescence. Once Sebastian is in French Morocco, he shows signs of outgrowing his imposed adolescence which is an

essential preliminary step for the resurrection of his fallen spirit. The teddy-bear Aloysius disappears and his affection, rather mercy, is directed towards a deserving German soldier, Kurt, who is lame and cannot support himself. The devotion with which he serves Kurt is no less than that of a true Christian. Instead of squandering his affection on a toy, he attains Christian humility in the service of the meek and the gentle. With this change, he shows signs of maturing into a true follower of his faith. Even though he continues to drink as hard as he did earlier, he is no longer deprived of the blessings of his church as it is longer for him a means of escape from the reality of God. Drinking, as Brideshead observes, is good as long as it leads to human fellowship, but when it becomes an end in itself, it is bad.
As wine is no longer an end in itself for Sebastian, it does not come in his way of being a true Roman Catholic. After his mother's death, Sebastian applies for entry into a monastery as a lay-brother. This signifies the ultimate triumph of the pious part of Sebastian's self over the heathen one and also his success in progressing towards the true goal of all human endeavours, the Roman Catholic hub of life. Waugh's comic vision of life reveals its profundity in showing how man, however fallen, can still reclaim himself by effecting religious change which liberates him from the absurdity of circular secular change.

Soon after the death of Lady Marchmain, Julia too begins to feel the pangs of conscience. She holds herself responsible for her mother's death. She realizes that her mother had been right in insisting upon their adherence to the values of Roman Catholicism and that by rebelling against her she had jeopardised her own peace and life. The failure of her marriage to Rex Mottram strengthens this feeling of remorse in her. It does not take much time for Julia to realize that her choice of husband has been a wrong one. Far from being a complete man, Rex is 'a few faculties of a man highly developed' which give the false impression of a whole man. Julia tells Charles about this late discovery of hers on board the liner.

"You know Father Mowbray hit on the truth about Rex at once, that it took me a year of marriage to see. He simply wasn't all there …. I thought he was a sort of primitive savage, but he was absolutely modern and up-to-date that only this ghastly age could produce. A tiny bit of a man pretending he was the whole."[385]

The marriage with Rex, however, helps Julia to understand the wasteful influence of the world of change on man. A marriage like this can never attain fulfilment and Waugh lends particularity to this idea by making Julia gives birth to a dead child. Realizing that God's vengeance is upon her, she wishes to put her life in order. Unfortunately, the corrective step she proposes to take is equally or perhaps more sinful; she reflects on the possibility of marriage with Charles Ryder, a man who is already married.

Hereafter, Julia's attempts at progressing towards the hub of life, signified by Roman Catholicism, though misdirected in the beginning, get intertwined with Charles Ryder's search for meaning and significance in earthly life. As discussed earlier, Ryder's association with Julia follows that with Sebastian as a sequel. This enables the novelist to give evidence of how Ryder comprehends and accepts the immutable truth of life embodied in the Roman Catholic Church. Notwithstanding the fact that he is an artist, Ryder is completely steeped in the world of change. This is evident from the subject of his paintings. The 'symptom of decline' that characterizes the dynamic world, is an important feature of his paintings as well. In his own words:
"…I was called to all parts of the country to make portraits of houses that were soon to be deserted or debased; indeed, my arrival seemed often to be only a few paces ahead of the auctioneer's a presage of doom."[386]

If the subject of his paintings is 'change and decay', the style of his painting is no less un-exalted. In his own words, his work 'had nothing to recommend it except [his] growing technical skill,

[385] Ibid., 193.

[386] Ibid., 216.

enthusiasm for …subject, and independence of popular nations.'[387] If art helps the artist to realize his own self, then what Ryder has achieved is decay and retrogression. Ryder's paintings register a new low when he goes to paint in the jungles of Mexico and Central America. The jungle is a symbol of anarchy and disorder in Waugh, as we have seen in the lesser comedies, and is an unvarnished mirror-image of the modern secular world.

In order that Ryder may discover his true self, he must re-connect with the Flyte family. This happens on board the ship to England. He meets Julia, who too is trying to find her way towards the hub of her life. Julia and Ryder drift into an intensely personal and sacrilegious relationship, mistaking it to be a step towards the right goal. Yet they have doubts about their love, right from its inception.

"'Oh, my darling, why is it that love makes me hate the world? It's supposed to have quite the opposite effect. I feel as though all mankind, and God, too were in a conspiracy against us'. 'They are, they are.'"[388]

A shadow hangs over their love as it runs counter to the eternal values espoused by the Roman Catholic Church, which for Waugh is a symbol of all-liberating and redemptive Truth. Jeffrey Heath has spoken of the manner in which Sebastian moves into the 'shadows' as he runs away from his vocation. The same may be said of their love as it always finds consummation in the dark ('Oh dear', said Julia, 'Where can we hide in fair weather, we orphans of the storm?'[389]).

At Brideshead, Julia is made aware of the mistake she is committing by the harsh remark of her fervently Catholic brother, Brideshead. He reminds her that what she is mistaking for an

---

387 Ibid., 216.

388 Ibid., 263.

389 Ibid., 244.

orderly life is the quagmire of sin. Ryder, who is still a stranger to Roman Catholicism, tries to comfort her, hut is unable to do so. He explains her feeling of guilt, in the manner of psychologists, as springing from 'the nonsense you were taught in the nursery'. Julia's reply, 'How I wish it was', shows her loss of faith in the modernist jargon of secular liberalism and progress. At first, Ryder cannot make out the significance of these sudden outbursts of her moods. But gradually, he has the foreboding that their love cannot last long.

"...perhaps all our loves are merely hints and symbols; vagabond-language scrawled on gate-posts and paving-stones along the weary road that others have tramped before us; ...each straining through and beyond the other, snatching a glimpse now and then of the shadow which turns the corner always a pace or two ahead of us."[390]

As the lines mentioned above show, Ryder seems to have a premonition of the goal to which he is headed. He, therefore, regards the human love with Julia as only a stepping stone towards a higher reality signified by the hub-like Roman Catholic faith. One other image that comes to his mind at this stage is that of an arctic hut within which the trapper feels warm and cosy so long as the weight of the snow piling on the hut and the heat of the sun do not make it 'open and splinter and disappear, rolling with the avalanche into the ravine'.[391] The hut that Ryder thinks of is no other than the shell of self-preservation that the worldly man constructs around himself. The snow and the sun breaking it down are the forces that break this shell to make him aware of the eternal reality around him. Harry Blamires explains the Christian significance of such an imagery in **The Christian Mind** in the following words:

"For all teaching of Christian revelation deals with the breaking-in of the greater supernatural order upon our more limited finite world. That conception is at the heart of the doctrine

---

[390] Ibid., 288.

[391] Ibid., 295-296.

of the Incarnation. It is at the heart of every claim to individual experience of God's love and power. The Greater breaks-in upon the smaller."[392]

Ryder and Julia are on the threshold of a religious transformation now and it is hastened by the arrival of the ailing and errant Lord Marchmain at Brideshead. He is afraid of the dark and loneliness. So, he keeps the lights of his room on and also makes someone sit in his room. These are the signs of Lord Marchmain's fear of death. With the burden of sin that he carries on his shoulders without repentance, he finds it difficult to reconcile to the idea of passing away to the other world. Ryder mistakes it for love of life because he has still not understood fully the significance of Roman Catholicism. Brideshead's attempt to make his father repent for his sins so that he may be at peace with God and overcome the fear of death meet with negative results as Lord Marchmain turns the priest out. The heathen spirit within Lord Marchmain holds him back from marching ahead to the hub of life. Ryder sees in this attempt, a threat to his imminent marriage with Julia. If Lord Marchmain accepts the Last Sacrament, Ryder and Julia's love shall stand condemned as sacrilegious, as it is not permitted by Roman Catholic Church. So, he is very happy when the attempt is aborted by Lord Marchmain himself.

"I felt triumphant. I had been right, everyone else had been wrong, truth had prevailed; the threat that I had felt hanging over Julia and me ever since that evening at the fountain, had been averted, perhaps dispelled for ever…"[393]

But Ryder is wrong in thinking so. The failing health of Lord Marchmain and the fear of an unavoidable death make him repentant for his sins. Even though the room he is in has all windows open, Lord Marchmain feels stifled to death in his own cellar of sin. Even the air that he breathes flows through a pipe; it is not free. Lord Marchmain notices the similarity between the state

---

[392] Harry Blamires, The Christian Mind, op. cit., 68.

[393] Ibid., 312.

of his soul and that of the air when he whispers to himself: 'Free as air; that's what they say- "free as air". Now they bring me my air in an iron barrel'.[394]Lord Marchmain is obviously referring to the philosophy of liberalism and rationalism inherent in the Humanist and Enlightenment historiography of the twentieth century. Realizing the hollowness of the liberalist claims of human progress that had spurred his rebellion against his wife and God, he becomes introspective and wistful ('They said we were fighting for freedom; I had my own victory. Was it a crime?'[395]).

To relieve her father from this pain, Julia goes to fetch Father Mackay. Sensing in it danger to his love life with Julia, Ryder enlists the support of Cara and the doctor against this move. When she arrives, he makes them speak out the dangerous consequences of such a step. The doctor forbids it as 'the shock of seeing a priest might well kill him'. Cara thinks similarly; though she is not against the idea of having a priest by his side when he is asleep and oblivious to whatever the priest does. As Lord Marchmain seems to be in a stupor at that time, so she does not object. Julia leads the priest in who administers the last sacred religious rites to him. The priest asks Lord Marchmain to make a sign in recognition of his being sorry for all the sins of his life. When the priest does so, Charles Ryder, who till now had been resisting it finds himself praying to God to make Lord Marchmain make the sign. In the beginning, his prayer is tinged with doubt ('O God, if there is a God, forgive him his sins, if there is such a thing as sin.'[396]). The second time, when he prays, there is no expression of doubt ('I prayed more simply: 'God forgive him his sins' and 'please God, make him accept your forgiveness'[397]). It is obvious that the novelist is tracing the evolution of Charles Ryder through the changes that the two important Flyte family embers are undergoing.

---

394 Ibid., 318.

395 Ibid., 318.

396 Ibid., 322.

397 Ibid., 322.

The result of these prayers, the earlier martyrdom of Lady Marchmain and the mysterious efficacy of the Sacrament is that Lord Marchmain at last makes the sign of the Cross with his hand and thus secures the blessings of the Lord he had abjured throughout his life. Yet, it is not so abrupt a change as has been alleged by critics. Lord Marchmain has, before taking this step towards the Roman Catholic hub of life, already realised the extent of his sin which only the Lord's blessings can wash off. The administering of the Last Sacrament, however, acts as a catalyst in this process as no rational realization not aided by divine grace can claim comprehension of the Christian truth.

For the first time, Charles Ryder understands the significance of the return to faith of the errant Flyte family members and is, therefore, impelled to reward the priest for the great service. The priest, however, knows that it has not been possible by virtue of his personal abilities; he has only acted as an agent of Divine Grace. So, he refuses it. That Ryder renews the offer but this time not for him but for the parish goes to show his growing understanding of a faith to which he was otherwise a stranger.

Ryder is not the only person affected by this change for the better in Lord Marchmain; Julia too is. Both realize that their ungodly and decadent love must now come to an end in order that it may be replaced by divine love. The death-bed scene sees three people forging their way ahead to the Roman Catholic hub of the wheel of life. It is one of the most significant scenes in the book as in the successful journey of three characters from the dynamic world of secular change to the stable hub of Roman Catholicism, Waugh suggests the broad parameters of his comic vision of life. The repetition of motifs closely following the changes in the scale of values is purposive and definitive. The change for the better discernible in Julia and Lord Marchmain and the endeavour to reach the Roman Catholic hub of life provide a means of gaining an aesthetic unity. Ideas like change and progress, decline or betterment appear over and over again, often varied a little in rhythm to avoid monotony but gloriously rising to a climax somewhere. The transformation in Lord Marchmain is really the transition of the baser self of a man to a higher self, the forward movement which provides an additional touch of unity to the novel and determines the direction usually found in a greater comedy composed by Waugh.

The ease and care with which Lord Marchmain and the other errant members of the Flyte family progress towards the Roman Catholic hub of life appears, however, to have received less than adequate attention from critics and reviewers alike. Edmund Wilson castigates Waugh for abandoning the lesser comic style as he believes that 'What happens when Evelyn Waugh abandons his comic convention… turns out to be more or less disastrous. The writer, in this more normal world, no longer knows his way'.[398]He goes on to add that the novelist has supplied 'mere romantic fantasy' in this novel. That the final scene of the novel is not 'mere romantic fantasy' is not only clear from the logical inevitability with which the scene and the story reach the climax but also from the fact that is based on a real life incident. In a letter to Ronald Knox, written from Pixton Park, Dulverton, on March 14, 1945, Waugh explains the genesis of this scene.

"I am delighted that you became reconciled to B.R. in the end. It was, of course, all about the death bed. I was present at almost exactly that scene, with less extravagant décor, when a friend of mine whom we thought in this final coma and stubbornly impenitent, whose womenfolk would only let the priest in because they thought him unconscious, did exactly that, making the sign of the Cross. It was profoundly affecting and I wrote the book about that scene."[399]

Stephen Spender, however, chooses to find the real fault not merely in the concluding scenes but also in the characterization of Charles Ryder. He is of the view that Waugh has failed in delineating his development from agnosticism to an acceptance of Roman Catholicism.

---

[398] Edmund Wilson, New Yorker, 5 January 1946, in ed. Martin Stannard, op. cit., 245.

[399] Ed. Mark Amory, op. cit., 206.

"The real failure of **Brideshead Revisited** is not confined, however, to these concluding scenes. It really lies in the character of Charles Ryder. Within his sensibility is the meeting of the minds of his Catholic friends and the agnostic views he supposedly represents. His development should record the emergence of the pattern of the true religion from the unsatisfactory lives of the Marchmains, and also from his own agnosticism."[400]

The discussion preceding the death-bed scene makes it amply clear that Spender's critical analysis is not supported by the narrative. The critic is oblivious to the gradual development of true religious feeling in Charles Ryder, a process that finds its ultimate and conclusive culmination in Ryder's attitude towards the administering of the Last Sacrament to Lord Marchmain. A.A. De Vitis has, therefore, rightly observed: "It does not come as a surprise to the reader that Ryder is converted to Roman Catholicism by the novel's end. It is Waugh's subtlest point of artistic merit that he makes his hero, his observer, the one on whom the events of the narrative leave the imprint of faith. Charles' conversion is not explained in words; it is explained by the action of the novel as he moves towards a keener understanding of the family with which his life is inextricably bound."[401]

De Vitis is clearly drawing attention here to the allegorical narrative of Charles Ryder's development. Inability to discern this has led critics to overlook the graph of Ryder's gradual upward movement. Ryder's success in touching the Roman Catholic hub of the wheel of life ensures for him freedom from the pointless and decadent nature of change as represented well by the circular motion of the wheel. It also signifies the resurrection of his life which had till then been deadened by the 'cultural water-wheal' of secular existence. The journey from incomprehension to comprehension of Roman Catholicism follows the pattern of a greater comedy as enunciated by Northrop Frye end Eric Bentley.

---

400 Stephen Spender, "The World of Evelyn Waugh", The Creative Element (London: Hamish Hamilton, 1953), 172.

401 A. A. De Vitis, Roman Holiday (London: Vision Press, 1958), 46-47.

Thus, Evelyn Waugh reveals his sublime and ultimate comic vision of life through the successful spiritual odyssey of Charles Ryder.

Brideshead Revisited has, however, had to face adverse criticism even for its professedly religious purpose. Rose Macaulay, who had praised the lesser comedies for no important merit than a seeming exaggeration of life, criticized this novel for its Catholic exclusiveness.

"No purpose can well have greater importance; no faith can be more asserting than that 'the human spirit, redeemed, can survive all disasters'. But, Mr. Waugh seems to equate the divine purpose, the tremendous fact of God at work in the universe, with the obedient membership of a church; the human spirit, if redeemed, must loyally conform to this church and its rules.... it seems to reduce the formidable problems of universe and the human spirit to a level almost parochial."[402]

Undoubtedly Evelyn Waugh measures the progress of humankind in terms of only one church, the one which he accepted, but he never fails to pay attention to the artistic quality in depicting the comic vision of life associated with the liberation of humanity from the shackles of constant meaningless motion, a theme that finds recurrent expression not only in the lesser comedies of Waugh but also in the plays of the Absurd Dramatists and early poetry of T.S. Eliot. Moreover, its exclusiveness does not violate the taste and refinement of discriminating readers. In John Bunyan's **Pilgrim's Progress**, there is open and oblique criticism of all denominations other than the one professed by its hero, Christian. Evelyn Waugh, on the other hand, has pitted his Roman Catholic hero not against any other sect but against the chaotic absurdity of the modernist way of life. His own words in this context prove revealing in more ways than one: "It seems to me that in the present phase of European history the essential issue is no longer between Catholicism, on one side, and Protestantism, on the

[402] Rose Macaulay, Horizon, December 1946, in ed. Martin Stannard, op. cit., 254.

other, but between Christianity and Chaos. It is much the same situation as existed in the early Middle Ages."[403]

The Protestant Rex Mottram is presented in an ugly light because Waugh felt that the unrestrained freedom granted by the Protestant faith was facilitating the growth of a spiritual crisis. It is in the context of 'the universal validity of his massage', as pointed out by A.A.De Vitis[404], that the novel must surely be understood. In a letter to his mother, Catherine Waugh, dated 05 Feb 1945, Evelyn himself succeeded in diagnosing the reason for the hostility of the critics to the underlying Catholic massage.

"The general criticism is that it is religious propaganda. That shows how opinion has changed in 80 years. No one now thinks a book which totally excludes religion is atheistic propaganda. 80 years ago every novel included religion as part of the normal life of the people."[405]

In fact, what Waugh attempts by bringing in religion in this novel is the opening up of a grand vista of opportunity of progress from the ennui of the modern and industrial societies. Having studied History at Oxford, he had closely examined the claims of the progressive liberal and Enlightenment historiographers and found them wanting. The lesser comedies fully present the absurdity implicit in this kind of life. The artist in him also wanted to present an alternative of hope to this absurdity. This he found in the faith to which he converted of his own choice. The greater comedies present the splendour of a life that conforms to eternal religious values. Waugh distinguished between a life lived according to secular principles and the one lived according to religious principles. He finds the former's emphasis on secular change as a

---

403 Evelyn Waugh, "Converted to Rome: Why it has Happened to Me", Daily Express, 20 October 1930, in ed. Donat Gallagher, The Essays, Articles, and Reviews of Evelyn Waugh (London: Methuen, 1983), 103.

404 A. A. De Vitis, op. cit., 53.

405 Ed. Mark Amory, op. cit., 200.

means to progress not only deceptive but also ludicrous. The desire to progress by undergoing religious change is, however, venerated and celebrated as it leads man from the world of deception to that of wisdom and reality. Thus, this novel completes the comic view of life that Waugh has presented in the lesser comedies. This development is as remarkable as that of Eliot in the composition of the poetic plays after poems like **The Wasteland.** This process of development did not escape the notice of one of Waugh's reviewers, John K. Hutchens. In the **New York Times Book Review** of 30 December 1945, he maintains:

"For Mr. Waugh is very definitely an artist, with something like a genius for precision and clarity not surpassed by any novelist writing in English in his time. This has been apparent from the very beginning of his career – a career in which **Brideshead Revisited** differs in setting, tone and technique from all his earlier creative work, is yet a logical development."[406]

The development of Waugh from the lesser comedies to the greater ones is reflected in the structure of this novel. Two kinds of plots co-exist in this novel, one that of the lesser comedies and the other that of the greater comedies. The image of the wheel of life referred to earlier explains this most fittingly. Just as the rotating portion of the wheel hems in its hub, so does the plot of the lesser comedies contain within it the plot of the greater comedies. The wheel of life with its circuitous motion brings Charles Ryder back to the place, Brideshead, that he had known once very intimately. Even the chapter classification is made to underline this fact. The novel begins with a 'Prologue' that is entitled 'Brideshead Revisited' and closes with an 'Epilogue' that is entitled similarly. The circular character of the plot provides the secular frame of the novel, reflecting the themes of stagnation and absurdity so successfully portrayed in the lesser comedies. Except for this, the narrative primarily indicates the progress of the hero, Charles Ryder who is also the narrator of the progress of the errant members of the Flyte

[406] John K. Hutchens, New York Times Book Review, 30 December 1945, in ed. Martin Stannard, op. cit., 242.

family from the degrading absurdity of dynamic life to the eternal stability of religious life. The motion described is similar to that that of a person moving from the circumference of the rotating wheel to its stable centre. While the earlier portion of the novel shows the drift of the characters away from the hub, the later portion shows the resurrection of hope in the renewed effort to reach the hub.

Waugh's architectonic skill in the work of encasing is illustrated by the use of Brideshead house itself. The gaunt and overwhelming façade of this house represents the fate of all secular efforts. Like Hetton Abbey, it is both the reconstruction of an older prototype and a product of later additions over the ages. Every generation of Flytes has made some contribution to the enhancement of its grandeur. In the days when the present generation of Flytes live here, it enjoys a splendour and architectural beauty of its own. But when Charles Ryder revisits it, the house appears useless, as Hooper too observes, and the efforts that have gone into its making appear futile.

"The builders did not know the uses to which their work would descend; they made a new house with the stones of old; year by year, generation after generation, they enriched and extended it; year by year the great harvest of timber in the park grew to ripeness; until, in sudden frost came the age of Hooper; the place was desolate and all work brought to nothing; *Quomdo sedet sola civitas*. Vanity of vanities, all is vanity."[407]

In fact, it meets with the same fate that most of the other ancient buildings in the novel undergo. Waugh's novel is thus a storehouse of recorded values. It springs from and perpetuates hours in the lives of exceptional people who lived in abodes like those of Brideshead House and Hetton Abbey when their control and command of experience was at their highest. Brideshead Revisited is unique is recording the changing phases of life lived by the Flytes through the ages and the author has clearly presented the varying possibilities of life in each age. The evaluation of this novel

---

[407] Evelyn Waugh, Brideshead Revisited, op. cit., 330-331.

and for that matter of subsequent novels will be rewarding when we take into account this measure of change and man's attempts to progress as greatly desirable and definitive.

Within the secular edifice of Brideshead House is, however, the changeless and eternal flame burning in the chapel. Notwithstanding the changes undergone by the house, it has remained unchanged over the years. The changing nature of Brideshead House is, therefore, comparable to the changing nature of the revolving wheel while the unchanging flame in the chapel compares well with the unchanging transcendental hub of the wheel of life. Ryder in his redeemed and elevated state is quick enough to notice this.

"Something quite remote from anything the builders intended, has come out of their work, and out of the fierce little human tragedy in which I played; something none of us thought about at the time; a small red flame – the flame which the old knights saw from their tombs, which they saw put out; that flame burns again for other soldiers, far from home, farther, in heart, than Aire of Jerusalem….."[408]

The flame plays up metaphorically the significance of the 'eternal perspective' without which life has no values and which, in the words of Harry Blamires, is a 'prime mark of the Christian mind'.[409]

In the light of the foregoing discussion, it can be safely inferred that Waugh has presented Ryder's "sacred" memories in a "profane" frame and not, as Jeffrey Heath[410] maintains, "profane" memories in a "sacred frame". The rejection of the secular way of life is clearly manifest in the plot of the novel and it should have itself absolved Waugh from the charge of snobbery levelled by

---

408 Ibid., 331

409 Harry Blamires, op. cit. 67.

410 Jeffrey Heath, op. cit., 52.

Donat O' Donnell in the article, 'The Pieties of Evelyn Waugh', published in **Bell.**

"In Catholic countries Catholicism is not romantic, not invariably associated with big houses, or the fate of an aristocracy.... but the Catholicism of Mr. Waugh, and of certain other English converts, is hardly separable from a personal romanticism and a class loyalty."[411]

However, T.J. Barrington, another reviewer of Waugh's novels, disputes this claim of Donat O' Donnell, as he finds it wanting in evidence. It is patent that Donat O' Donnell's article fails to prove the existence in Waugh's mind of a necessary connexion between snobbery and Catholicism. To lead us to believe, then, on the evidence produced that there is implicit in **Brideshead Revisited** an heretical private religion is to attempt to bamboozle us. Waugh's pieties have not been shown to have mingled with Catholicism to produce a private religion, 'a highly personal system of belief and devotion.'[412]
Donat 'O Donnell's arguments appear substantially fabricated and he succeeds in twisting the facts recorded in the novel. Not without reason, Waugh responded to it in right earnest and recorded his reaction thus:

"I think perhaps your reviewer is right in calling me a snob; that is to say I am happiest in the company of the European upper-classes; but I do not think this preference is necessarily an offence against charity, still less against Faith. I can assure you it had no influence on my conversion."[413]

Waugh is justified in making the remark as his decision to join the Roman Catholic Church was not, as Father D' Arcy admits, emotional but intellectual. It is the emotional part of his self

---

411 Donat O' Donnell, "The Pieties of Evelyn Waugh", Bell, December 1946, in ed. Martin Stannard, op. cit., 259.

412 T. J. Barrington, Bell, February 1947, in ed. Martin Stannard, op. cit., 265.

413 Evelyn Waugh, Bell, July 1947, in ed. Martin Stannard, op. cit. 270.

which enjoyed the company of the upper classes and not the intellectual or rational part which saw through this folly and accordingly, steered Waugh away from secular change to a religious change in the act of his conversion to Roman Catholicism. Waugh writes appropriately; "Nor does this preference unduly affect my writing. Besides Hooper there are two character in **Brideshead Revisited** whom I represent as worldly – Rex Mottram, a millionaire, and Lady Celia Ryder, a lady of high birth. Why did my reverence for money and rank not sanctify these two?"[414]

Waugh here suggests that life lived at the secular level of existence, however, resplendent and glorious apparently, is a prey to time and absurdity, whereas life lived religiously is alone progressive and significant. In conveying this vision of life, Waugh has used characters borrowed from the upper strata of life because they alone, and not the poor, have reached a stage of existence where self-realization and not self-preservation can dominate the thoughts of men. D.H. Lawrence in his study of Thomas Hardy's novels published in the collection of his posthumously published papers titled, Phoenix, supported the use of aristocratic characters in Thomas Hardy in a similar manner. Quite justifiably Waugh took offence about a similar accusation levelled by a close friend like David Pryce-Jones who in **Time and Tide** had observed, 'His essential view of society is indeed based upon a belief in the inherent superiority of one section at the expense of all others.'[415] Upon knowing, however, of Waugh's displeasure over it, he later on regretted his stand in the matter.

In **Brideshead Revisited**, therefore, Waugh said what he had left unsaid in the lesser comedies, that true progress constitutes a change in the very perspective of man. It is the carving of a path towards the stability of the hub of the wheel of life that is free from the delusion of secular progress induced by secular change. It is this message that forms an inseparable and essential part of his comic vision of life, and it is very vividly reflected in the greater comedies.

---

[414] Ibid., 271.

[415] David Pryce-Jones, Time and Tide 23 July 1960, in ed. Martin Stannard, op. cit., 274.

Furthermore, the use of a highly suggestive plot succeeds in shaping his thought in an aesthetically satisfying way. Waugh here sees life freed of irrelevancies and his task, we may safely conclude, is to clear away the ordinary trivia and distractions of our existence and lay bare the core of meaning concerning change and progress in an entertaining manner.

Helena

In **Helena** (1950) Waugh expresses his firm conviction that progress lies not in secular growth but in religious transformation in such a way that his thought creates a kind of compulsion upon the mind of the reader. Progress, as Frank J. Yarts has also maintained, 'involves breaking the cycle (of secular life) with novelty.'[416] Waugh's protagonist in this novel achieves it in two stages. In the first stage, she realizes the futility of secular change and in the second, she rejects it in favour of the path of the Messiah, Christianity, which promises eternal novelty in 'the Easter sense in which all things are made new in the risen Christ'.[417] As the dark recesses of her mind keep on getting enlightened with the flame of religious devotion, Helena forges ahead on a linear path towards the hub of the wheel of life which by its intrinsic nature not only transcends the relativism of the wheel but also supports that. In the triumphant conclusion of her progressive journey, not only does she elevate herself to the rank of a spiritual elite but she also gives expression to a fundamental tenet of Roman Catholicism: the historicity of the eternal Christian truth. Helena's transformation for the better is anticipated and conveyed through symbols and images which occur less frequently in **Brideshead Revisited** than in this novel. As the novel charts a movement from the insignificance of 'dynamic' existence to the significance of religious life, the novel may either be termed a divine comedy or a greater comedy.

---

[416] Frank J. Yartz, Alan L. Larson, and David J. Husserl, Progress and the Crisis of Man (Chicago: Nelson-Hall, 1976), 86.

[417] Evelyn Waugh, To Robin Campbell, 27 December 1945, in ed. Mark Amory, op. cit. 215.

In order that we may study the cohesiveness of the events narrated and also their relevance to the novel's thematic line of intention, a careful consideration of its plot becomes imperative. Like the eighteenth century 'histories' in English literature, the novel indicates a temporal movement in its plot. The loss of causality in such plots is made up by the close connection of the incidents narrated with the central character in whose life they invariably occur. As this novel has a 'Plot of character', to use Northrop Fry's terminology, sheer temporal progression does not come in the way of the novelist's thematic line of intention. The choice of such a plot liberates the novelist from the shackles of system-building logic, which is a human faculty and which incidentally was glorified by the Enlightenment historiographers as an agent of secular change. To unfold its greater comic vision of hope and resurrection, the novel uses the techniques of selective narration of incidents and the use of symbolic imagery. The unique aesthetic form, that is lent to the novel thereby, abjures logical argument even when it reveals the author's comic vision of life in the gradual emancipation of Helena from the yoke of sterile 'dynamic' existence. The novel should, therefore, be read not as a spiritual case-history of Helena's development but as an aesthetic expression of the theme of inevitability of progress through religious change. The recurrent image of the wheel of life plays as always a dominate role not only in conveying this theme but also in defining Waugh's ultimate comic vision of life. When the story opens, we are told that Helena is the daughter of the British King Coel, Paramount Chief of the Trivonantes. Christopher Sykes, Waugh's friend and biographer, gives the background to this aspect of Helena's story.

"Among the many unreliable accounts of St. Helena's origin, one of the most dubious is that she was a British princess, a daughter of the possibly historic king Cole after whom Colchester is said to be named. Evelyn decided that she should be a daughter of this British King."[418]

[418] Christopher Sykes, Evelyn Waugh (London: William Collins Sons & Co. Ltd., 1975) 318.

Waugh was a student of history at Oxford and it is curious that his historical sensibility was not offended in selecting a doubtful anecdote. In the 'Preface' to the novel, he explains, 'Where the authorities are doubtful, I have often chosen the picturesque in preference to the plausible'[419]. The reasons stated here hardly satisfy standards which one expects in historical exploration. That Waugh's statement is meant to mystify rather than clarify is obvious form his assertion in one of his letters to Nancy Mitford[420]. In fact, the idea of declaiming on one's works never gained favour with him[421]. For him, as for Eliot, a work of art is its own spokesperson. So, if one wants to know the reasons for such a choice, one needs to look for them within the aesthetic confines of the novel. Waugh also tells us that none of Helena's father's family 'had died naturally' and that one had gone crazy and died in a fit of abnormality. These details bring out the utter irrationality of world into which Helena was born. Waugh is obviously giving Helena the nativity of a dynamic world. In the lesser comedies, Waugh has already given us horrid as well as comic pictures of the dynamic world, such as the jungles of Brazil in A Handful of Dust and the disorganized city of Dierra Dowa in Black Mischief.. In fact, to the Romans of that time, Britain was as culturally backward a country as the African nations of early twentieth century. By granting a British origin to his heroine, Waugh has therefore placed her in the barbaric environs of the dynamic world. It is essential from the thematic pint of view as the novelist has to show Helena's rejection of the cramping confines of the dynamic world in order that she may break the cycle of the world of change by stepping out of it and make for the Roman Catholic hub of the wheel of life.

Helena's father's family traces its descent from the Trojans. But while her father is content with listening to songs that celebrate his proud pedigree, her imagination is fired with the desire to see Troy the original home of her valiant ancestors. Therefore, often in

---

419 Evelyn Waugh, Helena (Harmondsworth: Penguin, 1984), 9.

420 Ed. Mark Amory, op. cit., 273

421 Evelyn Waugh, The Ordeal of Gilbert Pinfold (Harmondsworth: Penguin, 1984), 9.

her conversations, she refers to herself as an 'exile'. With the help of irony, Waugh evokes one of the major Christian symbols in the book. It is a matter of common knowledge among the Christians, but not for Helena who is still a pagan, that man was exiled by God from the Garden of Eden for transgressing against His Will. The pagan world in which Helena is born is the fallen one and her exile gains significance from the Christian context, unknown to her at this stage of her life. The imagery of the wheel of life aptly embodies this distinction between the post-lapsarian world of mortality and the prelapsarian world of Eternal Truth. While the revolving wheel, with its relative states of motion and rest, represents the former, the hub of the wheel with its transcendental Absoluteness represents the latter. While Helena's quest for her true home holds the potential of the Christian quest for the prelapsarian world, it has a universal significance in the context of the wheel-imagery as it mirrors man's quest for the absolute transcendental reality. As the Roman Catholic Church is regarded by its followers as the temporal representative of God on the earth, Helena's progress is narrated in terms of her growing comprehension and acceptance of Roman Catholicism, her true home.

The other symbols that presage Helena's quest for the Roman Catholic home include the sexual reveries and fancies of her pagan youthful days. It goes to the credit of Waugh as a master story teller that he should have blatantly sexual fantasies into deeply eschatological symbols. Helena often pictures herself as a horse struggling for supremacy over its rider and then falling in line with the latter's wishes.

"Helena had galloped thus in solitude hours without number, but of late years, as her womanhood broke bud, a keener excitement infused the game. Two played it now. There was the will of the rider that spoke down the length of the rein, from the gloved hand to the warm and tender tongue under the bit; articulate, coaxing, commanding, now barely sensible, light as an eyelid, now steel-hard and compelling; that spoke in the stab of the spur and sudden double smart of the whip. And there was the will of the animal to shrink and start, to toss aside the restraint of the bridle and saddle and the firm legs across her, to shake the confident equipoise ... Then at the height of the play, in sweat and blood-flecked foam, came the sweet moment of surrender, the fusion, and the two were off together, single, full-stretched over the resounding earth... with none but the wind to oppose them. She took some handling, the chestnut."[422]

The symbolism evoked is overtly sexual. Waugh took pains, as is evident, to give a graphic and detailed account of it. It would not perhaps be out of place to mention here Waugh's indebtedness to Penelope Betjeman who upon his request supplied his imagination with the details given in the book.[423] Notwithstanding its sexual overtone, the imagery invoked here has a deeper symbolic significance hidden in the cloak of irony. The rider stands for the will of god and the horse for the unrestrained and blind human will. While God tries to lead man to the right goal, the will of man, out of its ignorance, struggles against its good and tries to lead man towards false goals. Unable to comprehend the spiritual significance of this struggle at this stage of her life, Helena relishes its overtly sexual value alone. The surrender of the horse to the will of the rider looks forward to the time when Helena will surrender her wild desires to the supreme will of God. Thus, Waugh very deftly prepares the reader for Helena's conversion to Roman Catholicism in the future.

Waugh introduces at this stage another symbolism, the allusion to the Helen of Troy. The story of Helen of Troy illustrates to good advantage the Christian symbolism contained in the horse imagery. The parallel between the two Helens is established through casual references and the naming of the second chapter, 'Fair Helena Forfeit'. While Paris abducted the Greek Helen to Troy, leaving her deceived husband, Menelaus, fretting and fuming, Constantius wins the hand of the British Helena with her father's consent though that is given very reluctantly. The naming of the second chapter thus intends to keep the parallelism between the two

---

422 Evelyn Waugh, Helena, op. cit., 24-25.

423 Ed. Mark Amory, op. cit. 207.

stories alive. The story of Helena's abduction is the story of carnal desires let loose and the comparison servers to highlight, on the surface, the grossness of the love between Constantius and Helena. But, the significance of this comparison does not end here. Dr. F.J. Stopp has rightly remarked in his essay, 'Grace in Reins':

"When Aphrodite first plucked at Helena's gown, it was in the guise of her natural love for Constantius. But the invitation to the mystical marriage of the soul was not for long able to disguise itself under the 'steadfast and bruised passion' of which Helena thought that Constantius was the only object."[424]

Thus, the Hellenic parallel evokes the deeper Christian symbolism of the mystical marriage of the individual soul with the spirit of Christ and prepares the readers as the other symbols employed in the novel do, for Helena's eventual spiritual odyssey.

In order that Helena may find her way to the hub of the wheel of life, she must first outgrow the static opinions of her adolescence. Until these are shattered, she cannot take the next step. The static opinions Helena nurses have grown out of her cloistered life in the nursery and school-room. These are embodied in the idealized images of her nurse's sapper-sergeant father and the scholarly Longinus. While the former represents the chivalric ideals which have little authenticity in the dynamic world of the Roman Empire, the latter stands for secular learning which bestows on man no immunity from the dangers that beset ordinary people. Dr. Frederick J. Stopp has rightly called them, 'powerful forerunners in the mind of Helena'.[425] Lionel Stevenson's[426] attempt to compare her to static characters like Paul Pennyfeather, Scott King and William Boot is, however, unjustified as unlike them Helena steps

---

424 F. J. Stopp, "Grace in Reins", Month, August 1953, in ed. Martin Stannard, op. cit., 332.

425 Ibid., 331.

426 Lionel Stevenson, The History of the English Novel, Vol 11 (New York: Barnes & Noble, 1967), 359.

out of the mould of a static character once her adolescence is over. Once in Rome, she sees her adolescent illusions melt away in the heat of the treacherous politics and warfare of the Roman Empire. Unlike the nurse's chivalrous sapper-sergeant father, her husband Constantius resorts to guile and deception to vanquish his enemy, Tetricus. She realizes that the world of Roman Empire has no regard for the code of chivalry to settle disputes. Of necessity, she must reject the inadequate and obsolete code of chivalry. Helena must look for ideals which are more permanent and real than these static ones, nurtured in her by her nanny. So, John Raymond's remark that 'Waugh's converts generally get to heaven the back way, through having had the right kind of Nanny'[427] is as much uncharitable as it is far from the truth. The death of Longinus shatters her last adolescent illusion about the potency of secular learning. Longinus' excellence in secular learning fails to save him from his death. Besides, with his death, all his scholarship comes to nought. With the death of Longinus, all her static opinions are shattered.

Helena now finds herself in the wilderness of the dynamic world of the Roman Empire. As it is itself devoid of order, it fails to provide her with an alternative code of conduct. The politics of Rome is full of intrigues and counter-intrigues. No sooner does a warrior ascend the throne as a king than news arrives that he has been killed by his own men. Moreover, every time an emperor dies, an internecine war among the claimants to the throne breaks out which takes a toll of both life and property. The instability of the Roman Empire is scarcely screened from her. Besides, the glamour of Roman court life doesn't dazzle her as it does her husband, who seeks a more important role in it. So, when her husband expresses his desire of becoming an emperor, she is not impressed. She is intelligent enough to realize that their paths are divergent. While her husband's lies round the wheel of life which promises no substantial progress, hers lies straight toward its transcendent hub. Even when Constantius turns to religion, he does so not for

---

[427] John Raymond, New Statesman, 21 October 1930, 374, in ed. Martin Stannard, op. cit., 321.

acquiring any permanent ideals but for earthly considerations. Thus, not even for once does he make an attempt to set his feet on the real path of progress as Helena does. So, Helena's estrangement from Constantius is both obvious and natural. Besides, it helps to clear her way for her next stopover on the road to her emergence as a spiritual elite. In order that she may realize the significance of the Mystical Marriage with Christ, she needs to eschew the pleasures of the Flesh. Pointing out their tempting nature, Harry Blamires observes, ' The magnitude and variety of the evil forces waiting to ensnare the human soul are hinted at in the triple formulation, the World, the Flesh and the Devil.'[428] Helena's ability to overcome these obstacles is anticipated in her decision to go hunting the very next day after her first nuptial night with Constantius.

"Next day, while Constantius dispatched the advanced-party and distributed the pack-loads, Helena went hunting once more for the last time over the familiar country."[429]

Hunting is an eschatological age-old metaphor used to convey man's pursuit of the immutable values of life, which Waugh associated with Roman Catholicism. By positioning this action, close to the nuptial night, Waugh is skilfully suggesting Helena's future emergence as a spiritual elite. While Helena will pursue Reality like the hounds, God like a good hunter will put the hounds on the right track. The comparison is appropriate from the Roman Catholic point of view which believes that the reality of God is unattainable to human reason unaided by Divine Grace.[430] The parting of ways between Constantius and Helena reaches the climax in their divorce and Constantius' second marriage. Helena's disenchantment with both the secular splendour of the Roman state and with her husband's obsession with temporal gains is reflected by what Waugh himself once experienced.

---

[428] Harry Blamires, op. cit., 86.

[429] Evelyn Waugh, Helena, op. cit., 32.

[430] The New Encyclopedia Britannica, Vol. 15 (Chicago: Encyclopedia Britannica Inc., 1981), 993.

"Those who have read my work will perhaps understand the character of the world into which I exuberantly launched myself. Ten years of that world sufficed to show me that life there, or anywhere, was unintelligible and unendurable without God."[431]

With the rejection of both the static as well as dynamic worlds, Helena is forced to explore the meaning of purposeful life elsewhere. She is aided in it by her common-sense. In one of her meetings with the Gnostic Marcias, who spins a long and convoluted narrative about the truth of existence like the Sophists, she demands answers to three simple questions: When did the events occur? Where did they occur? And how does he know them? By asking these child-like questions, she wishes to be sure about Marcias' version of Truth. Marcias evades these questions by discounting them as 'a child's question'.[432] Lanctatius, the Christian tutor of her grandson, however, answers them without any hesitation. He tells her where and when god was incarnated in the person of Jesus Christ. Upon being asked how he knows about it, he replies that he had got this information from the church which is the custodian of Christian truth and is therefore responsible for handing it down to posterity. He voices here the Roman Catholic belief in the 'body of truth transmitted to the church through the college of bishops preserved by oral tradition'[433] Satisfied with the authenticity of the Christian truth, Helena is eager to know whether Jesus Christ was a mere historical figure or he transcended the limitations of Time and Space to testify to the timelessness of the Christian truth. She, therefore, asks him whether he has been seen thereafter. To this, Lanctatius replies that saints and martyrs have seen him in their visions even after his Crucifixion. To be sure that Lanctatius is not hoodwinking her, she asks him to name one such saint. As the church had not yet come out into the open, this information was reserved only for the baptized to protect Christians

---

431 Evelyn Waugh, "Come Inside", in ed. Donat Gallagher, A Little Order (London: Eyre Methuen, 1977), 148.

432 Evelyn Waugh, Helena, op. cit., 84.

433 The New Encyclopedia Britannica, op. cit., 994.

from attacks by the pagan kings and warriors. So, he refuses to disclose the name of any such saint. Helena's discourse with Lanctatius, however, convinces her of the reality of the Christian truth. Helena likes the fact that unlike the truth enunciated by the Gnostics, it is real and verifiable historically despite its supernatural dimensions. It is analogous to the hub of the wheel of life which despite transcending the limitations of relativity produced by the circular motion of the wheel, is palpable and real. The exile finds her true home in the reality of Christian revelation and the conversion to Catholicism anticipated in the symbols mentioned earlier materializes now. Helena is redeemed from the sin of secular earthly life through her conversion to the Catholic faith.

Helena's acceptance of Christianity needs to be distinguished from that of Constantine, her son by Constantius. Though Constantine allows the church to operate without any persecution and even accords an honourable place to the Pope, he remains deprived of the Church's redemptive power as he does not accept it. In fact, Constantine's benevolent decision stems not out of any proper understanding of the church but out of his fear of it as an adversary. The reconciliatory approach towards it is thus born out of political expediency. Besides, he owes it to Pope Sylvester who cures him of an incurable disease. Even the Cross in whose name he wins his battles against his foes is a Labarum, seen in a vision, which is far from being a Cross. His misunderstanding of the redemptive power of baptism and admission to the church is such that it prevents him from being baptized; he only places himself under the protection of Christ. Constantine postpones his baptism to the last hours of his life because of the misconception that if he gets baptized earlier than that, he shall have time to sin and will thus become unworthy of Christ's mercy at the time of taking leave of this world. He, therefore, perverts the significance of Christianity, the way Mrs. Melrose Ape does in **Vile Bodies.** In this sense, he continues to be as far from the Roman Catholic hub of life, as his father Constantius was.

Again, the official recognition of Christianity scarcely has any impact on his mode of running the government. His kingdom is run by his pseudo-Christian wife, Fausta, who makes him kill anyone who earns her ill-will by suggesting that the person poses a threat to the stability of his crown. Constantine, as we know, had once told Helena that he must rule if he wants to live. The determination to rule for the sake of self-preservation is indicative of Constantine's exclusion from the Grace of God, When Fausta tries to incriminate even his mother, Helena, he realizes her Mephistophelean grip over his insecure mind. In a true spirit of savage ruthlessness, he has her roasted alive in her much-favoured bath. It contrasts with his mother's forgiving attitude and indicates his inability to comprehend the essence of Christianity. Even the house where he lives is a sort of Kafkaesque world. People do not speak each other's real name and disappearance of the members of the royal household is regarded as a regular phenomenon. So, in stark contrast with his mother, he is an epitome of Power without Grace and the world over which he presides continues to be deprived of the stability and order. Unable to see his mistake, Constantine is of the opinion that Christianity is not meant for the heathen-blooded Romans and he decides to shift his capital from Rome to a place which is free from the dark past of Rome. His decision is like that of his father who had wished to fence Rome from the onslaught of the marauding barbarians from the North. He fails to understand the significance of the Incarnation of Christ. Helena and Pope Sylvester, on the other hand, are aware that Christ came to redeem the fallen. Rome occupies a significant place in Christianity, as it has been a witness to the long and militant history of the church. In was here that men chose to part with their lives for the sake of devotion to the eternal truth contained in the arrival and resurrection of Christ. While the religious significance of Rome is unknown to Constantine, it no longer escapes Helena's notice who is now near the Roman Catholic hub of life. It is suggestive of Helena's spiritual development from the time when she considered Rome no more than a centre of secular human civilization. Yet, it is not altogether unexpected. Even when Helena as a pagan was making for her new home in the Roman Empire, she had questioned Constantius about the necessity of fencing Roman civilization from the onslaught of the marauding barbarians living in the north. A truly advanced society would indeed throw its doors open to all and sundry rather than shutting itself in for the test of civilization lies not only in the ability to withstand barbaric assaults but also in the ability to reform and sublimate the barbarism in man. By virtue of its transcendental orientation, Roman Catholicism for Waugh is capable of doing both and hence a Christian society does not have to shut its door upon the fallen. The philosophical background of Waugh's comic vision of life is, therefore, not exclusive but all inclusive.

Though Helena has found her true home in the transcendental city of God as represented in its temporal form by the church, she has not yet attained elevation to saint-hood that accrues from her mystical marriage with the Holy Spirit. The quest for the real Cross helps her attain this highest of ranks among the mortals. The person she meets in the course of her search for the Cross is Bishop Macarius, a person as simple as she has been yearning to meet for a long time. In him she finds embodied the true spirit of Christianity. He can distinguish between church as a community of the pious in communions with the Holy Spirit and the church as a mere temporal edifice in the shape of well constructed and architecturally splendid structures. While the former acts as a rock of faith, the latter is a victim of the depredations of time and perverse human will. In his enthusiasm to restore the see of Aelia Capitolina, the birth place of Jesus Christ, to its original glory and also to save its laity from the malefic influence of the Bishop of Caesarea, Bishop Macarius asks the Emperor to make it a full-fledged see. Impressed by the reality of the Christian truth, Constantine shows his devotion in the only way known to his secular mind: the excavation of the holy places and their decoration in the modern style by a new-fangled architect. Bishop Macarius is dismayed by this invasion of the secular spirit as it strips the holy places of their private purity and throws open the doors of desecration by the casually-interested tourist- public. The humility and concern for truth embodied in him is matched only by Helena, which shows the distance she has covered ever since she started moving away from the world of intrigue and savagery.

It is to his see that Helena repairs for discovering the Cross, unknown even to Pope Sylvester. It is interesting to compare her shift in interest from the excavation of Troy to that of the Cross, with Tony Last's fateful static quest for the lost City in the jungles of Brazil. Though both of them are explorers, Tony is incapacitated in his quest by his static opinions but Helena, who has outgrown them, is aided in her quest by her understanding of the Roman Catholic Church. So, while the former meets with a tragic end, Helena meets with success. Yet, when she seeks the advice of the army of speculative thinkers, they are unable to pinpoint the exact spot where the excavation could be started. So, she resorts to the best means of knowing it. She undertakes fasting during the Lent with a view to purifying her body for the descent of Divine Grace without whose aid revelation of truth is impossible. With this, Helena takes the final step towards acceptance by God. Renouncing the pleasures of the flesh, she perfects herself for the union with the Divine, a conclusion already foreshadowed in the parallel drawn with the Helena of Troy. The mystical marriage with the Divine grants her an insight into the working of nature and she is able to transcend the barriers of time and space, an idea deftly conveyed by Waugh in her dream about the Wandering Jew. The discovery of the Cross raises her to the ranks of the highest among mortals. In fact, she enters the select community of saints who form a vital link between mortals and God. In addition, her discovery bears testimony to the historical authenticity of Christian truth. Its significance is best expressed in Waugh's own words:

> "Everything about the new religion was capable of interpretation, could be refined and diminished; everything except the unreasonable assertion that God becomes man and dies on the Cross; not a myth or an allegory; true God, truly incarnate, tortured to death at a particular moment in time, at a particular geographical place, as a matter of plain historical truth." [434]

---

434 Evelyn Waugh, "St. Helena Empress", Month, January 1952, in ed. Donat Gallagher, The Essays, Articles and Reviews of Evelyn Waugh, op. cit., 410.

But the discovery also opens the possibility of an obsession with relics. It would not only commercialize religion but also erode the significance of relics in drawing attention to the historical veracity of the Christian truth. The most vulnerable will be the teeming majority, which often ignores the essence, and substitutes the ritual for the essence. Waugh does not gloss over this threat. Rather, he presents it very artistically in the form of the Wandering Jew, who appears in Helena's dream. The Wandering Jew is symbolic of man's insatiable quest for making profit out of everything, including religion, thereby profaning it with the love of the World. The Jew minces no words in enunciating his motives behind the discovery of True Cross. In the consequent popularity of Christian relics, he brazenly declares that he will make profit out of the sale of relics, real or fictitious. Finding that the supernatural context of these relics outweighs their temporal value, she goes ahead with the work of unearthing it. Waugh thus brings out the dual nature of the relics. As mere earthly things, they have no significance. But as participants in the historical basis of Christianity, they are significant. If man gives undue importance to the former, it does not inculpate them but degrades the stature of man himself. Christopher Sykes underestimates this significance when he comes down on the novel for playing up the significance of the discovery of the Cross:

"I think the book's weakness throughout lies in expression of a false estimate. Unlike Islam, another down-to-earth religion, Christianity does not depend on relics. They are regarded, and even in decadent times have always been regarded as 'aids to devotion', nothing more than that. Jerusalem is a holy city to Christians, but its total destruction would not disturb Christianity as the total destruction of Mecca and the Kaaba would disturb Islam."[435]

Waugh's own assertion of the point that has been made in our analysis of the novel also amply answers the charge made by Sykes.

---

[435] Christopher Sykes, op. cit., 320.

"It is not fantastic to claim that her discovery entitles her to a place in the Doctorate of the Church, for she was not merely adding one more stupendous trophy to the hoard of relics which were everywhere being unearthed and enshrined. She was asserting in sensational form a dogma that was in danger of neglect."[436]

Christopher Sykes has faulted the book even for the introduction of the Wandering Jew in the dream sequence of Helena.[437] The first objection to it concerns his characterization and Waugh's inability to make him rise 'above the music-hall original'. He goes on to say that it 'was not a type of comedy in which he was equipped to compete with the old hands'. His second objection to it stems out of a deeper cause. He maintains that 'the intrusion of the Wandering Jew seriously weakness the dominance' of the admirable theme concerning the literal reality of the Cross. While his first argument is plausible, his second objection is not. Far from weakening the theme, the introduction of the Wandering Jew strengthens it as it points out the danger of an attitude giving precedence to the Cross as a material object over its significance in paying attention to the historicity of the Christian Revelation.
The development of Helena from a static girl with romantic nations to a saint with *sub specie aeternitatis* vision is accomplished by Waugh not with direct authorial comments and exposition but with the help of images and symbols used sparingly and purposefully. The discriminating reader does not fail to trace different stages of her progress. There is no wobble in the line of development and the character of Helena has been depicted much more meaningfully than Charles Ryder's. It is somewhat intriguing that A.A. De Vitis should have been impressed by the latter's development and not by Helena's.

"In **Brideshead Revisited** it had not been necessary to describe the actual moment of Charles Ryder's conversion, though Waugh had done so subtly, meaningfully. In **Helena**, however, he asks his readers to accept the fact that an intellectually curious girl

---

436 Evelyn Waugh, "St. Helena Empress", op. cit., 409.

437 Christopher Sykes, op. cit., 320.

develops into a middle-aged woman who seeks a meaning to the riddle of life and through the grace of God is allowed to find religious conviction as well as the wood of the True Cross. These points are not consistent within the portrayal of her character."[438]

John Raymond's[439] dissatisfaction with the content of the novel stems out of his opinion that a 'Christian saint and empress is not perhaps the most suitable theme for a satirist' like Waugh. The remark is indicative of his inability to see Waugh's deft artistry in developing the plot along the lines of Helena's development as a spiritual elite. Like him, the correspondent of the **Time**, dated 23 October 1950, complained that not only **Helena** but even **Brideshead Revisited** was an unfortunate aberration from Waugh's normal vein of satiric fiction and he hoped that Waugh would return to his so-called original style.

"Several times in his writing life – in his study of Jesuit Edmund Campion, in **Brideshead Revisited**, and now in **Helena** – Author Waugh has tried to clear the satiric brambles out of his literary field, and to plant in their stead the herb of grace. He has had no very impressive crop so far, but most Waugh's readers don't mind. They can be pretty sure another season will bring forth a bucketful of raspberries on the old Waugh briers."[440]

The study of the novel's narrative pattern shows the consistent development in the character of Helena and also the use of selective imagery to further the novelist's thematic line of intention to show the grandeur of human resurrection through the working of Divine Grace. A. A. De Vitis has, however, castigated the novel for its loose construction. He maintains:

"**Helena** is more valid as an historical commentary and as an apology for Roman Catholicism than as a novel which creates an

---

[438] A. A. De Vitis, op. cit., 66-67.

[439] Ed. Martin Stannard, op. cit., 321.

[440] Ed. Martin Stannard, op. cit., 324.

experience of life. The religious theme is, of course, the controlling one; but it does not sustain the characterization or the plot incidents. Individual scenes are sharply drawn- Fausta's murder, Constantine's sermon- but the elements of the novel remain disparate. The theology underlying the structure is too apparent – too dogmatic, if possible. The religious theme fights for prominence, and it achieves it at the expense of art."[441]

His argument ignores the pivotal role played by the imagery of the wheel of life in shaping the novelist's comic vision of life and also in endowing its aesthetic expression with structural cohesiveness. Most of the characters and episodes, as has been made clear from the preceding analysis, help in the movement of the plot from the dynamic fringes of the British and the Roman societies, represented in the wheel-imagery by the revolving wheel, to the immutable reality of Roman Catholicism, represented by the hub that not only transcends the relativistic duality of the wheel but also supports its existence. Dr. F.J. Stop has rightly appreciated the movement of the plot along its thematic line of intention which culminates in Helena's supreme act of ascension to the status of Saints.

"But the special interest of this book is that, by choosing as the central character one about whose life almost nothing else is known but this one supreme, final and yet constitutive act, the author has a clear field in which to build up the total rounded picture of a life and a social and historical setting whose every line of development converges on to that point."[442]

David Lodge's criticism of the novel's structure springs out of according wrong priority to the themes inherent in this work. Though, the novel does intend 'to honor St. Helena, and through her to emphasize the historicity of the incarnation and the

---

441 A. A. De Vitis, op. cit., 67.

442 F. J. Stopp, "Grace in Reins", Month, August 1953, in ed. Martin Stannard, op. cit., 327.

common-sense reasonableness of Christian revelation'[443] but that is not its central theme and any attempt aimed at judging its structure by this yardstick is bound to mystify the nature of its plot and consequently, lower Waugh's master craftsmanship in it. The theme which structures the all-controlling comic vision of life implicit in the novel is that through religious change alone can an individual hope to progress and resurrect life, groaning in the grinding mill of the dynamic world. That Divine Grace is made to aid the intellectual efforts of the protagonist in achieving this change is because of the Roman Catholic nature of the religious change intended. Besides, in order that this theme may be plotted graphically, in the literal sense of the term, the protagonist has to be shown rejecting the dynamic world before she may realize the urgency of religious change. This calls for the portrayal of the world rejected. So, if the novelist has indicted the world of the fourteenth century Roman Empire and the modern world, through the suggestive use of a modern prose style, he has not, by any means, eroded the impact of the comic vision of life conveyed through Waugh's concept of change and progress. Thus, David Lodge's objection on the emphasis laid on the 'oblique comments on modern life,' is not justified. The message contained in Helena's life regarding the achievement of progress through a religious change is made more relevant to modern times by the use of a modern prose style which is nearer to modern man's pattern of thinking. Dr. Frederick J. Stopp[444] has offered another very interesting and plausible reason for its employment in narrating this 'venerable Christian story'. In his opinion, 'The alleged incongruity is in fact a congruity, that between the supernatural and the natural; and … this is a problem which will always face the 'Catholic' novel.' A little later, he goes on to suggest: 'Further reflection at a distance of time may succeed in revealing this incongruity as the key to Mr. Waugh's greatest success.' What he is trying to suggest can be understood clearly in the light of the wheel-imagery which moulds the structure of this novel. The hub of the wheel of life, representative of Roman Catholicism, is an eternal reminder of the

---

443 David Lodge, op. cit., 34.

444 F. J. Stopp, op. cit., 325.

manifestation of the transcendental reality in the sense-reality. Thus, it confirms the fact of the supernatural impinging on the natural, an idea basic to Roman Catholic theology. Harry Blamires has summed up this idea thus: "The conception of truth proper to the Christian mind is determined by the supernatural orientation of the Christian mind. When we Christians speak of "the great truths" of the Christian Faith, we mean especially those doctrines describing the meeting of the temporal and the eternal, doctrines testifying to a reality beyond our finite order, which has impinged upon that order and still impinges upon it; the doctrines of the Divine Creation, the Incarnation, the Redemption, the work of the Holy Spirit."[445]

The choice of a 'natural' idiom for the 'supernatural' truth highlighted by Helena's discovery of the True Cross is, thus, an admirable literary technique successfully made use of by Waugh. Asked by Christopher Sykes about its artistic merit, Waugh grew eloquent and ecstatic, comparing it to the best ever done by T.S. Eliot, who shared his concern with the aesthetic expression of religious values in life.

"I think you mean T.S. Eliot. It's just as good as anything he can do. In prose I mean. You've never written anything so good. I don't think Graham Greene has or Tony Powell. It's by far the best book I have ever written or ever will write. It's almost as good as Quennell."[446]

Waugh's enthusiasm is not as unjustified as Sykes[447] considers it. As an aesthetic expression of the novelist's concept of change and progress and an embodiment of his consequent sublime comic vision of life, the novel is without a parallel. The poetic brilliance with which Helena's progress from sterile paganism to

---

445 Harry Blamires, op. cit., 106.

446 Evelyn Waugh, quoted in Christopher Skypes, op. cit., 318.

447 Christopher Sykes, op. cit.

meaningful Roman Catholicism has been foreshadowed and conveyed compels critical commendation.

Helena may, therefore, be regarded as the best of all Waugh novels.

The Sword of Honour Trilogy

Originally published in the form of three novels, **The Sword of Honour Trilogy**[448] (1984) is best amenable to critical scrutiny as one literary work. The aggregative study of the Trilogy is feasible in view of the fact that it possesses not only one continuous narrative throughout but also one thematic pattern which together makes it one aesthetic work. Like the other greater comedies of Waugh, this novel too traces the movement of the hero from the state of comic error and ignorance to the state of sublime awareness, through a religious change in his life, which in Waugh is associated with Roman Catholicism. The action of this Trilogy plays out against the backdrop of World War II. One is reminded of the warnings of the destabilization of world order issued by Father Rothschild in **Vile Bodies** and also of the skirmishes beyond the out posts of secular civilization, in novels like **Black Mischief** and **Scoop.** In all these novels, war symbolises the precipitation of order into disorder, rationality into irrationality, civility into barbarity and stability into instability. As always in most Waugh novels, the wheel of life imagery helps in comprehending the significance of such a change. As secular change describes a circular path on the wheel of life, any attempt at quickening the pace of change tends to push human society away from its stable hub to its outermost orbit where the degree of susceptibility to instability becomes perilously high. It is such an extreme situation that Waugh tries to present in the outbreak of World War II. As the

[448] The three novels that comprise the *Sword of Honour* Trilogy (Harmondsworth: Penguin, 1984) were originally published separately at various points of time. While *Men at Arms* and *Officers and Gentlemen* were published by Chapman & Hall in 1952 and 1955 respectively, *Unconditional Surrender* was published after an unusually long interval of time in 1961.

outbreak of such a calamity conveys in Waugh, both the idea of the futility of secular change and that of its decadence to the barbaric level of existence, the enactment of the action of the Trilogy during the turbulent times of war enables Waugh to depict on an epic plane the irrationality and disorder that plague the 'dynamic' society of modern man. But as it is an aesthetic work rather than a mere period-piece, it shows how man can extricate himself from the morass of dynamism by resurrecting his dead and sterile spiritual life with the acceptance of a truly religious way of life, a step that would set him going on the linear path that leads to the stability of the hub of the revolving wheel of life. It is in this sense that the Trilogy needs to be studied as a greater comedy.

The man in whose life the drama of religious change and progress is enacted is Guy Crouchback, the chief protagonist of this Trilogy. Waugh's choice of the name is artistically significant as it reinforces with its rich associations and suggestions, the theme pursued in this work. Waugh's hero reminds one of the stooped Don Quixote; the ineffectual Catholic conspirator, Guy Fawkes; and Christ, bowed under the Cross of the sin of humankind. Like Don Quixote, Guy is oblivious to the real nature of the world he has launched himself into and has, therefore, to suffer his apotheosis's fate as long as his ignorance persists. Both plunge into the dynamic world armed with nothing but their obsolete static code of chivalry. Again, like the dynamic Guy Fawkes, Crouchback does not succeed in avenging the loss of his personal honour in the act of his wife's desertion, by fighting for the honour of the endangered Christendom. It is, however, in the allusion to the image of Christ bowed under the Cross, that Evelyn Waugh announces the significance of his life. Like Christ, Guy Crouchback willingly takes up the Cross of Virginia's sins when he agrees to father her child by Trimmer. Just as Christ did so in the face of public ignominy, he too does so in spite of the loss of face involved in it. So, by giving such a name to his central character, Waugh prepares us for the various stages of Guy's progress to the Roman Catholic hub of life.

The first novel of the Trilogy, **Men at Arms** (1952), presents Guy Crouchback in the style of the highly comic Don

Quixote. However, when the novel begins, we find Guy, a disillusioned person as his sense of personal honour has been wounded by the desertion of his coquettish wife, Virginia Troy. Waugh has a remarkable knack of giving very meaningful names to his characters; first, Crouchback and now Troy. It immediately calls up the allusion to the highly mercurial Helen of Troy, who deserted her husband, King Menelaus, for the dandy Paris, the son of King Priam. The allusion helps to accentuate the capricious character of Crouchback's wife, Virginia. The degree of her dynamic character can be gauged from the frequency with which she has been changing her husbands and paramours. Faith in Protestantism helps her to give unbridled freedom to her unrestrained individuality, as the Protestant Church was not rigid like the Roman Catholic Church in the matter of granting divorces. Guy Crouchback, in sharp contrast, is a static character. With his blinding faith in the outdated chivalric code of morality, he is no match for her. Like Paul, Adam, William Boot and Tony, Last, he is fit only for the life of the 'stands'. From there he can watch unhurt the acrobatics of dynamic characters on the ever-rotating wheel of life. His marriage with Virginia, like that ot Tony Last with Brenda, is a mistake. No wonder than that Guy flies to the secluded life of Santa Dulcina Delle Rocce after suffering a reverse at the hands of his dynamic wife, Virginia. In Italy, he is not a *sympatico* for the obvious reason that while the Italians, brimming with vitality, live in the midst of the world of change, Guy keeps aloof from it. So, when the war breaks out, Guy is living on the border of life, nursing his wounded personal honour. The outbreak of World War II offers Guy an opportunity of avenging the loss of his personal honour in the act of killing and exposing himself also to the risk of death just as Yeats' Irish Airman does in *An Irish Airman Foresees his Death.* Guy sees the Russo-German pact as a threat to the entire Christendom and as projections of the Modern Age, up in arms against the good old values of the feudal past. Like a true static character, his sense of justice gets offended by this pact and the zeal to protect his country against such monstrosity a sense of delight in making himself useful to his country. The sighting of the enemy gives him as great a satisfaction as his grand-parents had when they could consummate their love at Santa Dulcina Delle Rocce. Guy's decision to protect the honour of his country and that of the entire Christendom is not only an illusion fostered by the static code of his chivalric and rational attitude to life but also a device with which he can camouflage his real dynamic intention of justifying his manhood in the war. It draws him into the vortex of the secular/ dynamic world for the line of distinction that he draws between the champions of the Christian cause and the infidels hardly exists,

War in Waugh, as has been suggested earlier also, is an unbridled expression of the irrational and barbaric impulses within humankind . No degree of secular efforts towards modernization has been able to crush it. If the man living in the jungle makes an unabashed show of his barbarity, the man in the city cloaks it in urbane guile. Waugh calls both these sets of people dynamic as the dynamic world of secular humanity is characterized by these traits. Guy's crusade is bound to be abortive as it ignores the reality of the situation. This accounts for Guy's disillusionment and comic ineffectuality. But Guy transcends these feelings as he is much more than an ineffective Don Quixote. Participation in the war proves beneficial to him in so far as it makes him wiser about himself and the world; into which he has launched himself. Guy realizes not only the inadequacy of a rational and chivalric outlook on life but also the utter irrationality and valuelessness of the dynamic world. This saves him from the retrogressive step that William Boot takes in **Scoop** and he embarks instead on the odyssey of spiritual regeneration by dedicating himself to the true spirit of Christianity revealed to him by his sagacious father, Gervase Crouchback.

Guy's ineffectuality in the dynamic world and the prospect of his future progress on the path of religious transformation is suggested beautifully by the subtle parallel evoked in the mention of Sir Roger of Waybroke, the English Saint at Santa Dulcina Delle Rocce. Before leaving for England to join the war, Guy seeks his blessings by touching his sword. Sir Roger of Waybroke too had started from his home in England on a crusade to liberate the holy land of Jerusalem from the control of the heathens. But as fate would have it, he could never make it to Jerusalem. He died en route while fighting for a robber-baron, who had saved his life. Seen from the angle of the dynamic world, his mission was unsuccessful and abortive. But looking at his end from the Christian angle, one realizes that he proved himself worthy of being God's Chosen One by refusing to yield to the temptation of deserting his Italian saviour in order to earn for himself the fame of a crusader. Sir Roger was humble enough not to spurn the opportunity of proving himself useful to his benefactor by even performing, in comparison with the noble crusading cause, an insignificant act of fighting for him against his foe. Appreciating this act of gratitude on the part of Sir Roger, the people of Santa Dulcina Delle Rocce canonise him as a saint. By seeking Sir Roger's blessings, Guy seems to be seeking his guidance in finding his way out of the highly anarchic and unstable secular/ dynamic world.

He has forebodings of his folly ever since he lands in Britain. He finds that no one is rally sincere about the war as he is. The first place he visits upon his arrival in England is that of his sister, Angela who is married to Box-Bender, a Protestant M.P. Unlike Guy, Angela's husband considers war the right time to increase one's income and savings. He, therefore, has no qualms about making money during the war. In this sense, he represents the lowest level of politicking and profiteering that British society has sunk to. His son, Tony, who has already joined the army narrates incidents of irresponsible soldering and licentiousness in the barracks. Guy's romantic picture of a nation dedicated to defending Christendom against the heathen powers like Nazi Germany and Communist Russia is shattered.

However, far removed from this dynamic flock of people in Britain is the saintly old Mr. Gervase Crouchback. Though he has been a witness to many calamities in his family like the madness of one of his sons, Ivo; the untimely death of another son, Gervase, during the war; and the economic decline of the family; he has kept his cool and remained steadfast in his devotion to God.

"He was an innocent, affable old man who had somehow preserved his good humour –much more than that, a mysterious and tranquil joy - throughout a life which to all outward observation had been over-loaded with misfortune. He had like many others been born in full sunlight and lived to see night fall. England was full of such Jobs who had been disappointed in their prospects."[449]

The comparison with the Biblical character, Job, plays up old Mr. Crouchback's unswerving trust in God despite suffering many material and emotional setbacks. Notwithstanding his pride in his family which he, however, keeps to himself, he is 'quite without class consciousness' which is but natural for so sincere a Christian. Helena had similarly felt one with the multitude in the Christian sense of being one with the entire 'believing' humanity in the mystical Body of Christ. The reference to Job plays up the highest degree of stability that Gervase Crouchback has achieved in his life by virtue of his faith in the Roman Catholic Church. So, he may be regarded as a spiritual elite, anchored in the hub of the wheel of life. Commenting on his character, Frank Kermode rightly observes:

"... it must be added that Guy's father, humbly confident in his charity, his abstinence, and his view that there are really only two kinds of people, his kind and everybody else, is present almost throughout as a representative of this peculiar *noblesse oblige*."[450]

Even the thought of the lack of an issue to continue the name of this Catholic family in a largely Protestant country does not worry him, as much as it does Guy for the former gives precedence to the service of God rather than temporal considerations like the continuation of a family name. About him, Waugh Writes:

"All his pride of family was a school boy hobby compared with his religious faith. When Virginia left Guy childless, it did not occur to Mr. Crouchback, as it has never ceased occurring to Box-Bender, that the continuance of his line was worth a tiff with the

---

449 Evelyn Waugh, Men at Arms, The Sword of Honour Trilogy (Harmondsworth: Penguin, 1984), 28.

450 Frank Kermode, Partisan Review, 20 August 1962, in ed. Martin Stannard, op. cit., 445-446.

Church; that Guy should marry by civil law and beget an heir and settle things up later with the ecclesiastical authorities as other people seemed somehow to do. Family pride could not be served in dishonour."[451]

This makes it quite clear that old Mr. Crouchback's criteria of honour is not worldly but religious, a thing that Guy has yet to learn. Representing the hub of the wheel of life in these three novels, his advice steers Guy out of the wilderness of the World of Flesh and Avarice, once Guy begins to act on it, later in the Trilogy.

Through the good offices of Major Tickeridge, who is known to old Mr. Crouchback, Guy is able to join the Royal Corp of Halberdiers as a probationary officer. The former is not at all disturbed by his desire to expose himself to the peril of almost certain death in World War II. What he is concerned about, instead, is Guy's spiritual welfare. So, he gives Gervase's sacred medal of Our Lady of Lourdes to Guy before his departure. The medal had protected Gervase from sin when he was on the point of being seduced by a woman of loose morals. Not only did it protect Gervase but it also reformed that woman. She could not escape the sobering effect of the medal. Waugh suggests that if Guy has to achieve stable progress in his life, he must follow his father's example and choose religious change over the secular options offered by the world.

In order that he may embark on the linear path of progress, he must realize the folly of seeking justification for his personal honour in the options offered by the dynamic world of change, such as killing to prove one's manhood. But, even before that Guy needs to outgrow the static phase of a half-lived adolescence as it holds him back from gaining any mature insight into the world of barbarity around him. The irresponsible and gay abandon of pre-war army life helps Guy to do so. The narration of Guy's school boy pranks and quarrels in the army needs to be understood in this perspective. The regiment in which he serves is billeted in a school

---

[451] Evelyn Waugh, Men at Arms, op. cit., 29.

where 'the preparatory school way life of was completely recreated'. Ironically enough, Guy receives his first war-wound in the shape of an injury while playing football. It is here that a school boy war rages between Brigadier Ritchie Hook and Apthorpe, Guy's middle-aged companion-in-arms, over the 'thunder-box', a chemically operated portable field latrine. Viewed out of context, these school-boy pranks have drawn much criticism from critics like Christopher Sykes who complains against Waugh giving "sixteen pages to the adventure of Apthorpe's 'Thunder-Box'" and feels that the "joke, even to those who relish lavatory-jokes, becomes wearisome through repletion."[452]
If Apthorpe comes to represent one adolescent myth for Guy, Brigadier Ritchie Hook comes to stand for another. A veteran of World War I, Ritchie Hook takes immense pleasure in 'biffing' the enemy. Guy's admiration for him is revealed in his whole- hearted approval of Ritchie Hook's reckless adventure of Dakar Landing. In the words of A.A. De Vitis, 'The mission is a culmination of boyhood dreams of high adventure'.[453] Guy imagines himself playing the role of Truslove while embarking on this perilous adventure. Inspired by the foolhardy fancy of Ritchie Hook, Guy brings back the chopped off head of a negro sentry which he presents quite rightly to this symbol of destruction. As a result of this misadventure, Guy has his military career blotted and is recalled to England to face an inquiry.

To drive home the futility of a life lived by secular ideals, Waugh likens the pre-war effort to the circular motion of a wheel. Every time the men are asked to get ready to launch an offensive against the enemy, the call to arms is aborted as soon as the men are battle-ready. While the prospect of fighting a war fills their bosoms, including that of Guy with enthusiasm, the calling off the operation creates a sense of ennui and listlessness among them. The endless cycle of calls to arms and the putting off of those calls, along with the recurrent rise and ebb of passions is not dissimilar from the various images of the circularity of secular change shown in the

---

452 Christopher Sykes, op. cit., 418-419.

453 A. A. De Vitis, op. cit., 73.

lesser comedies. This lends the entire war effort an air of absurdity that Waugh has beautifully explored in the lesser comedies. The message is clear for Guy: that war, which is the ultimate point of rupturing of the world of secular change, cannot offer the redemption that Guy seeks from it. Soon after joining the army, Guy had disagreed with the dismal picture of war painted by the Catholic priest of the tin-Church, as he had then thought it a time of glory and dedication.

"The priest was a recent graduate from Maynooth who had little enthusiasm for the Allied cause or for the English army, which he regarded merely as a provocation to immorality in the town. His sermon that morning was not positively offensive; there was nothing in it to make the basis of a complaint; but when he spoke of 'this terrible time of doubt, danger and suffering in which we live', Guy stiffened. It was a time of glory and dedication."[454]

But now after having served the army for some time and undergone the charade of fighting a war against the enemies of his country, Guy feel otherwise. The invasion of Finland compels Guy to take a fresh look at the war. Though no one at Kut-al-Imara is affected by this invasion, Guy is. Not long before this disaster Poland had been invaded by Russia without even any protest from Britain. The sight of the Christian states being allowed to slip into the communist hold disconcerts Guy as it is a betrayal of all principles that had inspired Guy to fight for England. His earlier certitude about the nature of war abandons him now. Waugh writes: "No one at Kut-al Imara seemed much put out by the disaster. For Guy the news quickened the sickening suspicion he had tried to ignore, had succeeded in ignoring more often than not in his service in the Halberdiers; that he was engaged in a war in which courage and a just cause were quite irrelevant to the issue."[455]

---

[454] Evelyn Waugh, Men at Arms, op. cit., 49.

[455] Ibid., 112.

For the first time, Guy realises that the chivalric ideals which had inspired him to join the army were irrelevant in this war. The static characters before him in the lesser comedies could never realize the inadequacy of their static ideals and hence they paid a price for that. This movement from ignorance to knowledge is basic to the narrative of a greater comedy. As the circular motion of the revolving wheel of life also suggests, the dynamic mode of existence is wanting in a logical movement; the only motion it knows is temporal. In order that Guy may progress, he must extricate himself from the material concerns of a secular world whose change is counter-productive, instead of being progressive. The ultimate comic vision of life in Waugh derives its strength from such revelations.

Coupled with the growing disenchantment with the politics of the dynamic world is Guy's increasing awareness of his religious shortcomings. In the initial stage, he realizes that he has stopped saying his prayers ever since he had joined the army. Providence only saves him from a deadly sin he is on the verge of committing with his former wife, Virginia. Convinced by Mr. Goodall that there was no harm in the cohabitation of a divorced Catholic couple, Guy thinks of resuming sexual relations with her. In the eyes of his Church, however, such an act would be no less then committing adultery – Waugh uses the expression, 'auspicious pseudo-adultery' – as such a union would be confined only to the bodies, their souls being unaffected. It is only after his attempt aborts that he realizes the grave sin he was about to commit.

Waugh develops further the idea of irrationality in the 'dynamic' world in the lop-sided working of the counter-espionage department which opens a file on the patriotic Guy on the basis of an inadequate and insignificant piece of evidence. His past antecedents are held in suspicion and a nexus, which in reality does not exist, is established between him and Box-Bender, his brother-in-law.

"'But Crouchback's quite another fish. Until September of last year he lived in Italy and is known to have been on good terms with the Fascist authorities. Don't you think I'd better open a file for him?'

'Yes, perhaps it would be as well.'
'For both, sir?
'Yes, Pop'em all in.'''[456]

With this summary trial in absentia, Colonel Grace Groundling-Marchpole labels the patriotic Guy, a fascist. Such decisions were not uncommon during World War II. D.H. Lawrence, whose wife happened to be a German, was harassed much for the possible recovery of any incriminating document by the British police, during the war. Waugh himself was the scapegoat of such bear-baiting, though not by the police, but by his literary and journalistic detractors. In his reply to a query regarding which side he would support in the Spanish Civil War, he had, after suggesting the impossibility of such a hard choice, declared his support for the government of General Franco, as against that of the Communists, for the simple reason that an anarchic government is better than an irreligious and a wholly lop-sided government. A distortion of it helped them prove Waugh's fascist inclinations. Waugh thus made fun of such subversions of the rules of logic.

Men at Arms (1952) concludes with Guy Crouchback's return to England as a partially disenchanted and disgraced soldier. Guy is disenchanted with the entire war effort as one which makes no sense ideologically, especially after the invasion of Poland by Russia. To further complicate the situation, he has been sent back in disgrace from Dakar for participating in the preposterous offensive launched by his superior, Brig Ritchie Hook. So, when the first novel of the Trilogy ends, we have our hero down. It remains for the second and third novels in the Trilogy to complete the action and leave a feeling of splendid admiration in the readers. This accounts for Waugh's own lukewarm attitude to this work, as is revealed in one of his letters to Nancy Mitford: 'I have finished that novel-slogging, inelegant, boring-and what little point it has will

---

[456] Ibid., 126.

only be revealed in the fourth volume at least four year hence. Still there were some dunderheads who didn't appreciate **Helena**. Perhaps they will like it.'[457] Again in his letter of 8 January 1952 to Clarissa Churchill, Waugh writes, 'I have finished a novel-slogging, inelegant, the first volume of four or five, which won't show any shape until the end.'[458] Still again, in his letter of 1 September 1952 to Ann Fleming, Waugh reiterates his belief that the book must be seen as a preparatory part of a greater whole.

"The kindest way is to regard it as the first comic turn of a long musical-hall show, put on to keep the audience quiet as they are taking their seats. If I ever finish writing, and if anyone every reads, the succession of volumes that I plan to follow it, it will make some sense."[459]

Unmindful of this fact, Diana Cooper evaluated the novel as a complete work of art and consequently felt disenchanted with its literary merit. 'I thought', she told Evelyn, 'that you were going to give us a modern **War and Peace**, but it's much more like **Mrs. Dale's Diary'**[460] John Raymond's charge that 'Like every satirist at a loss for prey, the writer has made a temporary excursus into Myth. Mr. Waugh's myth ... is the English regimental tradition in 1940.'[461] That the novel's inconclusiveness owes to its incompleteness as a work of art has, however, been rightly perceived by Christopher Sykes who observers:

"The partial failure of the book was due to a familiar error of which Evelyn judging by his letter to Nancy Mitford, seems to have been partly aware; his writing was never amenable to

457 Evelyn Waugh, in Christopher Sykes, op. cit., 354.

458 Evelyn Waugh, in ed. Michael Davie, op.cit., 354.

459 Ibid., 379-380.

460 Diana Cooper, quoted in Christopher Sykes, op. cit., 354.

461 John Raymond, New Statesman, 20 September 1952, in ed. Martin Stannard, op. cit., 339.

publication by instalments, a large instalment of a very long book but an instalment nonetheless."[462]

Though Delmore Schwartz has been able to guess what the novel is about, he has done so in the wrong manner. He maintains; "Waugh appears to be saying to the reader: I see the tepidity, foolishness and triviality of human beings just as much as you, but I draw a different conclusion; human beings are ridiculous without religious belief and they are just as ridiculous when they are possessed by religious belief, but at least when they are truly religious, they have a touching pathetic, bewildered quality which makes possible a little comparison amid one's overwhelming contempt."[463]

While Waugh finds people without any religious beliefs ridiculous. But, he certainly does not think so about the religious minded, especially those who have comprehended the true essence of Christianity. The former are rendered ridiculous because of their inability to understand the futility manifest in the circular nature of secular change. The latter are not as they are coolly poised at the hub of the wheel of life where they are liberated from the deception of secular change. If Guy Crouchback looks ridiculous in this novel, it is because he has yet not outgrown his static personality which stands in the way of his understanding the nature of the dynamic world and also in his acceptance of the religious path of progress and honour.

However, despite its introductory character, the novel suffers from one serious blemish. It pays much greater attention to Apthorpe than to Guy Crouchback, the chief protagonist of the novel. In fact, all the three sections are named after him. In the biography of Evelyn Waugh, Christopher Sykes observes rightly, 'Its admirers were chiefly attracted by the character Apthorpe who

---

[462] Christopher Sykes, op. cit., 354.

[463] Delmore Schwartz, Partisan Review, 3 November 1952, in ed. Martin Stannard, op. cit., 345.

threatened to become the protagonist of the story.'[464] In fact, Waugh for once himself seems to be in doubt about who the actual hero of the novel is, when in one of his letters to Lady Mary Lygon, he writes: 'I have written a book in poor taste, mostly about WCs and very very dull. Well it is a dull subject isn't it. The only exciting moment is when a WC blows up with Capt. Apthorpe sitting on it. The shock & shame drive him mad. He is the hero.'[465]

The second novel of the **Sword of Honour Trilogy** is titled very meaningfully. Titled **Officers and Gentlemen** (1955), the novel throws us back in time to the days of the crusading knights, fighting for the liberation of the Holy Land. In those good old times, officers, read knights, were also gentlemen, as they subscribed to and upheld the ideals of chivalry. But, in modern times, when religion has been banished from the lives of people to make them progressive, there are no gentlemen officers as there is no holy war to be fought. As the first novel of the Trilogy has shown, the war has neither a religious purpose nor does it seem to have any logical rationale. Waugh seems to suggest that wars in our secular modern times are fought because there is a 'Death-Wish' in both people and nations.

Appropriately enough, the action of the second novel of the Trilogy opens with a grim and devastating picture of war-torn London. Waugh suggests that accelerated pace of secular change, in the form of beguiling narratives of modernization and development, lead ultimately to death and destruction. Such a life is really a tale told by an idiot, full of sound and fury, signifying nothing. London is being reduced to rubble by the German war-planes. Places of festivity have become the funeral piers of helpless humanity. The savagery of Seth's Azania or for that matter, Jacksons's Ishmaelia, fades into insignificance before this picture of wilful genocide precipitated by the developed world in its wild goose chase of secular progress. It is to such a London that Guy returns.

---

464 Christopher Sykes, op. cit., 354.

465 Evelyn Waugh, in ed. Michael Davie, op. cit., 366.

The mercurial Ritchie Hook, like Captain Grimes, not only saves himself from being court-martialled but also gets his admirer, Guy Crouchback, acquitted. In the absence of any particular official assignment, Guy performs an act of piety towards the deceased Apthorpe. The latter had asked him to trace Chatty Corner and hand over his gear to him. The interest with which he searches Apthorpe's legatee shows the change that has come over him. Guy does not mind caring for Apthorpe's gear, even though it hardly deserves his attention. Only after discovering Chatty Corner does he rest. As Guy begins to show greater signs of piety and Christian virtues, his interest in the war also begins to wane.

Posted at the Isle of Mugg as a commando, Guy has once again a first-hand feel of the futility of life, when he along with his fellow soldiers has to undergo a cyclical charade of preparing for an offensive and then abandoning it. Like Vladimir and Estragon waiting for Godot in Samuel Beckett's play, **Waiting for Godot**, they keep waiting for a ship that is supposed to ferry them near a Mediterranean island to be captured by them. The promised ship does not appear for days together so that officers and men lose all hopes of ever seeing it and wish they were back with their regiments. Waugh describes the impact of this recurrent cycle of rise and fall of their hopes in very telling words thus: 'This unvarying cycle of excitement and disappointment rubbed them bare of paint and exposed the lead beneath.'[466] The comparison with the circular motion of a ship on a rough sea recalls the image of the wheel of life. The wheel, as it revolves, creates an illusion of progress but when its circular motion brings the man standing on it back to his original position, the illusion is shattered. In other words, the dynamic mode of life cannot promise hope and progress but only despair and sterility. That quickening of the pace of the wheel of dynamic life only brings man back to this original position sooner is driven home in the abruptness with which military plans keep on changing. In the passage that follows, Ian Kilbannock tells Guy how many operations have been planned and then abandoned before even any one got scant of them.

---

[466] Evelyn Waugh, Officers and Gentlemen, The Sword of Honour Trilogy, op. cit., 257.

"(Guy): 'There was some loose talk about an island'.
(Ian): 'Operation Bottleneck? That was off weeks ago. Since then there's been Operation Quicksand and Operation Mousetrap. They're both off. It's Operation Badger now, of course'.
(Guy): 'And what is that?'
(Ian): 'If you don't know, I oughtn't to tell you'.
(Guy): 'Too late to go back now'.
(Ian): 'Well frankly it's simply Quicksand under another name'."[467]

It is indeed an artistic master stroke of Waugh that he should invest such situations of low comic fun with such abstruse significance as this one indicates. The entire exercise of planning and re-planning looks ridiculous in view of the fact that it lacks a progressive character. Waugh appears to be saying that all secular efforts meet with such fate. While the constant planning and putting off of plans discourages Guy, the bloodshed and utter chaos that accompanies the Crete expedition appeals to him. The army which to an outsider gives the appearance of a well organized and disciplined force is so only as long as it is under orders. The moment it is relieved of its orders, it becomes disorderly and unruly. The Crete expedition plays up the disorder and disobedience to authority that is rampant in any secular organization which has order superimposed upon it. Once the German war planes start hunting and decimating the British troops, chaos breaks out. In the scramble for the safety of their lives, Darwinian struggle for survival get graphically portrayed. Rank loses significance. The officers suspect their own men who in turn suspect their superiors. Authority is undermined and in the forced state of equality, soldiers at times even murder the latter. The animalistic spirit that possesses them is best presented in the person of Corporal Major Ludovic. Before and while escaping from Crete in a boat, he kills two soldiers, one of them being Major Hound, his superior. Ivor Claire, the man in who Guy had all along looked up to in giving the Germans a tough fight, shows his back. The nightmarish picture of war presented here is perhaps one of the best among the novels that have come out of World War II. Though Guy makes good his

---

[467] Ibid., 270.

escape, his psyche is substantially damaged as a result of this catastrophe. This foreshadows Guy's rejection of secular change as a means to progress and his consequent religious transformation.

While efforts are on to restore Guy to normalcy, the news of Russia's alliance with Britain is flashed. This changes the hue of the confrontation. Earlier, the war-camps were divisible ideologically. While the British and the other allies were Christians, the Germans and Russian were heathens. With this new pact, the rational distinction between the friend and the foe gets completely blurred. Political considerations gain ground at the expense of the religious, a fact which is not unnatural in the essentially secular dynamic world. Guy, who has been unaware of this fact and has consequently been fighting under the impression that it is a religious war, is unnerved by it. His illusion about the nature of the world, he has jumped into, is shattered. He realizes that the crusade upon which he had embarked does not exist. It is simply a figment of his imagination.

"Now that hallucination was dissolved, like the whales and turtles on the voyage from Crete, and he was back after less than two years' pilgrimage in a Holy Land of illusion in the old ambiguous world, where priests were spies and gallant friends proved traitors and his country was led blundering into dishonour."[468]

The new alliance is, however, in keeping with the socialist mood that was then seeping over England. The movement in favour of the common people and against the landed gentry was exaggerated to the point of absurdity in the suggestion that the upper classes stood for fascism. So, when Ian tells Guy that this is a People's War, he intends to suggest that this is a war not only against fascism but also against the upper classes. What happens, as a result of the obsession with having people's heroes rather than gentlemen heroes is that a nondescript and undeserving fraud like Trimmer shoots into prominence. Trimmer's unexpected and

[468] Ibid., 383.

meteoric success, as opposed to the defeat of many deserving soldiers, highlights the injustice that has crept into the fabric of dynamic world at every level.

It also drives home the difference between an unjust people's war and the chivalrous crusades of the past. By ridiculing the People's War, Waugh, however, does not show any predilection for chivalry as it is an institution which is unreal in the context of the world of change. Guy's disillusionment with it is a case in point. What Waugh is therefore trying to say is that Guy must bid farewell to war and the army so that he may seek his salvation in the real terms of Christianity which is not only an epitome of truth but also a true dispenser of justice. Had Waugh abandoned the Trilogy here, as he himself declared in the foreword to the first edition of this novel and in the letter of 16 Nov. 1954, written to Nancy Mitford[469], the entire work would have suffered the fate of a literary fragment, inviting misleading interpretations of the theme pursued. As Christopher Sykes has rightly remarked:

"The foreword was a great mistake. If it had been statement of the fact; if **Sword of Honour** had indeed ended with this second volume, then it would not have been a work to enhance Evelyn's literary reputation. Too many loose ends would have remained; the full intention would have but been remembered as a minor specimen... among those works of art which perplex and fascinate us *guia imperfectum*."[470]

Among the critics who perceived its incompleteness was Geoffrey Moore. Observing the 'tangle of loose threads' in the plot, he contended very rightly against Waugh's assertion that the first two novels of the Trilogy could 'form a whole'[471]. However, some

---

469 In the letter to Nancy Mitford, Waugh writes, 'It is short and funny & completes the story I began in Men at Arms which threatened to drag out to the grave.' (ed. Mark Amory, op. cit., 433.)

470 Christopher Sykes, op. cit., 322.

471 Geoffrey Moore, New York Times Book Review, 10 July 1955, in ed. Martin Stannard, op. cit., 375.

critics chose to assess the two novels as constituting one whole work. Cyril Connolly felt 'disappointed' as he found the characters 'too superficial to sustain the structure'.[472] Only Norman Shrapnel suggested subtly that 'Disorganization is more than merely a subject for his fierce brand of force; it is an expression of spiritual perversity.'[473] The other voice of appreciation was that of Kinsley Amis who appears not to have read the foreword carefully. He looked forward to 'the continuation of this saga' in order that 'the discursive and episodic' elements of the plot may fall in the right pattern'.[474]

One may, however, ask way Waugh issued such a declaration, knowing full well its adverse impact on the theme he was pursuing. Or was it a statement of Waugh's declining artistic abilities? The conversation between Graham Greene and Waugh, recorded in the former's review of the Diaries, is enlightening in this regard.

"I had asked him why there was no indication on the dust-wrapper of **Officers & Gentlemen** that a third volume of the Trilogy was to come. He said, I'm not sure that I'll be able to write it. I may go off my head again, and this time permanently."[475]

Waugh was understandably delighted when nothing of the kind happened and he could get down 'busily & happily ... [to] work on a sequel to those two war novels', and he goes on to add in his letter of 5 September 1960 to Ann Fleming, 'The trouble is that it is quite unintelligible to anyone who doesn't know them by heart. I have to keep dipping into them to find what I wrote seven or eight

---

[472] Cyril Connolly, Sunday Times, 3 July 1955, in ed., Martin Stannard, op. cit., 369.

[473] Norman Shrapnel, Manchester Guardian, 1 July 1955, 4, in ed., Martin Stannard, op. cit., 366.

[474] Kingsley Amis, Spectator, 8 July 1955, in ed., Martin Stannard, op. cit., 372.

[475] Graham Greene, Books and Bookmen, October 1976, 19-21, quoted in ed., Martin Stannard, op. cit., 47.

years ago. Otherwise it is a gripping tale.'[476] That the decision to terminate the Trilogy was taken solely because of the author's failing health and not because of Waugh's ignorance of the need of the final and culminating novel in the Trilogy becomes further clear from what he wrote after having written the third novel: 'In 1950 I wrote of **Officers and Gentlemen.** "I thought at first the story would run into three volumes. I find that two will do the trick". This was not quite candid. I knew that a third volume was needed.'[477]

Unconditional Surrender (1961), the third and the final novel of the **Sword of Honour Trilogy**, has a very suggestive title. The title alludes to the sermon of old Mr. Gervase Crouchback to Guy regarding serving God by saving even one life, despite the loss of face it may entail. That Guy Crouchback may ascend to the heights of Christian sublimity, he must learn to submit his personal honour to the will and service of God. This calls for an unconditional surrender of worldly attainments such as personal pride, about which Old Mr. Gervase catechises Guy.

When the novel opens, it is Christian Britain which is all set to unconditionally surrender to Communist Russia, but for politically expedient reasons. The exhibition of the 'state sword' near 'the shrine of St. Edward the Confessor and the sacring place of the kings of England', an expensive gift of the people of Britain to 'the steel-hearted people of Stalingrad' is an inversion of all religious values. That this sword is a symbol of the perversion of sacred Christian values, represented by Sir Roger of Waybroke's sword, is suggested by its reverse position: 'the escutcheon on the scabbard will be upside down when worn on a baldric.' It is, therefore, ironical that this sword, which is an image of political expediency and barbarity, should have been offered a place so close to a shrine and, more than that, worshipped. Ludovic, who is thoroughly steeped in the destructive spirit of this pseudo-civilized world, does not hesitate in having a close look at it in order that he

---

476 Evelyn Waugh, in ed., Michael Davie, op. cit., 548.

477 Evelyn Waugh, quoted in Cyril Connolly, Sunday Times, 29 October 1961, 31, in ed. Martin Stannard, op. cit., 430.

may celebrate its ignoble glory in a poem for a literary competition. Guy, on the other hand, refuses to pay homage to this sword as he regards it as a symbol of dishonour and destruction. Guy feels that by giving away their 'state sword' to a heathen nation, Britain was dishonouring its Christian heritage and cause. Guy's refusal to be drawn into this dishonourable war is aptly and subtly suggested by his aversion for the 'state sword'. It marks an end of his love affair with the army and psychological association with the dynamic world that has gone berserk.

The association with Guy Fawkes here becomes prominent. Just as Guy Fawkes had failed in the mission of dethroning Queen Elizabeth to install the Catholic Mary in her place, Crouchback has failed in defending the endangered Christendom from heathen forces as years of secularization have eclipsed the Christian outlook of the pseudo-Christian societies of the West. Disillusioned with the irrational ways of the dynamic world, Guy sulks in the absence of an alternative ideal that can redefine an otherwise wasted life. Old Mr. Crouchback reads it on his face and is worried as before about his spiritual welfare. Earlier, he had given him a sacred medal for the purpose. This time, he offers advice that drastically alters Guy's perception of the world and the individual's role in it. In his letter to Guy, old Mr. Crouchback writes, though in the context of the Lateran Treaty: 'Quantitative judgments don't apply. If only one soul was saved that is full compensation for any amount of loss of face.'[478] This advice is at once Miltonic and simple. Till now, Guy believed that honour could be reclaimed by fighting for big causes, like crusading for Christendom. The belief led him into a cul-de-sac that offers no hope. The Christendom that he set out to defend no longer exists. It has long ago vanished and has been replaced by the secular world's dazzling artefacts of modernity and development. So, old Mr. Crouchback's simple Christian advice comes at the right time. But, for this Guy has to develop the level of faith which can give him the strength to bear the Cross of other people's sins.

---

[478] Evelyn Waugh, Unconditional Surrender, The Sword of Honour Trilogy, op. cit., 400.

If Guy can accomplish this change in his personality, he can pull himself out of the Slough of Despondence that the loss of his manhood has been making him to suffer. It is this movement from illusion to reality that lies at the heart of an Evelyn Waugh greater comedy. The Evelyn Waugh protagonist rises like a phoenix from the ashes of a sterile dynamic life to touch the sublime heights of the all-embracing and eternal truth of the Roman Catholic hub of life. Unlike the circular movement of the comic hero in the lesser comedies, the graph of his progress from illusion to truth is linear and therefore amenable to value judgement.

Guy gets the opportunity to justify his faith in the shape of owning up of his ex-wife, Virginia's illegitimate child by Trimmer. If Guy does not accept Virginia as his wife, the child shall not only be born a bastard but he will also be deprived of the Grace of God. If he does, the child shall be saved but Guy himself shall lose face in the society. Guy agrees to undergo personal humiliation for the sake of redeeming the nascent life in the shape of little Trimmer. This is in shining contrast with his past motives in possessing Virginia. Secular considerations such as the perpetuation of the family line with a son of his own fade into insignificance before the religious ones. By emulating his father old Mr. Crouchback who himself is a spiritual elite, in the true sense of the world, Guy has not only discovered, to use Jeffrey Health's term, his 'vocation', but has also raised himself to a pedestal near that of his father. In other words, Guy has started seeing life from the *sub specie aeternitatis* perspective of the hub of the wheel of life. Bernard Bergonzi appears to be oblivious of this change in Guy's perspective when he suggests, ' Guy Crouchback embodies the nostalgic myth of so much of Mr. Waugh's writing, the notion that true value lies in a combination of Catholicism and the aristocratic virtues.'[479] His suggestion, similar to that of Donat O Donnell, disregards how Guy willingly undergoes public humility, which includes foregoing his family pride, in the act of accepting Trimmer's child. V.S. Pritchett's defence almost admits the presence of class-snobbery in Waugh and

---

479 Bernard Bergonzi, Guardian, 27 October 1961, 7, in ed., Martin Stannard, op. cit., 423.

thus is equally unjustifiable. He maintains, ' To object to his snobbery is as futile as objecting to cricket, for every summer the damn game comes round again whether you like it or not.'[480]
An extension of Guy's newly discovered 'vocation' is the help he extends to the Jews trapped in Yugoslavia. Posted as a Liaison officer there, he does his best to help them get out of the Communist controlled country. The persecution of the Jews, a subject quite ancient in human history and glaringly particular during World War II, fills Guy with pity for them, even though they are not Christians. This should be a case in point for those who have accused Waugh repeatedly of being exclusively Catholic in his art. Guy's efforts do not yield fruit for a long time as the air-lifting of the Jews is repeatedly put off because of bad weather. Despite most of them finding their way out, the Kanyis do not as they are executed for their proximity to Guy. This is the little task that Guy could perform in the service of God and he does not flinch in doing it. This shows the level of humanity that he has come to embody ever since his adherence to his father's advice. Guy's firm pursuit of his Catholic ideals contrasts sharply with his previous comic capers when he sought to justify his own and the secularized Christendom's honour by joining the war. By submitting his personal ego and pride to the service of God through his acts of benevolence, he ceases to be an anti-hero and he assumes the stature of grand comic heroes such as Henry in T. S. Eliot's **The Family Reunion.**

While Guy has surrenders himself unconditionally to the Divine will, the other characters in the novel have submit themselves to the soul-grinding speed of the wheel of irrational world of change. It is on the crest of such a change that Ludovic rises to the rank of a Major and even becomes the Commandant of a Parachute Training Centre where Guy comes as a trainee officer. The appearance of Guy disturbs his peace. He feels haunted by Guy's awareness of the double murders he had committed during the Cretan retreat. Fleeing from his past, he first shuts himself in his

---

480 V. S. Pritchett, New Statesman, 27 October 1961, in ed. Martin Stannard, op. cit., 425.

room and afterwards, at the end of the war, leaves England for good, buying Guy's Castello at Santa Dulcina Delle Rocce to stay there forever. Ludovic's decision to quit England plays up, in terms of the imagery of the wheel of life, his decision to quit the constantly revolving wheel, representative of the world of secular change, and take a seat in the stands. It is a regressive step as it leads him from a dynamic state of existence, however vile and futile, to a static one. Meanwhile, he also publishes a book, entitled 'Death Wish'. Way back in 1924, Waugh had perceived such a fatalistic attitude among the youth of his own generation. In "A Letter of Exhortation from an Undergraduate to a Friend Abroad", he observes:

"You know, Bill, what we want is another war. I become more and more convinced of that every day. These tiresome historians always find causes for their wars in national expansion and trade rivalry and religion and such things. I don't' know about these because, as you know, I am never up in time to read the newspapers, but I gather from those who do that things are pretty unsettled .... we have a great body of young men of all sorts of education just longing for another general disturbance."[481]

A little ahead in the same letter, he expresses the willingness of these young men 'to fight for any institution or party that would pay them handsomely and offer them a good chance of speedy death'.[482] Ludovic's book draws attention towards this death-wish as the raison d'être of the outbreak of World War II.

Virginia's life, like that of Ludovic's, is both unsettled and unsettling. Her inconstancy deprives her of the possibility of any stable marital relationship. Her marriage with Guy falls a prey to this element of fickleness in her character. Her affair with Trimmer helps to cure her of this inadequacy in her personality. He not only dins into her ears his repetitive 'you, you, you' but also impregnates

---

[481] Evelyn Waugh, "A Letter of Exhortation from an Undergraduate to a Friend Abroad", in ed. Donat Gallagher, A Little Order, op. cit., 4.

[482] Ibid., 4.

her with his child. When she is unable to get rid of the nascent life within her womb, she tries to deceive Guy into marrying her again. Though Guy had felt deeply hurt when she had deserted him, he is by now a changed man, under the tutelage of his father old Mr. Crouchback. Guy's willingness to accept Trimmer's child not only redeems the unborn child's life but redeems Virginia from the stranglehold of her inconstant passions. Waugh indicates this change in her by showing her conversion to the Roman Catholic faith, which Waugh regarded as a genuine form of Christianity. Her death as a Catholic guarantees the descent of the Grace of God upon her as in Lord Marchmain's case. The linear graph of her life from the most unsettling fringes of the wheel of life to its ever-stable hub is the characteristic of the typical narrative movement of an Evelyn Waugh greater comedy.

Acting upon his father's desire that he should stay at Broome after his death, Guy sells the property in Italy and raises a family of his own with Dominica Plessington at Broome. Waugh deleted the happy ending in the succeeding edition of this book as he felt it detracted attention from the novel's real thematic line of intention. His letter dated 31 October 1961, to Anthony Powell makes this explicit. It reads:

"I am disconcerted to find I have given the general impression of a 'happy ending'. This was far from my intention. The mistake was allowing Guy legitimate offspring. They shall be deleted in any subsequent edition. I thought it more ironical that there should be real heirs of the Blessed Gervase Crouchback dispossessed by Trimmer but I plainly failed to make that clear. So no nippers for Guy & Domenica in Penguin."[483]

Most critics, however, interpreted the perpetuation of Guy's own family line by Domenica as a sign of Waugh's eagerness to make Guy comfortable not only spiritually but also materially. Box -Bender's envy over Guy's own progeny was cited as an evidence of this intention. The second edition rectified the happy ending by

---

[483] Evelyn Waugh, in ed. Michael Davie, op. cit., 579.

leaving Guy issueless by his marriage with Domenica Plessingtion. This leaves little Trimmer, an outsider, the sole heir to the impeccable family name of the Crouchbacks, a fitting rebuff too to his self-opinionated reviewers. Besides, it redeems the evaluation of Guy's progress to the hub of the wheel of life from any material or secular criteria.

The second-home coming of Guy is markedly different from the earlier one. While earlier, he had come as a static person, unaware of the dark nature of the dynamic world that is spreading out like a wild fire at the opportune time of the war, he now returns for good as a spiritual elite, anchored peacefully wisdom of the Roman Catholic hub of the wheel of life. We can say, the native has returned home from his self-imposed exile. Waugh has, thus, successfully steered the development of Guy crouchback from the time he was an ineffectual Don Quixote or Guy Fawkes to the time when he becomes the sagacious Christ bent under the Cross of humanity's sin. To those who view the story of his life from a secular angle, it is a tragedy. But to those who view it from the eternal perspective of Roman Catholicism, it is a magnificent and 'divine' comedy. Indeed, the pattern of Waugh's greater comedy is somewhat similar to that of Eliot. Eliot's chief protagonists also achieve epiphany or resurrection the way Guy does. Waugh, therefore, succeeds like Eliot in showing that abiding progress is possible only though religious change.

So, Bernard Bergonzi's contention that 'the defeat and disillusion of Guy Crouchback seems to indicate the total collapse of Mr. Waugh's dominating myth'[484]is hardly substantiated by the change Guy undergoes in the Trilogy. His suggestion that 'the modern world has triumphed and the implications of the book's title are everywhere apparent'[485] ignores the reality of Crouchback's transformation into a true Christian, ready to bear the Cross of others' sins. In contrast, Christopher Derrick rightly observes the graph of Guy's gradual progress towards the status of a spiritual elite when he says: "… the Italian peasants canonised the English

---

484 Bernard Bergonzi, op. cit., 423.

485 Ibid., 423-424.

Knight, and we can provisionally make a kind of saint out of Guy, whom we leave at the end of the Trilogy restored like Job to something better than his former condition, the heavenly visitation over and done with, the sacrifice accepted in tongues of fire, the books balanced, the past still there to be lived with."[486]

But, he too falls into the trap of the happy ending and fails to see the point of the irony in it. Similar mistake is committed by Simon Raven who sees in Guy's spiritual journey a sign of 'private salvation through private good faith'.[487] He clarifies this in the following remark:

"There is more than a suggestion that what Crouchback will righteously resist is not merely Nazism but the whole apparatus of modern and secular progress as promoting religious apostasy and social change- two calamities which Mr. Waugh does not, it is true, equate but sees as intimately connected."[488]

The metaphorical representation of Roman Catholicism as the hub of the wheel, precludes the possibility of such interpretations, as the hub of a rotating wheel transcends the various stages of change that is circuitous. So, the conscious decision to accept Roman Catholicism in Waugh represents a rejection of all projects of secular efforts, be it chivalry or modernism. The ultimate comic vision of life in Evelyn Waugh steers away from this emphasis on the pursuit of secular progress which is shown to be deceptive and comically absurd. Regarding Waugh basically as a satirist, Gore Vidal considers the affirmative aspect of Waugh's fiction, as revealed in this Trilogy, no more than romantic day dreaming and hence a drag on him as a critic of life. He observes: "Waugh . . . in the military trilogy , which **The End of the Battle** (the title of the American edition of

---

[486] Christopher Derrick, Tablet, 28 October 1961, in ed. Martin Stannard, op. cit., 428.

[487] Simon Raven, Spectator, 12 June 1964, 798, in ed. Martin Stannard, op. cit., 449-450.

[488] Ibid., 448.

Unconditional Surrender) completes, indulges himself in romantic day dreams which are not only quite as unpleasant as the things he satirized, but tend in their silliness to undermine his authority as critic, Juvenal would not have made that mistake."[489]

Far from indulging in romantic day-dreams, Waugh rejects them, a point that is clear enough in Guy's realization of the inadequacy of the obsolete code of chivalry. Moreover, Waugh shows realism of *par excellence* when he makes his protagonist not only comprehend the deep rooted depravity in the dynamic world but also withdraw from its concerns. So, it is not Waugh but Juvenal, who committed a mistake in not outgrowing a mere negative attitude in his artistic expressions. Commenting on the Trilogy, Christopher Sykes observes, 'As hardly needs saying, after a long withdrawal from the subject and preoccupation with work of a different kind, Evelyn eventually and triumphantly finished the trilogy.'[490] His appreciation owes to the perception that 'In this work Evelyn attempted to achieve a great ambition: to describe in terms of a fictional experience close to his own the significance to men and women of the ordeal of the crisis of the civilization which reached its climax in World War II.'[491] He, however, punctuates his praise with the question, 'Whether he succeeded; or whether, among others who tried to reflect the Hitlerian catastrophe in fiction, he merely over-reached himself, is the subject of this chapter.'[492] Though his perception is not wrong, it would yet be wrong to judge the artistic merit of the book on this basis, as it tells only half the truth about the book's thematic line of intention. Far from being a mere account of the significance of the crisis of civilization, the narrative of the novel aims at showing Guy's progress to the religious hub of life from the irrationality and corruption signified by the bestiality of the second Great War. In

---

489 Gore Vidal, New York Times Book Review, 7 January 1962, 1, in ed. Martin Stannard, op. cit., 439.

490 Christopher Sykes, op. cit., 375.

491 Ibid., 415.

492 Ibid., 415.

the successful completion of this spiritual odyssey, the hero undergoes a renewal of life that is implicit in the Christian view of progress.

Thus the novel, instead of being a static portrayal of life, charts the movement of the central character from insignificance to significance. This movement is at the heart of all 'great comedies', whether written by Waugh or Eliot. The central character extricates himself from the absurd monotony of a circular secular change in order to discover the true meaning of his existence. His success forms the essence of the triumphant conclusion of any greater comedy. Christopher Sykes appears to be ignorant of this change in Guy when he objects to his delineation as an 'ineffectual' person.

"... in the first sentence, there occurs the worst blemish on the whole undertaking: the ineffectual hero, Guy Crouchback. He is not something new in Evelyn's writing, he is the victim as the hero again, making a late though not his last appearance. He had first appeared not as farcical in himself but as an effective stimulator of farce ... in **Decline and Fall** and then much later as a stimulator of unorthodox tragedy in **A Handful of Dust**. His appearance had all been successfully contrived, and they had all followed, with amazing originality, a well-worn path; that of the character who is not interesting in himself but to whom interesting (and horrifying) things happen. Here his appearance as Guy Crouchback was not successful."[493]

Guy's ineffectuality, far from being a blemish, is only a part of an essential stage in his spiritual development. It sheds light on the inadequacy of his static chivalric code which he must outgrow in order that he may become an effective instrument of Divine Grace on the earth. In this sense, he is certainly a development over static characters like Paul Pennyfeather and Tony Last. His development parallels that of Helena, who similarly reposes faith in the redemptive power of the Church after outgrowing her static opinions. Cyril Connolly has rightly observed the graph of Guy

---

[493] Ibid., 415-416.

Crouchback's progressive life when he enunciates the theme that his life embodies:

> "I have left out what is perhaps Mr. Waugh's major theme: the recovery of Crouchback's faith, of the sense of joy and purpose in life which he had lost when his marriage broke up, and which had invalidated his scrupulous orthodoxy."[494]

In fact, Waugh has brilliantly portrayed the theme of progress through religious change in the character of Guy Crouchback, as he did in that of Helena. Together, the three books show Waugh's ultimate comic vision of life, which is affirmative and poised in the resurgence of life. No wonder than that Cyril Connolly felt impelled to make a request for the immediate publication of all three novels in one volume.

> "I strongly urge the publisher to issue all three books in one volume immediately; the cumulative effect is most impressive, and it seems to me unquestionably the finest novel to have come out of the war."[495]

From an examination of the narrative concerning Guy Crouchback's spiritual odyssey, it become clear that the **Sword of Honour Trilogy**, though written and published in three parts, is one work with one vision and one structure. Evelyn Waugh's comic vision envisages the journey of his protagonist from the world of illusion associated with his static ideals of chivalry and his participation in the dynamic world of secular change to his resurrection as a spiritual elite. The graph of this narrative is linear and it begins with Guy leading a static life in his villa in Italy and ends with his final return to Broome, the traditional home of the Catholic family of Crouchbacks, as a spiritually enlightened and reformed character. That this change in Waugh is invariably Roman Catholic in character does not in any way discount the

---

494 Cyril Connolly, Sunday Times, 29 October 1961, 31, in ed. Martin Stannard, op. cit., 432.

495 Ibid., 430.

universality of his vision. The employment of the wheel of life imagery to communicate this vision endows his works an appeal that is at once universal. Guy Crouchback describes a linear movement away from the periphery of the wheel to its transcendental hub as he begins to comprehend the meaning of service of God and the significance of humility. The artistic harmony achieved between content and form here speaks of the artistic maturity Waugh had achieved by the time he came to write this Trilogy. The reputation of Waugh as a literary genius must, therefore, rest on the ease with which he has crafted the greater comedies.

Chapter 4

Conclusion

The study of Evelyn Waugh's comic vision and art is an uphill task. Not because of any complexity in the production of his works, but because of the complexity of his public persona. Waugh valued the entertaining aspect of art too much to let the profundity of his vision to impact upon the simplicity of the form of his works. Unlike his illustrious contemporaries like James Joyce and Virginia Woolf who reflect in the forms of their works the discursiveness of the reality they were writing about, he was content to leave alone the style of his works so that it could reach out to the least common denominator of his audiences. What makes the enterprise tough is his public persona. Waugh, as we have seen, was a stickler for aristocratic manners and life style. To compound the problem, he was on the wrong side of the religious temper of the times. For one, religion was on the wane and those who did pay attention to it in their lives were non-Catholics. Though born an Anglican, he converted to Roman Catholicism, which had long lost its flock in England. That made him a kind of social outcast. To further complicate the matters, he lashed out at the dominant ideology of the times in his works. This made him an ideological pariah. It was difficult for people to digest his stinging black humour at the revered icons of modernity, the child of Enlightenment philosophy. To top it all, like an expert magician, he kept the critics wondering about the meaning of his works by throwing them off the scent with his artistic sleights of hand. With so many odds weighed against him, it was not surprising that he received very cold critical attention. He was dismissed as a minor writer, compared to his contemporaries or else a major writer offering a minor interest in his dated works.

This study attempts to tear through the foggy veil of such critiques to revisit and redeem the real Waugh as represented in his creative works, especially the thirteen major novels that he wrote. The study argues that the claim of Evelyn Waugh to be recognised as a major twentieth century novelist in English literature rests on his creative use of comedy to convey his vision of life. That this vision is critical of the gains of modernity and all secular values in the lesser comedies and celebratory of the transformative character of religious change in the greater comedies, shows the range and depth of his comic art. Furthermore, the unobtrusive use of the metaphor of the ever-rotating wheel of life to communicate this vision speaks of his creative genius which could embed like a seed his metaphorical vision within the metonymy of his narratives. That this all-pervasive metaphor is revealed in the very first work, **Decline and Fall**, through a character most ill-suited for the job, is a masterful act of unobtrusive story telling.

The presiding image of the wheel of life informs not only the theme of change and progress at the base of his comic vision but also the movement of his narrative. Waugh leans towards the cyclical historiographers in questioning the Enlightenment philosophers' faith in the linearity of secular change. Like an iconoclast, he hammers down all the celebrated icons of secular human effort. He shows how the Enlightenment philosophers' cocksure confidence in the progressive nature of secular change has led man into the trap of Sisyphean absurdity and instability. Waugh likens secular change to the circular movement of a rotating wheel, which flings away all parameters of value judgement. Not only does it not offer any value judgement on its circular circumference, but it also induces a high degree of instability as it accelerates its pace of change. Besides, the circuitous nature of secular change ensures that man returns to his original state of existence, no matter how much he may try to get away from it. Waugh suggests that progress can never be achieved through secular human efforts. And the sooner man realises this the better. Or else, he will expose himself to comic ridicule for his misplaced faith in secular change and also to his own annihilation due to the release of the barbaric forces in the guise of development. This comic vision of absurdity pervades all the lesser comedies of Waugh.

Waugh sees hope for the redemption of humankind in religious change. In sharp contrast with secular change, religious change alone is linear in character. In the presiding image of the ever-rotating wheel of life, it translates into the movement towards its ever-stable hub, which transcends the circuitous motion of the wheel. As a Roman Catholic Christian by deliberate choice, Waugh sees the hub of the wheel of life in the Roman Catholic Church as it is for him the eternal reminder of the immutable reality of God on the Earth. The passage from the outermost periphery of the rotating wheel, which is most unstable, to the stable hub is, therefore, not unlike the passage from the world of secular change to the world of religious change. As such a change enhances the degree of stability in human society, it alone rescues man and his world from the ignominy of absurdity and perils of war. So, by embracing religious change, which in effect means conversion to Roman Catholicism, the individual makes his life meaningful and also at times ascends to the heights of human excellence through unconditional surrender to the Will of God. The sense of joy that accompanies this change is palpable in all the greater comedies.

But if the image of the wheel of life defines Waugh's comic vision of life adequately, it also endows it with an equally expressive form. While the absurdity of secular change is underlined by a circular plot in the lesser comedies, the purposefulness of religious change is conveyed by linear plot in the greater comedies. In the lesser comedies, the comic fun that arises is of a grim nature for while we laugh at the ignorance of people gullible enough to rely on secular change as a means to progress, we also sympathise with them when their illusions take the toll of their lives, physically or spiritually. The perpetual cyclical motion that the characters undergo on the ever-rotating wheel of life defines both the comic vision of absurdity in the lesser comedies and their individual form. In **Decline and Fall** (1928), Waugh's first major novel, secular achievements are shown to be no more than an eye-wash. British society, despite its vigorous programme of modernization, is shown to be simmering with the corruption of moral values. Britain emerges no better than a remote barbaric society of Africa. The idea of secular progress epitomized in the modernity of Britain is ridiculed through Paul Pennyfeather, a static character, whose picaresque journey through Britain proves as futile as its history. Paul returns to the point from where he began his journey. By ending the novel with the same situation with which it began,

Waugh endows it with a circular plot that immediately makes the reader recall the absurd cyclical motion of the wheel of life. Despite the comic vision of absurdity unfolded here both at the thematic and structural level, the central character, Paul Pennyfeather is not a flat character. Waugh traces his development from the time when he was ignorant of his real identity to the time when he beams with self-knowledge. At the beginning of the novel, Paul Pennyfeather does not know that he is a static character unfit for participating in the process of secular change. But at the end, he is fully aware of this reality. Accordingly, he retraces his steps into the static environs of an academic institution like Oxford.

In **Vile Bodies** (1930), the focus becomes more concentrated as the central character Adam Fenwick-Symes' repeated attempts to marry Nina Blount describe a circular pattern. In the secularized world of modern Britain, even sacred institutions like marriage have been divested of their religious essence. Marriage here has become a social institution based solely on such secular factors as the monetary status of the individuals wishing to tie the nuptial knot. As Adam's repetitive attempts to marry are not inspired by any eschatological considerations, they are as good as any secular attempts to progress in life. Episode after episode renders Adam comic in has misplaced confidence in secular change as a means to bettering his lot. The comic vision of absurdity unfolded here is underlined by the circular plot of the novel which makes no material alteration in Adam's lot. There is, however, a hint of large-scale devastation in the outbreak of the Second World War which Waugh sees as a direct consequence of the acceleration of the rate of secular change. The movement away from the Roman Catholic hub of the wheel of life represents in Waugh a drift towards a state of anarchy and chaos indicated by the high degree of instability at the outermost orbits of the wheel of life. Adam does not achieve the self-knowledge that his predecessor in **Decline and Fall** does. Nevertheless, Waugh's second major novel is a strong indictment of the progressive historiographers' reliance on secular change as a means to progress.

By the time, Waugh came to write **Black Mischief** (1932), he had already got converted to Roman Catholicism. His conversion is a landmark in his artistic growth. Till now, Waugh had only an intellectual conception of the kind of thing that could redeem man from the vicious and absurd circle of temporal change. The evidence is irrefutably there in Otto Silenus' discourse on the nature of life in **Decline and Fall**. Waugh saw in the hub of the wheel of life a temporal indicator of eternal reality. Despite its historical existence, the hub is beyond the reach of historical change. As a consequence, it is a reminder of eternal reality. With his conversion to Roman Catholic faith, the hub of the wheel of life came to stand for him for the immutable reality of the Roman Catholic Church. Accordingly, Waugh surveys the temporal world steeped in historical change with renewed vigour and greater insight in the novels beginning with **Black Mischief.** Temporal change now signifies, in no uncertain terms, the quest for secular progress through secular change and the movement towards the hub of the wheel of life, man's willingness to conform to Divine Order and Harmony, which alone guarantees true progress.

In **Black Mischief,** Waugh unmasks the absurdity of pursuing progress through secular change by debunking the Enlightenment historiographers' claims to development through the agency of secular human efforts on the vast historical canvas of an African nation on the threshold of the experiment with modernization. The African state of Azania has been a living case study of pre-historical barbarism under its early rulers until Emperor Seth, with his Oxonian Bachelor of Arts degree descends on it to transform it into a modern state. Seth's successive efforts, to transform his people and his country into a modern progressive state, end up in comic failure. The macabre end of Seth, the very epitome of this misconceived quest, points to the absurdity of seeking progress through secular change. With Seth's death, the thin veneer of civility is ripped open and Azania returns to its original state of barbarity. Waugh drives home the absurdity of the repetitive secular efforts with a plot that too is circular. The action of the novel begins with a war in Azania and ends too with a war. Waugh seems to suggest that barbarism can never be defeated with such secular efforts and that if man wishes to progress, he needs to look for answers elsewhere.

In **A Handful of Dust,** Waugh set out to demolish the belief that if he was against modernity, he must by default then favour the chivalric values of the bygone past. The price that Tony Last, a static character, pays for persisting with his static illusions of chivalry is reading one by one, in a perpetual cyclical motion, the gothic novels of Dickens to a half-crazy hybrid, Mr. Todd. In his tryst with Mr. Todd, Tony clashes with the unabashed barbarity of savages unredeemed by religion and the menacingly comic guile of secular western civilization. The absurd cyclical motion that his life is condemned to is not unlike that of Sisyphus. The absurdity of clinging on to the dated values of the past highlighted in the death-in-life existence of Tony Last leaves no room for doubt regarding where Waugh's sympathies lie. In fact, the novel reiterates the thesis contained in the metaphor of the ever-rotating wheel of life that secular values of life, whether ancient or modern, can never substitute for the religious ones and that man can hope to redeem himself only by accepting religious change. Any quest for the Eternal City in the secular world is foredoomed to failure as Tony Last's fate at the end of the novel shows.

In **Scoop**, Waugh explodes the myth of human reason being the sole agency of change and development as the Enlightenment and Humanist philosophers would have us believe. Waugh effectively communicates this through the highly entertaining farce of William Boot's rise to fame as a successful journalist. William Boot, a novice journalist, is catapulted into fame as a leading investigative news reporter by a series of incidents that hardly show any causal sequence. The reader can scarcely repress his laughter over the gullibility of the secular world for being taken in by the apparently logical nature of secular change in William's career. The sense of absurdity that characterizes Waugh's comic world of secular change is conveyed through a circular plot that first substitutes John Boot with William Boot and then, as if to make amends, substitutes William Boot with John Boot, most surreptitiously. This ensures William Boot's return to his original static world of Boot Magna while John Boot basks in the glory of borrowed plumes. However, unlike other static characters of Waugh, William Boot is aware of his personal limitations from the beginning and never for even once gets deluded by his inadvertent success.

In **Put Out More Flags** (1942), Waugh once again invokes the presiding metaphor of the ever-rotating wheel of life, to indicate the dangerous level of instability that the secular efforts of modernization and development can lead to, in the outbreak of the World War II. Waugh suggests that just as the outermost orbit of the rotating wheel is most dangerously unstable for any man to hold his own on it, so is the acceleration of pace of secular change, which creates the disorder and chaos of the war in human society. Waugh is obviously hitting out at the Enlightenment historiographers who maintain that secular change can bring about modernization and development. Waugh conveys his unique comic vision of absurdity through a plot that is circular in nature like the wheel. At the beginning of the novel, Basil Seal flees from the fate of conscription in British army during World War II to his sister's secluded place, Malfrey. Basil detests the order imposed by the discipline of military life. Being a dynamic character, he has a predilection for chaos and anarchy. These conditions aid him in carrying out ruthless exploits with impunity. One of his first war-efforts is, therefore, the exploitation of the static characters of Malfrey. It is followed by his operation-persecution against the static Ambrose. The novel returns to its original situation when Basil Seal decides, at the end of the novel, to join the war so that he may enjoy killing Germans. The circular course of Basil's life offers no redemption of even the slightest improvement in his personality. The circularity of the plot is further reinforced with the temporal framework of the cycle of seasons.

In The **Loved One,** just as in **Decline and Fall**, an entire secularized society is brought under the focus of Waugh's serio-comic vision of absurdity. The absurdity of pursuing progress through secular change is driven home through the perversion and inversion of religious values of life in the secular institutions of developed America. The fragility of these products of secular human endeavour for progress becomes clear in their inability to serve as a life-buoy to the people who repose faith in them. When the testing time arrives, these false values desert man and he, perforce, is left in the arms of the barbaric past. Aimee Thenatogenos' death at the end of the novel amply testifies to the veracity of this fact. Unable to seek support from the false religion of Whispering Glades, Aimee turns to her barbaric ancestors for help and eventually, commits suicide. The return of men and women of the secular Western civilization to the ways of their ancestors in their hours of crisis shows the absurdity of man's quest for secular progress. Waugh's comic vision of absurdity makes us laugh at Aimee for her excessive and misplaced faith in the inverted values of Whispering Glades and feel sympathetic simultaneously over her gruesome end. The absurdity of elevating transient secular values to the level of eternal religious ones in America is reinforced by a circular plot which begins with Dennis's arrival in America and ends with his departure to England, the place of his nativity.

In **The Ordeal of Gilbert Pinfold,** Waugh touches the heights of artistic maturity, when he ruthlessly holds up to ridicule his own individual predilection for the secular values of the past. It is interesting to note here that the way in which Waugh comes down on his own inadequacies endorses the thesis that the narrator-author in Waugh transcends the limitations of Waugh, the aristocratic and Catholic snob, something that the critics and reviewers have failed to observe. That Waugh should have used the metaphor of madness to drive home this dissonance between the two aspects of his chief protagonist, Gilbert Pinfold, shows the command Waugh had come to acquire over his art by this time. In the ordeal of Gilbert Pinfold on board the ship, S. S. Caliban, Waugh masterfully communicates the extent of depravity and disorder in the secular world when he dramatises the conflict between the static Pinfold-Waugh and the dynamic swashbuckling people-of-the-world inhabiting the world of his hallucinations. But, even as he comes down upon these ogres of his hallucinations, he also holds up to ridicule the static Pinfold-Waugh. Waugh underpins the lack of order in Pinfold-Waugh's world of hallucinations with a circular plot that first throws the schizophrenic Pinfold into the dynamic world of his own hallucinations aboard the ship, S.S. Caliban, and then brings him back, at the end, to his native static world of Lychople. As in **Decline and Fall**, the novel ends with the protagonist gaining an insight into his real nature. Accordingly, he rejects the dynamic world and accepts the static world. It is a regressive step and not progressive one. Hence, the comic vision of absurdity revealed in the valuelessness of the dynamic world remains central to the meaning of this novel.

The study contends that these eight novels constitute what may be called lesser comedies by virtue of their preoccupation with a similar concern and the use of a similar form. The study shows that the lesser comedies of Waugh concern themselves with exploring the comic absurdity of pursuing progress through secular human values of life. Contrary to the claims of the Enlightenment and Humanist ideologues of modernity, Waugh showcases in each of these novels that secular change is a delusion and that man can never progress by ignoring the religious perspective of life. Such a change, as we have seen in these novels, is both comically absurd and also comically gruesome at times in its end. By virtue of the vision of absurdity revealed in these novels, they have been classified as lesser comedies. It goes to the credit of Waugh that he conveys the lesser comic vision through the presiding metaphor of the ever-rotating wheel of life. Waugh shows in the successive lesser comedies that man returns to the point from where he starts the journey of his life just as the circular motion of the wheel brings the person standing on it back to his original position. The circular plot employed in the lesser comedies, therefore, underscores the vision of absurdity that these novels reveal. The balance achieved in the lesser comedies between the vision and the form, however, does not sacrifice easy comprehension on the part of the reader. The temporal movement of the plot ensures the accessibility of the reader to its entertaining flavour. It speaks highly of Waugh's artistic genius that even when he conveys the vision of absurdity and chaos, he does not allow the form of his novels to lose their classical perfection. He is, therefore, a post-modernist writer with a difference.

Unlike other writers who have explored the absurdity of human existence in the modern times, Waugh also offers hope out of this comic despair in the five other novels that he wrote. It is by virtue of the superior vision of regeneration and redemption offered in these five novels that I have called these greater comedies. The fact that Waugh gave expression to self-realization and redemption from the ennui of an absurd and sinful world, shows how he transcended the comic vision of absurdity that circumscribes the entire literary output of the theatre of the Absurd, and existentialist writers.

Brideshead Revisited is a transitional novel. The development of Waugh from the lesser to the greater comedies is reflected in the structure of this novel. Two kinds of plots co-exist in it: one that of the lesser comedies and the other that of the greater comedies. The presiding image of the ever-rotating wheel of life explains best the action of this novel. While the rotating part of the wheel captures the lesser comic action of Charles Ryder's return to Brideshead, the linear motion towards the ever-stable hub of the wheel captures the transformative change in the hero and the errant members of the Flyte family from a state of sinful error and confusion to a state of acceptance of religious conversion to Roman Catholicism. The circular plot is reinforced through chapterization that begins with a 'Prologue' that is entitled 'Brideshead Revisited' and closes with an 'Epilogue' that is entitled similarly. The circular character of the plot provides the secular frame of the novel, reflecting the themes of stagnation and absurdity so successfully portrayed in the lesser comedies. Except for this, the narrative primarily indicates the progress of the hero, Charles Ryder who is also the narrator of the progress of the errant members of the Flyte family from the degrading absurdity of dynamic life to the eternal stability of religious life. The novel is appropriately sub-titled "Sacred and Profane Memories of Charles Ryder", with profane memories represented by the secular edifice of Brideshead Revisited that has witnessed many renovations and sacred memories represented by the sacred flame in the chapel of the gothic building. While the profane memories relate to the depravity of the world of secular change in which the errant members of the Flyte family and even Charles Ryder lose themselves, the sacred memories relate to their gradual emancipation from the world of sin to the world of redemption. In **Brideshead Revisited**, Waugh was, therefore, testing the waters to see how well he could attempt to portray the grand eschatological theme of the sublimity that people attain when they surrender to the eternal Truth as represented in the Church.

By the time Waugh came to write Helena, he was a mature artist, confident of portraying the theme of ascension from the ranks of the ordinary to the ranks of the blessed and exalted. Milton attempted it in Paradise Lost, but ended up creating a far more powerful character in Satan than in the All-Merciful and Pious Christ a case of failed vision indeed. But when we come to Waugh's Helena, we read a narrative that beautifully and powerfully describes the spiritual journey of Helena as the princess of a chieftain from Britain, the then barbarous outpost of Roman Empire, to the holy precincts of the Roman Catholic Church as a Saint. Appropriately enough, there is a single plot that displays the progressive nature of religious change in the liner spiritual odyssey of Helena. As the dark recesses of her mind keep on getting enlightened with the flame of religious devotion, Helena forges ahead on a linear path towards the hub of the wheel of life which by its intrinsic nature not only transcends the relativism of the wheel but also supports that. In the triumphant conclusion of her progressive journey, not only does she elevate herself to the rank of a spiritual elite but she also gives expression to a fundamental tenet of Roman Catholicism: the historicity of the eternal Christian truth. Helena's transformation for the better is anticipated and conveyed through symbols and images which occur less frequently in **Brideshead Revisited** than in this novel. As the novel charts a movement from the insignificance of dynamic existence to the significance of religious life, the novel may either be termed a divine comedy or a greater comedy.

Waugh's third and the last greater comedy, **The Sword of Honour Trilogy**, is spread over three volumes, **Men At Arms, Officers and Gentlemen,** and **Unconditional Surrender**, each published separately and at separate points of time. Like all other greater comedies, its narrative too runs along a plot which is linear in character. Guy Crouchback, the chief protagonist of this trilogy, is a victim of the dynamic world and is, therefore, living as an exile in Italy. The outbreak of world War II offers him an opportunity of reasserting his lost self-esteem under the pretext of protecting the honour of Christendom. His knight- errantry comes to a naught when he realizes that the war is being fought for no such reason. Even he has been hoodwinking his own self by thinking so. Deep in the mind of every soldier, he included, is an irrational and barbaric desire to kill and be killed. Confronted with this knowledge, Guy Crouchback sloughs off both his static mental sheath and dynamic emotional covering. He realizes the inadequacy of a static attitude to life and the absurdity of the dynamic world's obsession with secular change. Acting upon his father, old Mr. Gervase Crouchback's advice, he submits to the will of God so much so that he is willing to undergo worldly humiliation for the sake of giving Trimmer's child a Christian birth. This act of humility in the service of God, disregarding the public humiliation that it would earn him, is indicative of the religious transformation in Guy and his elevation in God's eyes. Taken together, the Trilogy is a masterpiece of epic proportion, but when analysed as three separate novels, it loses its thematic unity and appeal. That Waugh should have thought of narrating the story of spiritual regeneration of an individual against the backdrop of the greatest war in history is a sign of his artistic mastery and his ability to handle the two themes together.

The three greater comedies are in fact a necessary sequel to the lesser comedies. Having shown the futility of secular change as a means to progress, Waugh, as a committed Christian writer, had to show the comic vision of life implicit in the religious transformation of the individual and the society. While the circular motion of the wheel of life helped him convey the first view, the linear motion towards the ever-stable hub of the rotating wheel helped him in conveying his ultimate and Christian vision of life. While the circular motion of the rotating wheel indicates hopelessness, the movement towards its ever-stable hub offers hope of redemption and rebirth. It is this movement that the greater comedies capture and present in their narratives. Just as the lesser comedies reveal a balance between their form and meaning, so do the greater comedies. The structure of these comic novels coheres with the vision emerging out of them. Each of these novels possesses a linear plot which adequately indicates the logical development present in religious change. The central character begins his life with static nations of life, confronts the dynamic world, and discovers the inadequacy of his static attitude to life and the absurdity of the dynamic mode of existence. Eventually, he rejects both and makes for the Roman Catholic hub of life which he selects as the ultimate goal of his life. The achievement of this goal redeems him from the absurdity of secular change and uplifts him to a state of existence which is both exalted and abiding. He realizes, so to say, the bliss of the prelapsarian state of existence. It is most often indicated by admission to the Church and elevation to sainthood.

The comic vision of life unfolded in the greater comedies is, however, never allowed to touch the borderland of didacticism. Waugh was no explainer of things. He was, as a novelist should be, a describer of events. Consequently, his narratives do away with the causal sequence of the traditional nineteenth century novel. In order that his comic vision of life may emerge unobtrusively, Waugh made innovative use of English language and its literary techniques. It is quite obvious from the central role played by the metaphor of the ever-rotating wheel of life, to be found ubiquitously present in all his novels. It is not without reason that the grater comedies of Waugh have an aura of poetic charm about them. His post-modernist emphasis on objectivity does not, therefore, stand in the way of his artistic achievement. Instead, it aids him in gaining a universal appeal.

Rene Wellek and Austin Warren describe a successful literary work of art as one in which the materials are completely assimilated into form. Waugh too held the belief that properly understood style was not a seductive decoration added to a functional structure, but the essence of a work of art.

The balanced inter-relationship between subject and form achieved in Waugh's comic novels bears testimony to this assertion. And it is by virtue of this achievement that Waugh's major literary output is one luminous mass of order aesthetic beauty. We, thus, conclude that while there may be many useful approaches to the study of Waugh but the one approach that touches the heart of Waugh's creative works and uncovers his artistic genius is the study of his comic vision and art. It is only by placing the comic vision of life in Evelyn Waugh in the centre of our study of Waugh that we discover the comic thematic concern running through the entire canon of Waugh literature; be it the lesser of the greater comedies. The superior comic vision of life unfolded in the greater comedies, as a way out of the absurdity of life, depicted in the lesser comedies, without being didactic at the same time, shows the heights of artistic perception achieved by Waugh. Again, the creative use of language and literary tools made for its artistic expression attract attention towards the artistic excellence achieved by Waugh. Thus, Waugh emerges as a major post modernist novelist who felt and lent an abstruse artistic utterance to his perceptions and vision.

***

About the Author

A topper in B. Com and Master's in English from the University of Jammu, Ravi K Dhar did his PhD from the North-Eastern Hill University (NEHU), Shillong. Dr. Dhar started his career as a Lecturer in English at North-Eastern Hill University, Nagaland Campus, Medziphema. Thereafter, he went on to work as an Assistant Professor of English and Associate Professor of Journalism in the Dept. of Journalism, Languages and Culture of Punjab Agricultural University, Ludhiana. He went on deputation to Ethiopian Civil Service College, now University, Addis Ababa, where he worked for over a year. Since June 2006, he has been working as Professor of Media and Communication Studies and the Director of Jagannath International Management School, Vasant Kunj, of Guru Gobind Singh Indraprastha University, New Delhi.

Dr. Dhar has been a member of a number of academic bodies in various universities, including his own, where he has been a member of the University Court and the Academic Council. A keen researcher, he has published and presented papers in the areas of Modern English Novel, Communication Policy, Online Communication, Communication Rights and Child Rights. He is the Founder Editor of Mass Communicator, an international journal of Communication Studies. He has also come out with three edited books, Indian Management: Theory & Practice, Media in the Swirl, and Perspectives on Thought Leadership. He has also published Orphans of the Storm, a novel; The Chant of Vitasta, a collection of poems; and 101 Thoughts to Light up your Path, a collection of mystical aphorisms.

Dr. Dhar has also launched a YouTube Channel, The Mystic Mariner. He has traveled to Sweden, the Netherlands, Germany, Austria, Slovakia, Czech Republic, Hungary, Korea, Singapore, Malaysia, and Thailand. He has a personal website, ravikdhar.in.